MUSIC

A Way of Life for the Young Child

FIFTH EDITION

MUSIC

A Way of Life for the Young Child

Linda Carol Edwards

College of Charleston
Charleston, South Carolina

Kathleen M. Bayless

Kent State University, emerita

Marjorie E. Ramsey

Georgia Southwestern College

PEARSON

Merrill
Prentice Hall

Upper Saddle River, New Jersey
Columbus, Ohio

Library of Congress Cataloging-in-Publication Data

Edwards, Linda Carol.
   Music, a way of life for the young child / Linda Carol Edwards, Kathleen M. Bayless,
   Marjorie E. Ramsey.—5th ed.
      p. cm.
   Includes indexes.
   ISBN 0-13-111676-2
      1. Music—Instruction and study—Juvenile. I. Bayless, Kathleen M. II. Ramsey, Marjorie
   E.- III. Title.

MT1.E346 2005
372.87—dc22

2003069014

Vice President and Executive Publisher: Jeffery W. Johnston
Publisher: Kevin M. Davis
Editor: Julie Peters
Editorial Assistant: Amanda King
Production Editor: Sheryl Glicker Langner
Design Coordinator: Diane C. Lorenzo
Photo Coordinator: Kathy Kirtland
Production Coordination: Linda Zuk, WordCrafters Editorial Services, Inc.
Cover Designer: Terry Rohrback
Cover Image: Getty One
Production Manager: Laura Messerly
Director of Marketing: Ann Castel Davis
Marketing Manager: Autumn Purdy
Marketing Coordinator: Tyra Poole

This book was set in Times Roman by Carlisle Communications, Ltd. It was printed and bound by Courier
Kendallville, Inc. The cover was printed by Coral Graphics Services, Inc.

Photo Credits: Art Brewer/Getty Images, Inc.–Stone Allstock, p. 111; Paul S. Conklin/PhotoEdit, p. 64
(top); Scott Cunningham/Merrill, pp. 9, 23, 53; Laima Druskis/PH College, pp. 26, 79, 80; Ken Karp/PH
College, pp. 55, 119; Jose Luis/Getty Images, Inc.–Taxi, p. 15; Anthony Magnacca/Merrill, p. 97; L. Morris
Nantz/PH College, p. 8; Pam Seabrook Ohlandt, pp. 4, 10, 20, 63, 123, 126, 136, 196; Barbara Schwartz/
Merrill, pp. 83, 85; Steve & Mary Skjold/PH College, p. 77; Teri Leigh Stratford/PH College, pp. 41, 44;
Anne Vega/Merrill, pp. 24, 27, 43, 99, 101, 138, 195; Susan Woog Wagner/PH College, p. 39; Todd
Yarrington/Merrill, pp. 45, 64 (bottom), 102, 193; David Young-Wolff/PhotoEdit, pp. 1, 104.

Pearson Education Ltd.
Pearson Education Singapore, Pte. Ltd.
Pearson Education Canada, Ltd.
Pearson Education—Japan

Pearson Education Australia PTY, Limited
Pearson Education North Asia Ltd.
Pearson Educacion de Mexico, S.A. de C.V.
Pearson Education Malaysia, Pte. Ltd.

PEARSON
Merrill
Prentice Hall

10 9 8 7 6 5 4 3 2 1
ISBN 0-13-111676-2

To Mama, Sarah Cameron Edwards,
my first music teacher.

Thank you for instilling in me a love of music and dance
that stays with me always.

Educator Learning Center: An Invaluable Online Resource

Merrill Education and the Association for Supervision and Curriculum Development (ASCD) invite you to take advantage of a new online resource, one that provides access to the top research and proven strategies associated with ASCD and Merrill—the Educator Learning Center. At **www.EducatorLearningCenter.com** you will find resources that will enhance your students' understanding of course topics and of current educational issues, in addition to being invaluable for further research.

HOW THE EDUCATOR LEARNING CENTER WILL HELP YOUR STUDENTS BECOME BETTER TEACHERS

With the combined resources of Merrill Education and ASCD, you and your students will find a wealth of tools and materials to better prepare them for the classroom.

Research

- More than 600 articles from the ASCD journal *Educational Leadership* discuss everyday issues faced by practicing teachers.
- A direct link on the site to Research Navigator™ gives students access to many of the leading education journals, as well as extensive content detailing the research process.

- Excerpts from Merrill Education texts give your students insight on important topics of instructional methods, diverse populations, assessment, classroom management, technology, and refining classroom practice.

Classroom Practice

- Hundreds of lesson plans and teaching strategies are categorized by content area and age range.
- Case studies and classroom video footage provide virtual field experience for student reflection.
- Computer simulations and other electronic tools keep your students abreast of today's classrooms and current technologies.

LOOK INTO THE VALUE OF EDUCATOR LEARNING CENTER YOURSELF

A four-month subscription to Educator Learning Center is $25 but is **FREE** when used in conjunction with this text. To obtain free passcodes for your students, simply contact your Merrill/Prentice Hall sales representative, and your representative will give you a special ISBN to give your bookstore when ordering your textbooks. To preview the value of this website to you and your students, please go to **www.EducatorLearningCenter.com** and click on "Demo."

Preface

Music is our universal language, the language of our imaginations, of musicians and dancers, composers and performers, orchestras and operas. Music is the rhythmic language of the dancing 5-year-old using her body to recreate the graceful movements of a swimming dolphin. Music is the lullaby of a father singing to his infant while communicating tenderness and love. The language of music is revealed through the dancers who choose not to be restrained by convention as they represent their understanding of space, time, and form in ways that are personally satisfying and pleasing. Music is the language of children adding original lyrics and new melodies to a familiar song.

This new edition presents a comprehensive and up-to-date survey of professional research while continuing to provide links between theory and practice. It encourages teachers and caregivers to attend to the importance of research and contemporary thought regarding music education. At the same time, the narrative frames theoretical ideas in meaningful ways for the adult who has chosen teaching as a profession.

The songs, ideas, suggestions, and musical concepts are time tested. Parents, teachers, student teachers, caregivers, and students have aided in compiling and assessing the contents of this edition. Musical concepts and activities appropriate for each age level have been included to accompany some of the songs and rhythms. I do not believe, however, that music experiences provided for young children must always be used to teach them something. Children's awareness and understanding of the concepts and skills presented should grow out of natural encounters with the musical selections and activities. At each age level, enjoyment of the music should be paramount, and teachers are encouraged to use music

in creative ways. I hope that as you discover the materials, you will enjoy the musical activities whether in your home or in the larger community where children gather. Become an advocate for music in the lives of young children. Even though you may feel you lack experience, just begin! Young children are not critics of your expertise with music; they enjoy, participate, and thrive as you do the same.

Throughout the book, the word *teacher* is used to describe the adult who is charged with the care and well-being of children. This includes the preservice college student enrolled in a teacher education program, the student teacher embarking on a teaching career, practicing teachers, master teachers, college professors, and other professionals who are dedicated to enriching the lives of children.

NEW TO THIS EDITION

Many changes and major revisions to this fifth edition provide a comprehensive look at music, children and teachers, and how music can expand our understanding of the teaching and learning process.

Music in a Cultural Context

Music is suited to address the wonderful diversity of children in today's schools. Music provides teachers with a multicultural context for seeing diversity from viewpoints different from their own and provides some of the tools needed to meet the different learning modalities of children. A new focus on viewing music through a multicultural context is included in this fifth edition. New sections entitled "Music from Around the World" highlight music's great potential as a resource for musical expression and an awareness of the diversity of music.

Multiple Intelligences Theory

Howard Gardner's eight intelligences provide a framework for approaching multiple intelligence theory and the implications this theory has for music education. His theory recognizes eight intelligences: linguistic, logical-mathematical, spatial, bodily-kinesthetic, musical, interpersonal, intrapersonal, and naturalist. In this edition, the coverage of these intelligences includes an in-depth focus on musical, bodily-kinesthetic, and logical-mathematical intelligences because our own success as adults in these areas may have been helped or hindered by experiences during our early childhood years.

National Standards for Music Education

Sections on the National Standards for Music Education, written by the National Association for Music Educators, provide in-depth coverage on why we must look to these standards as challenges for bringing music back into the mainstream of essential subject areas. This content also addresses how we, as teachers and teacher educators, are in a unique position to do just that.

Research

More than ever before, research studies and theoretical contributions provide a comprehensive view of why music is an integral component of education for all learners, especially children. To accurately reflect this growth, current and relevant research is included in this edition to provide the foundation for continued study of music. Also cited are practical articles and references to which teachers can refer for additional information.

Developmentally Appropriate Practice

The term *developmentally appropriate practice* (DAP), as reported by the National Association for the Education of Young Children, focuses on the ways in which teachers implement the curriculum, the organization of the classroom environment, the materials and equipment, and the children's interactions with the teacher and with one another. This edition presents new information on DAP as it relates to music education for young children.

Quotations

The powerful words of philosophers, musicians, and dancers at the beginning and end of each chapter promote new ways of thinking about music. Some quotations are presented to provoke serious thought, while others use humor to convey a musical message. All provide inspiration to teachers for including music education in the lives of young children.

SPECIAL CONTENT COVERAGE

Sections on developmentally appropriate practice present concrete experiences and ways to use music that are appropriate to the developmental levels of children. Several sections discuss how to provide music experiences for *all* the children in your classroom in an inclusive environment. These sections focus on the need for sensitivity when caring for and sharing music with young children with special needs.

You will also enjoy additional special content coverage on opera, classical music, and folk music. A bonus to this edition is the inclusion of new content about Ella Jenkins and the invaluable contributions she has made to music education for young children. Think of her as the music educator who changed the course of music education in this country and abroad.

Each chapter also includes coverage of global music to introduce you and your children to the richness of music from around the world. In light of the increasing awareness of and changing populations of our world today, I hope you will pay special attention to the references to "the tourist approach to diversity." It may well extend your views.

ORGANIZATION AND STRUCTURE

Chapter 1 of the text presents an overview of the central themes and ideas about music that are woven throughout the book. Chapters 2 through 6 focus on specific age levels and children's growth and development in music and music understanding. Chapter 7 emphasizes music in an integrated curriculum, with suggestions and songs suitable for other content areas, including language arts, science, mathematics, and social studies. Expanded material on "Stories That Sing" and using music to promote language development have been added to Chapter 7. It is here that those who work with young children can realize the opportunities for using music through the day. Chapter 8 considers the professional responsibilities of teachers and how we must remember the importance of music in all aspects of our lives.

APPENDIXES

The extensive appendixes at the end of the book provide a wealth of additional resources and information. **Appendix A, "Music from Around the World,"** includes over 25 songs from many different countries and cultures. **Appendix B, "Music Terminology and Approaches to Music Education,"** introduces musical concepts, a glossary of terms, grand staff and piano keyboards, music fundamentals, and information on the Orff and Suzuki approaches to teaching and learning to play musical instruments. **Appendix C, "Resources for Teachers in Early Childhood Classrooms,"** provides a quick reference for professional organizations, newsletters, and journals; sources for ordering instruments; books on making instruments; songs for listening and music appreciation; an extensive list of recordings appropriate for encouraging movement and music in the learning environment; and a list of wonderful children's books that involve music. **Appendix D, "Learning Autoharp® and Guitar for the Classroom,"** introduces the basics of playing the autoharp and guitar. There is also a fingering chart for the guitar. **Appendix E** provides an overview of percussion, melody, and chording instruments. It also presents ideas and illustrations on how to make homemade musical instruments.

REFERENCES

More than 90 new references to the professional literature are cited in this edition, and a complete list appears at the end of each chapter. These reference lists compile recent research and reflect the expansion of the base of theory and research that supports music education for young children.

ACKNOWLEDGMENTS

Many people inspired me as I was writing this fifth edition, and it has been enhanced by the combined efforts of a talented team of professionals at Merrill/Prentice Hall. I want to thank Ann Davis, who urged me to consider this revision and then gave me the guidance and support to do so. I am also grateful to Kevin Davis for his insight and encouragement. In addition, my special thanks to Julie Peters for her valuable assistance and interest and knowledge of music education. I wish especially to thank Sheryl Langner, who made the publication of this book possible. Kathy Kirtland

is acknowledged for her creative artistry in selecting wonderful photographs to illustrate the book. I am also very grateful to have been able to work with Linda Zuk of WordCrafters. She provided me with guidance throughout the production process. Her attention to detail and professionalism are very much appreciated. They are a wonderful group of professionals and have been a pleasure to work with throughout the book's publication.

In addition, I appreciate the input from those who provided timely and helpful reviews of the manuscript: Nanci Donato, Clarion University of Pennsylvania; Carolyn Hildebrandt, University of Northern Iowa; Pat Hofbauer, Northwest State Community College; Margaret Kelly, Illinois State University; and Margery A. Kranyik, Bridgewater State College, Curry College.

I appreciate and wish to acknowledge the support of friends and colleagues who provided guidance during the writing process: Dr. Susan Gurganus, for her important contributions to the section on children with special needs; and Dr. Robert Fowler, for his professional expertise and for leading me through the complex world of technology. I wish also to thank my graduate assistants, Mollie Hedden, Cara Spitz, and Sara Burton, who were often given the impossible to do and who did it. I feel blessed to have had the opportunity to collaborate with these wonderful students; they were always ready to find obscure articles and to tackle any tasks I sent their way. Thanks to all my students in the creative arts classes. In their field experiences and student teaching they have demonstrated their commitment to music education through the many ways in which they have planned for and implemented music in the curriculum.

Finally, I wish to express my appreciation to Linda Kay Kauffman for her continuous and unwavering support while I was writing and revising this edition. Her professionalism has brought clarity and cohesiveness to the book. I also owe much to Margaret Humphreys, Karen Paciorck, and Cavas Gobhai for their wisdom and guidance throughout the process and for their encouragement and understanding during the time it took to develop this fifth edition.

Linda Carol Edwards

Statement of Beliefs

Music is a vital part of daily living. It becomes a part of life as opportunities are provided for experiences in singing, responding physically to different rhythms, creative expressions, playing instruments, and quiet listening. A well-organized musical environment provides for a wide range of musical activities and experiences adequate to meet the needs and interests of all children. It also supports and strengthens learning in the other areas brought into the unified experience. Music helps children understand other people and their cultures and gives increased opportunities for social and emotional development. Music also provides a means for the aesthetic enrichment and growth of every child.

WE BELIEVE

Young Children Have a Right to

- have a variety of musical experiences that will bring pleasure and enjoyment to them throughout their lives
- experience musical activities and materials that are appropriate to their age level and developmental needs
- engage in musical experiences that are based on an action art, not a performing art
- be guided to the fullest development of their musical potential
- have the opportunity for support and/or extension of content areas throughout the medium of music
- express themselves musically in an atmosphere of freedom and trust, where divergent and creative interpretation is encouraged
- be involved in the full gamut of musical experiences, regardless of physical, social, emotional, or intellectual limitations

- have sufficient time provided each day for the exploration of musical experiences

Adults Working with Children Will

- provide both planned and spontaneous musical activities as a part of each child's day
- offer opportunities for listening, creating, singing, moving rhythmically, and experimenting with sound
- place emphasis on the child's enjoyment of the musical experience rather than on an expected outcome
- provide musical activities that will enhance other learning, such as acquisition of language, listening skills, auditory discrimination, and social understanding
- arrange an environment in which children will feel free to explore and engage in a variety of musical experiences that represent contributions from a variety of ethnic groups and cultures from around the world
- recognize and plan for well-balanced musical experiences for all children, adapted to physical, social, emotional, and intellectual capabilities

Because

- one of the main goals for music is to make children's lives richer through musical experiences that will help develop their aesthetic senses
- a balance of musical activities can contribute to the development of all children according to their individual patterns of growth and development
- music can support concepts and skills that children are developing, but enjoyment of music should hold priority

- children are natural musicians and, given the opportunity, will express themselves musically in a variety of creative ways

In 1898, Sarah E. Sprague, State Institute Conductor and Inspector of Graded Schools for Minnesota, wrote:

> Life's Song, indeed would lose its charm,
> Were there no babies to begin it;
> A doleful place this world would be,
> Were there no little people in it.

Sarah Sprague concluded,

> Home, nature and school are the three influences in a child's life, and when these are harmoniously blended it is the "World Beautiful" realized for him, wherein he may grow, as a plant does, always toward the light.

Discover the Companion Website Accompanying This Book

THE PRENTICE HALL COMPANION WEBSITE: A VIRTUAL LEARNING ENVIRONMENT

Technology is a constantly growing and changing aspect of our field that is creating a need for content and resources. To address this emerging need, Prentice Hall has developed an online learning environment for students and professors alike—Companion Websites—to support our textbooks.

In creating a Companion Website, our goal is to build on and enhance what the textbook already offers. For this reason, the content for each user-friendly website is organized by topic and provides the professor and student with a variety of meaningful resources. Common features of a Companion Website include:

FOR THE PROFESSOR—

Every Companion Website integrates **Syllabus Manager™,** an online syllabus creation and management utility.

- **Syllabus Manager™** provides you, the instructor, with an easy, step-by-step process to create and revise syllabi, with direct links into Companion Website and other online content without having to learn HTML.
- Students may logon to your syllabus during any study session. All they need to know is the web address for the Companion Website and the password you've assigned to your syllabus.

- After you have created a syllabus using **Syllabus Manager™,** students may enter the syllabus for their course section from any point in the Companion Website.
- Clicking on a date, the student is shown the list of activities for the assignment. The activities for each assignment are linked directly to actual content, saving time for students.
- Adding assignments consists of clicking on the desired due date, then filling in the details of the assignment—name of the assignment, instructions, and whether or not it is a one-time or repeating assignment.
- In addition, links to other activities can be created easily. If the activity is online, a URL can be entered in the space provided, and it will be linked automatically in the final syllabus.
- Your completed syllabus is hosted on our servers, allowing convenient updates from any computer on the Internet. Changes you make to your syllabus are immediately available to your students at their next logon.

FOR THE STUDENT—

- **Introduction**—General information about the topic and how it will be covered in the website.
- **Web Links**—A variety of websites related to topic areas.
- **Timely Articles**—Links to online articles that enable you to become more aware of important issues in early childhood.
- **Learn by Doing**—Put concepts into action, participate in activities, examine strategies, and more.

- **Visit a School**—Visit a school's website to see concepts, theories, and strategies in action.
- **For Teachers/Practitioners**—Access information you will need to know as an educator, including information on materials, activities, and lessons.
- **Observation Tools**—A collection of checklists and forms to print and use when observing and assessing children's development.
- **Current Policies and Standards**—Find out the latest early childhood policies from the government and various organizations, and view state, federal, and curriculum standards.
- **Resources and Organizations**—Discover tools to help you plan your classroom or center and organizations to provide current information and standards for each topic.
- **Electronic Bluebook**—Paperless method of completing homework or essays assigned by a professor. Finished work can be sent to the professor via email.
- **Message Board**—Virtual bulletin board to post and respond to questions and comments from a national audience.

To take advantage of these and other resources, please visit the *Music: A Way of Life for the Young Child,* Fifth Edition, Companion Website at

www.prenhall.com/edwards

Brief Contents

Contents

NOTE: Every effort has been made to provide accurate and current Internet information in this book. However, the Internet and information posted on it are constantly changing, and it is inevitable that some of the Internet addresses listed in this textbook will change.

About the Authors

Linda Carol Edwards is a professor of early childhood in the School of Education at the College of Charleston, Charleston, South Carolina, where she teaches both graduate and undergraduate courses in the visual and performing arts. Her degrees include a BA from Pembroke State University and an MEd and EdD from the University of Massachusetts at Amherst. Before moving to the college level, she taught kindergarten for 12 years in the public schools of North Carolina.

Dr. Edwards is the author of *The Creative Arts: A Process Approach for Teachers and Children* (Merrill/Prentice Hall), which is now in its third edition. She has been published in *Young Children, Science and Children, Journal of Early Education and Family Review, Dimensions in Early Childhood,* and the *Kappa Delta Pi Record.* She also serves on the advisory board of *Annual Editions: Early Childhood Education.* In addition, Dr. Edwards's experience has allowed her to create graduate programs in early childhood education that have received NCATE/NAEYC approval.

As an advocate for arts education for young children, she takes the opportunity to present at local, state, and national conferences about the importance of the visual and performing arts in the lives of young children.

Kathleen M. Bayless is currently professor emerita of teacher development and curriculum studies at Kent State University. Since her retirement, she has been teaching early childhood music courses, supervising student teachers, and assisting with a class of special learners. She served on the National Association for the Education of Young Children's Commission on Appropriate Education for Four- and Five-Year-Old Children. She serves as a consultant and presenter for school systems, teacher organizations, and preschool parent groups in the field of music for young children. Her current research interests involve using music with the special-needs child.

Marjorie E. Ramsey is a freelance writer, consultant, and lecturer, having retired from the University System of Georgia. She served as chairman of the Division of Education and director of teacher education for Georgia Southwestern College until July 1988. She has shared her experience as a classroom teacher, principal, supervisor, and college administrator in numerous publications, lectures, workshops, and professional organizations. Dr. Ramsey has traveled extensively in Europe, the Far East, the People's Republic of China, and Taiwan as lecture tour director and liaison to educational systems. Her present research interests center on leadership, language development, and creativity.

CHAPTER ONE

Beginning the Musical Journey

We are the music makers,
And we are the dreamers of dreams. . .

Arthur O'Shaughnessy, 1881

It was time for the annual holiday program. Because I had a background in music, my principal appointed me chair of the program committee. I was excited! This was my first year teaching, my first class of 5-year-olds, and the principal wanted me to be in charge of the program. I decided that our whole K–3 school would perform *The Nutcracker Suite,* complete with costumes, music, props, and all the embellishments. I was eager to impress the parents and the other teachers, so I decided to teach my kindergarten girls the ballet, "The Waltz of the Flowers," and my kindergarten boys, "The Dance of the Toy Soldiers." For weeks I taught these children perfect steps, perfect timing, turn right, stand still, curtsey, and step and turn. At first my kindergartners seemed to enjoy it, but as the days and weeks went on, they started resisting going to practice or would actually beg not to have to do "the program" again. On several occasions, some complained of being tired, while others had great difficulty with self-control . . . disrupting, acting inappropriately, hitting, and being generally unhappy; however, we did make it to the big night. The parents loved the performance. We all congratulated ourselves on a wonderful program. I remember talking with a first-grade teacher about how much the children loved it and what a good time they had. The truth is that the children were exhausted. They were fidgety and irritable, tired and pouty. Some even fell asleep before the program ended.

After a long weekend, the children returned to school and seemed to be the happy, well-adjusted children they had been before I had this brilliant idea of producing *The Nutcracker.* Young children, as we all know, are so resilient. In the weeks that followed, they didn't want me to play any music during center time. I would put on a Hap Palmer album, and they would argue about the right and wrong way to "get up in the morning." Why would kindergartners turn against the sacred Hap Palmer? I tried playing more of their favorites, Prokofiev's *Peter and the Wolf* and Debussy's *La Mer* and, of course, the music from *The Nutcracker.* My children didn't want to hear the music from the ballet; they didn't want me to play any music at all. Just the mention of the words dance or costume or program would change the mood of our whole classroom environment. Although it took some time— several weeks as I remember—my children finally came back to music. By early spring they were again requesting their favorite music and especially enjoyed listening to the "Spring" movement from Vivaldi's *Four Seasons.* (Edwards & Nabors, 1993, p. 78)

When thinking about how to begin this chapter, the story you just read seemed most appropriate. These events actually took place in a kindergarten classroom. This was obviously a performance-based experience, or product-oriented approach, to music in early childhood.

These little children had been forced to perform (under the name of "music" and, more specifically, "dance") in ways that were totally inappropriate for children their age. Not only were these children involved in inappropriate practice, but teacher-centered ideas had been imposed on these children, forcing them to become waltzing flowers and toy soldiers without regard as to how they might interpret or create their own ideas, thoughts, images, or forms of expression.

How do you feel about expressing your ideas through music, creative movement, or dance? Are you musical? Do you enjoy singing "Happy Birthday" to loved ones or dancing with friends when the music is so good you just can't sit still? Have you ever noticed yourself tapping your foot in rhythm with a great band or standing to applaud for an encore at the end of a beautifully orchestrated symphony? Most of us probably have some of these musical competencies, while others have a deeper connection with music either as consumers or performers. Whatever our current level of musical involvement, any effort we make toward increasing our musical abilities and talents certainly falls under the broad definition of being creative.

Chenfeld defines a creative teacher as "a person who is open, flexible, willing to try new things and risk their failing, honest, responsive to people and situations, and welcoming of new experiences" (1978, p. 39). Most of us who have chosen teaching as a profession are willing to venture into new and different situations. In this case, the adventure involves exploring music. After all, musical happenings occur spontaneously as we hum a familiar melody or sing along with a favorite recording artist.

However, if you are saying to yourself, "I really can't sing," don't worry. A beautiful singing voice is not a requirement for bringing meaningful musical experiences to young children. You can recite or chant fingerplays and action songs. The rhythm is more interesting to children than the melody. You can use recordings, simple instruments such as an autoharp or melody bells, or the talents of a musical volunteer. If your body just doesn't feel rhythm in movement or dance, begin slowly by experimenting with the different types of movement presented in this book, and open yourself to the possibility of discovering something new about yourself and your musical creativity. Your children will respond to you, their teacher, and your enthusiasm, interest, and spontaneity. If you trust yourself enough to try, your children and their responses will help build your confidence.

Now let's take a look at how children respond to music and movement. More specifically, how do young children enjoy music and movement?

MUSIC AND MOVEMENT: ENJOYMENT AND VALUE FOR CHILDREN

Young children are action oriented. Not only are singing, moving, and dancing fun, but they also provide young children opportunities to listen, respond, imitate, and use their voices, fingers, hands, arms, and bodies in ways that are creative and uniquely theirs.

In his classic book, *Teaching the Child Under Six* (1981), Hymes writes about the "style and swing" of the young child in one of the clearest, most articulate descriptions ever written. Hymes must know more about the qualities of young children than most people in our profession. He reminds us of the following ways in which young children "flow" differently from their older brothers and sisters:

- Young children are not good sitters.
- Young children are not good at keeping quiet.
- Young children are shy.
- Young children are highly egocentric.
- Young children want to feel proud, big, and important.
- Young children have their private dream world.
- Young children are very tender.
- Young children are beginners.
- Young children are hungry for stimulation.
- Young children are earthy, practical, concrete-minded.
- Young children are acquiescent.
- Young children are illiterate. (pp. 38–46)

Hymes also says that our capacity and willingness to live with these qualities makes the crucial difference between a good classroom (and teacher) and one that does not fit the age or provide child-appropriate experiences for young children.

How does Hymes's description of the style and swing of young children apply to music and movement? The answer lies in our approach and our attitude toward developing musical experiences for children who are action oriented. They need room to move both indoors in the classroom and outside in the play yard. Dancing, rhythmic movement, and action songs all provide ample opportunity for action. A former graduate student coined a phrase that seems especially appropriate here: "Sitting still and being quiet is not a marketable skill" (R. W. Cain, personal communication, 1984). Since young children are not good at being quiet, they need the freedom to make a joyful noise by singing, playing instruments, and making up sing-songs and chants as they play and work.

Shy children should be given opportunities to play with musical ideas in small groups. Hymes calls these groups "safe personal clusters." When you see or hear shy children gingerly exploring the properties of a triangle and mallet or singing quietly to themselves during center time,

remember that they are tentative in their efforts and may not yet be ready to join the whole-class activities.

The egocentric nature of young children will show in their excitement when they stop you in the middle of an activity and say, "Watch me do the little rabbit song all by myself," "I can move just like a butterfly," or "I went to the circus, and they had a band that played clown music." They begin their sentences with *I*, and the sensitive teacher takes time to listen to the musical news children bring to the classroom.

The main purpose of including music and movement in the classroom is enjoyment. Through music and movement, young children express themselves, explore space, develop language and communication skills, increase sensory awareness, and express themselves through rhythm, gesture, time, and space.

Four Important Reasons for Including Music in the Classroom

Van der Linde (1999) outlines six reasons why the importance of music and movement activities should not be underestimated. Among these are four that are particularly relevant here:

1. *Mental capacity and intellect.* There is a connection between music and the development of mathematical thinking. Mathematical concepts are developed as children sing counting songs.
2. *Mastery of the physical self.* Children develop coordination, which aids muscular development. They begin to understand what they can do with their bodies as they run, balance, stretch, crawl, and skip.
3. *Development of the affective aspect.* Through music and movement, children learn acceptable outlets to express feelings and relieve tension. Music may also convey a specific mood through which children reveal their feelings and emotions.
4. *Development of creativity.* Music can create an imaginary world that stimulates a child's creativity. A box can become a drum, a stick can be transformed into a horn, or a broom can become a dance partner. Children make up songs or give new words to old songs for pure enjoyment. (pp. 2–5)

It is sometimes all too easy to miss the opportunity to expand on the music and movement experiences of a child's budding musical awareness. The imaginary world, the dream world, is a private place where children can sort out ideas before actually implementing those ideas. They can imagine how a butterfly moves from flower to flower before re-creating their own interpretation of pretending to fly like a butterfly. Teachers must encourage imagery and fantasy throughout music and movement activities. It is a natural resource that children bring with them to the classroom and one that encourages the development of musical processes that are foundational to future thinking and perceptual organization. Tender children who are just beginning to discover their ability to soar like an eagle, dance with the flowers, sing for the pure joy of hearing their own voices, or pretend to gallop swiftly like a pony look to their teacher to provide a safe place where they can explore all the possibilities their bodies, minds, and voices hold for musical and bodily-kinesthetic development.

Young children love to repeat things. They want to "sing it again!" and "move like a zigzag!" They are hungry for ideas that tap into their curiosity of how the Eensy-Weensy Spider goes up the water-spout; they want to move and dance when the spirit strikes them. They need teachers who will design a variety of rich musical experiences to help them test out things for themselves. We can play a recording by Hap Palmer or Raffi, but we must give children permission to test out their own ways of interpreting what they hear in ways that are right and personal to them.

A good classroom is geared to music. A sensitive teacher celebrates the clumsy and often awkward beginnings children make in their attempts to move rhythmically. Caring about the whole child means honoring all aspects of their musical expression. An awareness of the values of musical encounters provides the wise teacher with many choices and worthwhile possibilities for immersing children in a rich variety of songs, fingerplays, and other musical experiences.

A child's awareness of music begins very early. Infants can be comforted by quiet singing, music boxes, and musical toys. As they make cooing sounds and begin babbling, infants experiment with different tones and rhythmic patterns. Typical toddlers can frequently be observed clapping, dancing, or parading around the room, trying out different ways of moving to musical beats and rhythmic patterns. Young children are sensitive to musical sound and respond freely and joyfully to different tempos and beats. At the same time, they discover new and different ways to use their bodies and voices.

Throughout the childhood years, children's major accomplishments in musical development in turn support many developmental milestones. One important byproduct of exploration of music and movement is language development. Communication for the very young child is largely nonverbal, and music and movement can enhance and expand the child's repertoire of communication skills and abilities. Children experiment with familiar word patterns as they combine words with a tune. They imitate rhythmic patterns and combine these with physical activity as they communicate through move-

ment or dance. Children play with words as they change the lyrics to familiar songs or make up chants to accompany their play activity. Verbal and motor cues help children remember new words or sequences of words. They experience regular beats, changes in tempo, accents, and synchronization, all of which are an integral part of communicating in words and sentences.

As with all areas of the curriculum, developmentally appropriate music and movement activities will be successful only if you, the teacher, understand why music and movement are important tools for assisting children in constructing knowledge about their world and helping them make sense of their experiences. Admittedly, music and movement *can* be used in an integrated curriculum to enhance other subject areas, such as the language arts, but as Metz (1989) cautions, "Simply using music in an educational setting does not insure that children's musical perceptions are developing. . . . We need to focus on music as 'an end in itself'" (p. 89).

We further believe that, as teachers, we must be well versed in not only *how* to bring musical experiences to

Keep a camera loaded with film so you can capture a creative moment in progress.

children, but also *why* music is so essential to the young child's overall development. One way to facilitate our understanding of the "why?" is to look at the perspective that developmental theory has to offer. The next section provides some insight into why children need music in their lives and why music stands alone as an important subject area.

Beginning the Process of Planning

Children need to be provided with the circumstances for the development of all of their capabilities. When nurturing children's musical intelligence, we should provide a variety of experiences to support musical expression. For example, sing simple songs or let your children hear you humming, listen to music throughout the day, and play instruments to signal transition periods or to announce special happenings. Play background music in the classroom, and play special recordings regularly during specific times, such as after lunch or just before the children leave at the end of the day. Select many different varieties of musical compositions and styles to encourage your children to use their imaginations to see musical imagery. Introduce musical concepts that focus on the great classical composers and how classical compositions sound different from, for example, commercial musical jingles. Use music to help children relax after a period of high-energy activity. Play Debussy's *La Mer* (The Sea) before reading *One Morning in Maine,* or play a lively jazz recording just before you read *Ben's Trumpet.*

Educators have intuitively emphasized musical and physical activity as a part of children's learning experiences, but until recently, we have perhaps failed to realize fully the musical and bodily-kinesthetic learning that can take place when we purposely and systematically offer activities and experiences that nurture and support these two important areas of learning and knowing. The theory and educational philosophy supporting every person's capacity to develop a wide range of human intelligence reflects the influences of Howard Gardner. (Chapter 5 presents a comprehensive discussion of Gardner's theory of multiple intelligences.) Curricula designed to facilitate the development of musical and bodily-kinesthetic intelligence must be promoted through child-appropriate learning activities and teaching methods. At a very early age, children can begin to form concepts of music, movement, and dance that will serve as the base for later intellectual growth. Moreover, all children deserve opportunities to learn in ways that suit their individual and highly personal modes for knowing, learning, and processing information.

BASIC STAGES OF EARLY MUSICAL DEVELOPMENT

Before you begin thinking about ways to plan and implement music and movement experiences for young children, it is important to have an understanding of the basic stages of early musical development. Figures 1-1, 1-2, and 1-3 provide a descriptive overview of musical development and suggest ideas for music and movement activities for children from birth to 6 years.

This overview of early musical development provides you with an important framework for developing goals for music and movement experiences with your children. Another very important point for you to consider in this process is the National Association for the Education of Young Children's position statement on developmentally appropriate practice.

Music Skills Development from Birth to Six Years

The following material, written by Cohen and Gross, first appeared in "Let's Make Music" in the March 1982 issue of *Parents.* These developmental tables (Figures 1–1 through 1–3) show when one might expect a child to begin new music skills. It's important to remember, however, that every child develops at a unique pace. While the order of these sequences is generally the same for all children, the age at which a particular child progresses from one stage to another may vary.

Whatever their age, children need to be actively involved in making music. As you become familiar with the way they are progressing through their musical development, you'll become more adept at recognizing the signals they give you about their musical interest and inclinations. You don't have to be a trained musician to help children explore their musical potential in the early years. You'll find plenty of opportunity to provide them with encouragement. And whether or not they are destined to become musical "greats," they can still enjoy the tremendous rewards that music brings and can spend a lifetime exploring and expanding the natural music abilities that are part of all of us.

DEVELOPMENTALLY APPROPRIATE PRACTICE

The concept of developmentally appropriate practice provides a clear description of appropriate practice for programs serving the full age span of early childhood. A

Figure 1-1   Listening and Moving to Music

Birth to 4 Months
Awareness of music starts almost immediately. The baby may show his early awareness by responding differently to different kinds of music; he quiets himself to a soothing lullaby and becomes more active when lively music is played.

4 to 8 Months
Musical awareness becomes more active. The baby now enjoys listening intently to all types of sounds in her environment. She begins showing more active awareness of musical sounds by turning her head or face toward the source of the music.

10 to 18 Months
Expression of musical preferences begins. The infant may begin indicating the types of music he likes best—many at this age prefer vocal to instrumental—as well as showing clear displeasure at music he does not like. He rocks or sways his hips to a familiar tune, although not necessarily in time with the music, and claps his hands to a pleasing song.

18 Months to 2 Years
Exploration of musical sounds increases. Sounds in her environment continue to captivate the toddler. Her developing language skills and increasing mobility allow her to seek out sounds that please her most. She may especially enjoy music on daily TV or radio programs or commercials and may watch with fascination as a family member plays a musical instrument.

2 to 3 Years
Dance begins. The toddler now attempts to "dance" to music by bending his knees in a bouncing motion, turning circles, swaying, swinging his arms, and nodding his head. He especially likes a marked rhythm, so band music, nursery songs, or catchy TV jingles may be favorites. He shows an increasing ability to keep time and to follow directions in musical games, which he loves. You'll also notice that he can now pay attention for longer periods. While easily distracted in the past, he can now lie or sit down quietly and listen for several minutes at a time.

3½ to 4 Years
Self-expression through music increases. At this stage, a very significant change takes place. As the child listens, she is increasingly aware of some of the components that make up her favorite music. She may love to dramatize songs and may also enjoy trying out different ways of interpreting music (for example, experimenting with different rhythms). She shows marked improvement in keeping the beat, although she is still not always entirely accurate. (Music is now an important means for her to express and communicate ideas and emotions that may be beyond her developing language skills.)

4 to 5 Years
Ability to discuss musical experiences expands. By now, the child can talk about what a piece of music suggests to him, and he is able to tell you in greater detail what he is hearing. This is the stage of the "active listener." With encouragement, the child's desire to listen to music will increase.

5 to 6 Years
Actual coordinated dance movements begin. The child's increased motor control and ability to synchronize his movements with the rhythm of the music are evident as one watches his attempts to dance. He can actually synchronize hand or foot tapping with music and can skip, hop on one foot, and make rhythmic dance movements to music. He may begin to show an interest in dance lessons.

Source: Marilyn A. Cohen and Pamela J. Gross, *The Developmental Resource,* Grune and Stratton, Inc., 1979. Copyright © 1982 Gruner & Jahr USA Publishing. Reprinted from *Parents* Magazine by permission.

summary of these important guidelines, as they relate to music, dance, and other musical experiences, is provided in Figure 1-4. Use this information to further your understanding of the role you play in providing musical experiences that match your children's developmental levels.

Remember that these developmentally appropriate practices represent the minimum that we should be doing to expand children's musical and movement experiences (Bredekamp, 1987; Bredekamp & Copple, 1997).

Figure 1-2 Singing

Birth to 4 Months
Crying is a baby's first "musical" sound. A baby's cries are her first and most important means of expressing early needs and feelings. They vary in pitch, loudness, and rhythmic patterns, making them musical in a very real sense. Gradually, she begins to experiment with other sounds; she coos, gurgles, squeals, and begins to "babble," repeating long strings of sound, such as "ba-ba-ba."

6 to 18 Months
Babbling increases, taking on more pronounced musical characteristics. As the baby continues to experiment with his voice, babbling becomes a favorite activity. As the infant's range of pitch, tone, and voice intensity widens, this activity comes to resemble song. Don't be surprised if at some point the baby is able to repeat the pitches you sing to him on exactly the same notes.

18 Months to 3 Years
Real singing begins. The baby's tuneful jabbering during play now sounds more like real song. She may chant a catchy rhyme, using nonsense syllables or even her own name as she plays, but she is still unable to sing a song like "Farmer in the Dell" completely accurately. She may join you in favorite nursery rhymes or songs; she especially enjoys familiar tunes and asks you to sing then repeatedly. (Although she'll sing along with you or a family member, she's still hesitant to sing in front of other children and may balk at a solo performance in preschool.)

3½ to 4 Years
Accuracy in matching simple tunes begins. Now the youngster starts to approximate adult singing. He may spontaneously make up his own songs, although the words are often repetitive and the tune may closely resemble one he already knows.

4 to 5 Years
Singing accuracy increases. The child shows increased voice control and a closer approximation of pitch and rhythm. She may sing an entire song accurately. Sometimes she creates songs during play and may use these songs to tease others. She shows more responsiveness in group singing and may even enjoy taking a turn singing alone. She takes great pride in her ability to identify favorite melodies.

5 Years and Older
Song repertoire expands; recognition and appreciation increase. Most children now produce simple tunes accurately. The child's expanded vocal range should allow him to reach higher notes more easily, and his rhythmic accuracy is noticeably improved. He pays more attention to a song's "dynamics" and tempo and is able to add subtleties to its rendition, expressing meaning and emotion with his voice.

Source: Marilyn A. Cohen and Pamela J. Gross, *The Developmental Resource,* Grune and Stratton, Inc., 1979. Copyright © 1982 Gruner & Jahr USA Publishing. Reprinted from *Parents* Magazine by permission.

Figure 1-3 Playing Musical Instruments

6 to 9 Months
Baby enjoys creating sounds with any object available. The infant's eye-hand coordination is rapidly improving. She loves to manipulate objects within reach and is fascinated with her newfound ability to make sounds with objects. She will tap, kick, or hit almost all objects with which she comes in contact, delighting in the sounds she creates.

18 Months to 2 Years
Toddler seeks special objects to make sounds. You may notice the toddler's repeated efforts to locate particular objects—pots and pans, cups, bowls, and other utensils—for his sound-making activities.

2 to 3½ Years
Interest in real musical instruments increases. At this stage, when the youngster is beginning to show interest in listening to musical instruments and recordings, provide her with toys that make interesting musical sounds, such as toy xylophones, drums, pipes, tambourines, or maracas. Musical toys needn't be expensive. In fact, you can easily make your own coffee-can drums, bottle-cap tambourines, soup-can shakers, or pot-cover cymbals.

4 to 5 Years
A child begins experimenting with real musical instruments. At this stage, the youngster can identify certain sounds made by selected instruments and can play many rhythm instruments, both to accompany songs or instrumental pieces he hears and to create tunes of his own. He may also enjoy trying out some of the instruments he has seen others play.

Source: Marilyn A. Cohen and Pamela J. Gross are educational consultants and coauthors of *The Developmental Resource,* Grune and Stratton, Inc., 1979. Copyright © 1982 Gruner & Jahr USA Publishing. Reprinted from *Parents* Magazine by permission.

Figure 1-4   Developmentally Appropriate Practice

- Teachers must sing with the children, do fingerplays, and take part in acting out simple stories like "The Three Bears" with children participating actively.
- Adults have to structure the physical environment to provide plenty of space and time indoors and outdoors for children to explore and exercise such large-muscle skills as running, jumping, galloping, or catching a ball. We also need to stay close by to offer assistance as needed. The old days of the teacher sitting in a chair during outdoor activity has, fortunately, disappeared.
- Adults in the classroom provide many experiences and opportunities to extend children's language and musical abilities. We introduce children to nursery rhymes and fingerplays; encourage children to sing songs and listen to recordings; facilitate children's play of circle and movement games such as "London Bridge," "The Farmer in the Dell," and "Ring Around the Rosie"; and present simple rhythm instruments as *real* instruments.
- Children must have daily opportunities for aesthetic expression and appreciation through hearing a variety of musical forms and compositions.

Babies enjoy listening to songs sung by a loving adult.

PLANNING FOR CHILDREN WITH SPECIAL NEEDS

It is very important to remember that *all* the children in your classroom can enjoy movement and music activities. Children with disabilities should never be excluded from experiencing the joy that music can bring to their lives. You might have to modify some activities to help your children with disabilities enter into the process, but you must view this extra planning as yet another way of giving special gifts to each child entrusted to your care. Moomaw (1984), Gee (1997), and S. Gurganus (personal communication, 2002) offer the following suggestions for engaging children with disabilities in music and movement activities.

Children with Physical Disabilities

Make sure that your children with physical disabilities are comfortable, feel balanced, and are positioned so that they can see and move their arms, hands, legs, or heads. Also, make sure that there is an adult near the children to observe them and make sure they are comfortable throughout the activity. Introduce songs that use the children's names or allow them to sing about what they are wearing or how they are feeling. Remember to focus on aspects of who they are as people rather than on their disabilities. Select movement songs that use the parts of the body that the child with physical disabilities *can* move so that they can participate fully. For example, if a child has difficulty with arm movement, plan an activity that allows for total body swaying or activities that emphasize head movements. If she is working on speech sounds, motor skills, eye-hand coordination, or other particular skills, design your activities in ways that allow her to practice these skills in a pleasurable and non-threatening manner.

Children with Hearing Impairments

For hearing-impaired children, plan rhythmic activities like clapping and chanting to help them develop a feel for rhythm. Use visual clues so that they can clap along with the other children. Children with hearing impairments should also have opportunities for free movement that is not related to sound or visual clues, so that they can experiment with different ways of creating their own movements. Let your children play instruments and feel the vibrations that come from striking a triangle or strumming an autoharp. Xylophones and melody bells are excellent instruments for children with hearing impairments because of the different vibrations each produces. Wood blocks, sticks, and maracas also enable children to feel vibrations. Although they may not hear the sound of the blocks or the click of the sticks, they can feel the vibrations as the blocks pass over each other and as the sticks strike, and they learn to play them rhythmically. Maracas have tactile appeal, and children can feel the vibrations as they shake these instruments. Many children with hearing impairments can hear good-quality, low-pitched drums. As they listen to these low pitches, they can also notice the feel of the vibrating drumhead. When hearing-impaired

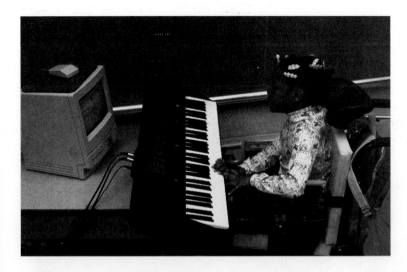

It is very important that teachers remember to plan music activities for all children, including children with special needs.

children place a hand on a portable tape player, they can feel the vibrations of a deep-bass pulsation through their hands. You may also gently take the child's hands and assist him or her during a clapping activity.

Gurganus (personal communication, 2002) recommends placing a compact disc player on the floor and turning the bass to the maximum volume. Invite hearing-impaired children to take off both shoes so that the vibrations of the bass can be felt through the feet. This enables them to feel the beat of the music so that they can move their bodies, arms, and heads to the rhythm of the musical beat. The children's own experiences when feeling rhythm and beat through vibrations is more important and meaningful than teacher-assisted instruction.

Children with Visual Disabilities

You will want to give special consideration to your children with visual disabilities when planning music and movement activities. Make sure they are seated next to an adult and that they have their own physical space. Talk about the music, describe the instruments, and encourage the children to explore the physical properties of a variety of instruments. You may need to show the children how to hold and play an instrument since they cannot use visual clues to learn these techniques. Playing instruments that require children to coordinate one hand with the other, such as rhythm sticks or triangles, may be difficult for children with visual disabilities. You can help a child succeed by holding the instrument still while he or she plays it. Movement activities are often frightening to children with visual disabilities. You must be sensitive to this fear and design movement activities that begin with stationary movements, such as bending or swaying. Once your children are comfortable moving in one spot, you

can gradually extend the movement experiences to safe ambulatory motions, such as crawling or rolling, since these keep the child in contact with the floor. Children with visual disabilities *can* learn how to hop and gallop or perform other more complicated movements, but you may have to guide them physically as they learn to do these movements. The important thing is to make sure the child with visual disabilities feels safe and knows that you or another adult are always close by. Figure 1-5 provides an overview for music and movement for children with disabilities.

Many elements of the music and movement curriculum are evident in current early childhood programs. Teachers who know how to plan for singing, dancing, playing instruments, and expressive movement to emerge are those who achieve the most important goals of music and movement activities. You will have to decide how to best arrange your environment so that it presents your children with an imaginary stage that invites them to enter freely into the music and movement activities you design. Your own resources and creative approach to musical experiences are the keys to a successful music and movement curriculum.

MUSIC AND MOVEMENT FOR YOUNG CHILDREN

There are a wealth of music and movement experiences that are appropriate for young children. Children move their bodies in expressive ways, they dance to the beat of the rhythms they hear, and they sing with a spontaneity unmatched by even the most melodic adult voices. Music and movement activities fill the early childhood classroom with radiant happy faces and laughing, joyful children. This section explores music

Figure 1-5   Music and Movement for Children with Disabilities

Music and movement experiences are as important to children with disabilities as they are to all the other children in your classroom. You must make modifications in your activities to help these children express themselves as freely as they can, while deriving all the benefits the musical experience provides. The following general guidelines will help you begin to plan music and movement activities for children with disabilities:

- Provide helmets as safety devices for children with limited balancing skills.
- Give hand signals as well as verbal signals, and face children each time you make a suggestion.
- Encourage children in wheelchairs to use facial expressions to represent how they feel as they move themselves or are pushed by you or others in the group.
- Provide tactile clues for children with visual disabilities and visual clues for children with hearing disabilities.
- Allow children with limited finger movements to use other body parts when mimicking fingerplays.
- Provide carpet squares so children will have an awareness of boundaries in the general space.
- Pair children who are visually impaired with other children who can provide personal, verbal clues (Broughton, 1986).
- When you are unsure about how to plan music and movement experiences for children with disabilities, seek the advice of the specialist in your school or district.

Providing props and open-ended materials is the teacher's responsibility. The availability of a variety of materials enables children to make choices.

and movement for young children and introduces several aspects of music and movement, including dance, singing, playing instruments, dramatic movement, and action songs.

Children and Dance in the Classroom

Isadora Duncan, one of the greatest dancers of the twentieth century, is credited with having announced before a performance: "If I could *tell* you what I mean, there would be no point in dancing." Her powerful statement certainly exemplifies how young children approach the process of movement and dance.

As teachers, our prime concern should be to nurture, develop, and deepen children's abilities to respond affectively to the sounds, melodies, and rhythms generated by music. Music and movement represent ways of knowing as well as ways of expressing feeling, and they allow children to move beyond the common ways of experiencing their world and expressing what they know

about it. Dancer Martha Graham once said, "The reality of the dance is its truth to our inner life; dance is the hidden language of the soul" (Brown, 1979, p. 50). "A dance is one instant of life—a vibratory piece of energy. A great piece of sculpture is never contained; it reaches out to affect the space around it. We exist in space—that is the energy of the world, and each of us is a recipient of that energy, if he so wills" (Mazo, 1991, p. 34).

With all of our understanding and acceptance of music, movement, and dance, it is of vital importance for the early childhood teacher to have both the willingness and sensibility to provide experiences in these ways of knowing for young children. To be better prepared to plan music, movement, and dance activities for your children, you should be aware of how young children explore these creative processes and how you can begin to stretch their horizons.

Basic Dance Movements

When movement experiences and the sensations of moving are connected to the expressive and imaginative powers of the mover, we have dance. Dance involves a heightened kinesthetic awareness, a bodily intelligence, and a sharpened perception of movement as an aesthetic experience.

While dance may be an eloquent art form, it is nevertheless a form of expression that can be made easily accessible to young children. There is general agreement among practitioners, theorists, and writers dealing with the nature of dance as to what basic movements form an overall conceptual framework for dance and dance education (Barrett, 1977; Dimondstein, 1971; Downey, 1995; Gensemer, 1985; Laban, 1948). All dance movements are a blending of three basic qualities: space, time, and force. Other factors that influence movement are flow, weight, body awareness, and relationships with others or objects. In addition, movement can occur through locomotion, nonlocomotion, representational responses, or a combination of two or more body movements. If all this sounds a bit complicated, relax. One of the most effective ways you can help children to develop the art of dance is to promote significant discussion about the meaning of these terms.

It is important to talk with children about the vocabulary of music and movement. Young children may not have the language skills or knowledge to use words like *time* in a musical context. They may relate time only to when they get up in the morning or to adults giving a clock significant meaning. Introduce music and dance vocabulary while your children are listening to music or exploring rhythm and beat so that the words are connected to their actual activity. Do not "lecture" children or teach them words and terminology out of context; instead, use accurate vocabulary unobtrusively as a means of describing what your children are experiencing.

The other thing you can do to expand your awareness of the language and the meaning of these words in a musical context is to respond to the creative movement process, not as a dance-educator "giving" dance to children, but rather as a regular classroom teacher who is actively involved in sensing your own feelings for creative movement: "When children see adults working creatively, they understand this is something that people do in real life, something that gives enjoyment and satisfaction, and is not just a classroom exercise. In this way, children are able to move away from relying entirely on explanations and secondhand information, and have the chance to witness the behaviors and even the physical movements involved" (Dixon and Chalmers, 1990, pp. 16–17). Again, it is important to remember that we are focusing on the *process* of movement, not on the *product*.

Following are descriptions of common terms used in movement and dance:

Space

This word refers to the manner in which we use an area for movement. This can be either a "personal space" that no one else can enter or a more expansive area of "general space," which is everywhere else. Children need to be aware that once they are in a space, whether standing or sitting, that space becomes occupied. In movement and dance, the perception of space is viewed in relation to the body, the space of others, and the unoccupied place or general space.

You can help children define their personal space by asking them to extend their arms while turning around and around to make sure they can't touch anyone else. You might tap their imaginative powers by asking them to pretend that they are moving inside a very large bubble. Young children can carry their personal space with them as they move during locomotor activities. Leaping, jumping, skipping, and sliding are examples of locomotor activities that involve moving from one place to another.

Locomotor activities require a large, uncluttered space. You don't need a space as large as a gymnasium; a large open area in your classroom or even outdoors is more than adequate. It is important to remember that your children need to hear you and your suggestions during movement activities. In a large, oversized room, the children will have difficulty seeing and hearing you. If you find, however, that a large area is the only space available to you, you can easily solve the problem of the children not being able to hear you by using a percussion instrument (drum or tambourine) to signal to children that it is time for them to stop and listen. Movement invites squeals of delight, laughter, and many other appropriate "child sounds." A signal can provide structure and predictability to music and movement experiences, both of which are important in establishing and maintaining a secure and trusting environment in which your children feel safe to explore the process.

Time

Time is a quality of tempo or rhythm. A movement can be slow or fast (time) and a succession of muscular relaxations and rests (rhythm). The speed of movement can change from faster to slower. A child's sense of tempo can be facilitated by a simple, percussion accompaniment that provides beats or a grouping of beats. In movement and dance, rhythm comes from two sources: either from music where children hear rhythm as it is produced through sound, or from dance, where children create rhythm from their movements. Moreover, the tempo of a movement can be a series of rhythmic changes involving a total kinesthetic response by which a child organizes and interprets tempo and rhythm through both internal and external stimuli (that is, what they hear in the music and the spontaneous feelings and emotions they feel in their bodies).

Time for young children is *not* "keeping time" or "being in time" with the music. Rather, it is an opportunity for children to be involved in exploration and improvisation of the qualities of tempo and rhythm. Dimondstein

(1971) cautions us to not ask children to "dance by the numbers." Allow children to respond in ways that they can control their bodies and broaden the scope of their rhythmic expression.

Force

The concept of force is also important in movement and dance. Children experience light, heavy, sudden, or sustained qualities of movement that require varying degrees of muscular tension. As children explore different qualities of force, they can experience the difference between pushing and pulling and between heaviness and lightness. They become aware of balance and the transference of body weight. Most important, perhaps, is that through an exploration of force, children may begin to understand the idea of being "centered," controlling their bodies from a place of balance from which energy is released and controlled.

Gensemer defines *force* as "the amount of tension or stress of a movement; the flow and control of energy" (1985, p. 39). For example, there are sustained movements expressed as smooth, easy-going flows of energy, such as lifting an imaginary heavy object. There are swinging movements where one part of the body moves around another, such as swinging our arms in a circle over our heads. Percussion movement requires a sudden, quick, sharp release of energy, as when we shake a hand or a leg or our whole selves. Percussion movement can be facilitated by using instruments that produce sounds by hitting or beating. Children can discover the amount of force they use when beating a drum or hitting a triangle.

Locomotor Activity

Locomotor refers to the quality of moving through space. Walking, running, jumping, hopping, skipping, leaping, sliding, and galloping are examples of locomotor movements. Nonlocomotor movements are stationary. Children move in ways that do not require them to move away from their area. Examples of nonlocomotor movement include stretching, bending, turning, twisting, swinging, and curling.

Throughout all of these expressive movement and dance encounters, children explore direction (straight, forward, backward, up, down), levels (high, low, or somewhere in between), relationships (above, below, over, under, through, around), and position of movement (horizontal, vertical, diagonal). Children also learn to organize the available space in relation to themselves and to objects and other individuals. As children experiment with and explore all of these different ways of creative movement, they are developing body control and confidence in the power and ability of their own bodies. Best of all, they are finding intrinsic

pleasure in "being" the creator of movement and dance rather than "imitating" a prescribed, "follow me and do as I do" approach.

Young children are beginners; they are just beginning to make discoveries about the vast repertoire of expression that comes through movement and dance. There will be plenty of time for them to take formal dance lessons in the next 20 or more years of formal "schooling" that lie ahead.

SELECTING SONGS, FINGERPLAYS, AND INSTRUMENTS

Singing songs, moving to music, and transforming little fingers into birds, rabbits, or falling rain form the basis for many types of musical expression. Young children who have positive and pleasurable experiences with rhythm and movement will want to repeat these experiences. Young children sing spontaneously while they play. They make up nonsense chants and songs as they experiment with variations in rhythm, pitch, and volume: Jane listens as her teacher magically transforms his fingers into two little blackbirds, one named Jack and one named Jill. She attends to the story line and the actions of this fingerplay and begins to respond with a few words and finger movements of her own. When she moves to the outdoor classroom, she lifts her arms and flies around the play yard singing, "This is Jack, and this is Jill!"

This 4-year-old finds intrinsic pleasure in learning a new fingerplay, and the enthusiasm of her teacher and his seriousness about the process have transcended circle time. A simple fingerplay has become a part of this child's universal experience—in this case, that of flying around the play yard.

Singing with Young Children

Songs for toddlers should be short, easy to sing, and have a steady beat. Songs should also have a lot of repetition, as these children will often remember the chorus of a song long before they learn all the words to the verse. When pitching songs for young children, be sure that the range is well within their vocal abilities. Try pitching songs in the range between middle C up to G, a fifth above. If you don't know where middle C is located on the piano keyboard, find someone in your class who can find middle C on a piano, or ask your professor to show you how to find a middle C chord on an autoharp. Or find a piano and, beginning at the far left of the keyboard, count the white keys until you get to the 24th white key: this is middle C!

As children develop their singing voices, their range extends, sometimes by as much as an octave above and below middle C. Remember that even if you don't like your singing voice, you can still introduce and sing songs with your children. There are not many of us who have beautifully trained singing voices, so if you don't relish the idea of strumming a guitar as you sing to a group of children, you are most likely in the majority! Your children will always be more interested in the interaction than they are in your perfectly pitched, or unpitched, singing voice.

Young children enjoy a variety of songs and especially seem to like songs that have personal meaning, such as songs about their names, body parts, clothes, feelings, and special occasions like birthdays. Songs about children's interests—home and family, things that happen at school, and animals and pets—are appealing. Songs about animals, in which children can imitate or make animal sounds, capture children's interest and encourage them to become involved in singing activities.

It is very important for you to have a large repertoire of songs and chants available "in the moment." Teachers must constantly search for new songs and fingerplays, as they are an invaluable resource in the day-to-day happenings in the early childhood classroom.

Selecting Songs for Singing

Out of the hundreds of songs that you can introduce to children, several categories of songs are used most often in the early childhood classroom. You might consider learning songs from the following categories before your singing debut with young children. For your children, singing and moving must be a purely pleasurable experience and not a "teaching method" for activating budding young composers or maestros.

Old Traditional and Folk Songs
Many traditional and folk songs come to us from all around the world, and most tell a story or convey a simple message that children can understand. Some favorites include the following:

"Where Is Thumbkin?"
"This Old Man, He Played One"
"I'm a Little Teapot"
"Two Little Blackbirds"
"Miss Mary (Molly) Mack"

Nursery Rhymes
The melodies of nursery rhymes are always favorites of young children. Because of their simple and catchy melodies, they are easy to sing and most appropriate for the young child.

"Mary Had a Little Lamb"
"Twinkle, Twinkle, Little Star"
"London Bridge"
"Here We Go ' Round the Mulberry Bush"

Lullabies
Lullabies are wonderful for quieting and calming children after active periods or before nap time. They are also useful when encouraging children to imagine that they are rocking a little bunny or a baby doll to sleep. It's very special to sing lullabies to children and watch their sweet eyes close for some much-needed sleep.

"Hush, Little Baby"
"Rock-a-Bye Baby"
"Are You Sleeping?"
"Lullaby and Good Night"

Fingerplays and Action Songs

Fingerplays are, in a sense, a type of rhythmic improvisation. They have strong appeal to young children because there is usually repetition of melody, words, and phrases. There seems to be some magic in transforming a tiny finger into a "Thumbkin" or a rabbit, or "shaking all about" during "The Hokey Pokey." In fingerplays and action songs, the words provide suggestions or directions on what, how, when, and where to move. In general, children enjoy the continuity of hearing and playing with the fingerplays and action songs from the beginning to the end. If the fingerplays are short (or led by a teacher) and action songs are simple and repetitive, children can learn the actions or movements after doing them a few times. With longer action songs and fingerplays, it is still important that children first hear the entire song. When children are familiar with the content, lyrics, and melody, you can always divide the song or fingerplay into smaller, more manageable parts. Echo chants and fingerplays, such as "Let's Go on a Bear Hunt," are very easy for children to respond to because they are led by the teacher. The teacher chants a phrase, and the children chant it back. Echo chants are popular among young children because all they have to remember is one short line or simple phrase.

Fingerplays and other action songs can relate to curriculum development and can be used to enhance a young child's understanding of concepts. For example, the action chant "Let's Go on a Bear Hunt" reinforces the concepts of under, over, around, and through. At the same time, action songs and fingerplays that directly relate to the children can provide personal, concrete experiences that are relevant and meaningful to the young child. "Where Is

Thumbkin?" is an all-time favorite of young children. It is their fingers and arms that are the center of attention and the stars of the play.

Fingerplays and songs that encourage full-body movement are also helpful when it comes to transition times. "Teddy Bear, Teddy Bear, Turn Around" can be used to redirect children's energies when they need help to calm them down during transitions. The movement is fun, and children pick up cues from the words and move through transitions with ease and pleasure. The process is so much gentler to young children than ringing a bell or switching the lights off and on.

The traditional song "Come Follow Me in a Line, in a Line" is a delightful little tune that can also be used to assist children through transition periods. The teacher moves through a group of children while singing or chanting the verse in Pied Piper fashion and, one by one, touches the head of each child. As the children are touched, they join one hand and follow the teacher until they are all in a long, connected line. This is especially effective for moving children into a circle or a different area of the classroom. This calm process of forming a line and moving to a repetitive song allows you and your children to gather together or form a circle without the confusion that this request often causes!

COME FOLLOW ME IN A LINE, IN A LINE

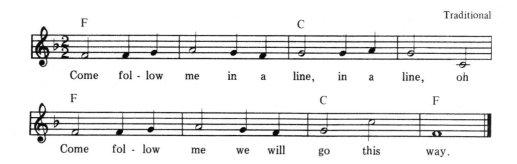

It is very important that we not limit the use of fingerplays and action songs to very young children. Children's abilities to elaborate and expand their movements, actions, and singing abilities increase with age and experience. Three-year-olds may sing or chant short melodic songs informally as they move through an activity. These young children may not remember all the words or even understand the exact meaning of some words, but they often remember the feeling they experienced during a song or fingerplay.

For the older child, fingerplays and songs offer great potential for learning new words, rhyming, and alliteration; developing language and verbal skills; and forming concepts. Teachers can also use songs and fingerplays to expand children's awareness of tempo, accent, rhythmic patterns, and intensity, all of which are part of the language and reading process.

Before using fingerplays and action songs with young children, you must learn and practice the words and movements until they are committed to memory. Fingerplays, especially, should involve a warm, intimate exchange between you and your children. This atmosphere can be lost if you have to read or refer to written notes during the play. You must be enthusiastic about sharing

fingerplays and action songs with your children and must be involved with both the play and your children. Learn and practice a few fingerplays until you are totally familiar with the words and actions. Once you are comfortable with the words and actions, you can present them with the warmth, naturalness, and spontaneity needed to give them excitement and life.

Feel free to change or revise the basic forms to create your own versions or to accommodate the ages or abilities of your children. Approaching action songs and fingerplays from this perspective will allow you to use your own creative abilities and should limit the potential stereotyping of having all of your children doing the exact same thing at the same time. Your children should make their "Eensy Weensy Spider" move the way they want it to move. And, if you'll think about it, all children shake their "Hokey Pokey" in individual and different ways!

Musical Instruments for Young Children

Making music by playing instruments can be one of the most exciting parts of the musical experience. Children are responsive to musical instruments, and they love to experiment with the different sounds and tone qualities

Drums are usually children's favorite instrument. One child told me that she feels special playing the drums.

of sticks, drums, cymbals, bells, and a variety of other instruments. Rhythm instruments, which are real musical instruments, provide rich and varied opportunities for young children to focus on creative exploration. Each instrument is different, they are simple to use, and they can be played in many interesting ways.

Appreciating Musical Instruments

While it is important for children to be free to manipulate and experiment with instruments, it is equally as important that we, their teachers, provide guidance and structure when introducing instruments. One of the first things that we must do is adopt the attitude that percussion and tuned instruments are real instruments. All major symphony orchestras use drums, triangles, bells, and other instruments in the traditional early childhood rhythm band sets.

Each instrument in your commercial rhythm band set can produce a distinctive and unique sound quality. Tuned instruments, such as resonator bells, have their own particular rich and resonating tone qualities. Young children stand ready to model our behavior and take our word on things, and our treatment of instruments and our attitude toward them can have a lasting effect on the way children handle and play all instruments.

Introduce one instrument at a time. If possible, have several identical instruments so that all of your children can explore and discover what sounds the instrument can make and how to produce these sounds. Young children

are not good at waiting. They want to play the instrument now! Encourage your children to try different ways to produce sounds. Give them the time they need to get to know the instrument. If you have only one set of instruments, try placing an instrument in a music center and introducing it as a small-group activity.

By introducing instruments one at a time, you allow your children to develop a musical sensitivity to each instrument gradually. When children have experimented with several instruments, you can encourage them to make rhythmic patterns or melodies. Give your children this type of respectful introduction to musical instruments. You will be opening an avenue for them to respond to rhythm, tone, melody, and harmony—an avenue to music. Figure 1-6 illustrates and explains the rhythm instruments that are appropriate for use with young children.

While the music and movement ideas presented above are good ways of getting you and your children started on the road to a music program, you should also consider some of the excellent recordings available. One advantage of using compact discs, or cassette tapes is that the songs are usually grouped and classified for specific purposes. It would be impossible to provide you with a complete list of what is suitable and available for use in the early childhood classroom, but you will find many suggestions throughout the book.

Give children music made all around the world as a way of beginning a lifetime discovery of other cultures and countries, from the reggae of Jamaica to the jigs and reels of Ireland to the zydeco of Louisiana. A wide variety of music and movement from across the globe can be a springboard for children's introduction to multicultural education in the classroom. Later in this book, you'll be introduced to many music and movement activities from cultures on opposite sides of the globe.

Classical Music and Children

Musical experiences for young children must include classical music in addition to the music we usually associate with the early childhood classroom. Some children in your classroom may be growing up in homes where classical music is played and appreciated. These children are indeed fortunate. For those children who are growing up on a minimal musical diet of rock-and-roll, rap, or "oldies," you may be the only resource for extending their musical experiences and the appreciation that comes from exposure to classical music. Research indicates that early association with classical music can increase children's enjoyment of music as an art form and increase children's aesthetic awareness (Cecil and Lauritzen, 1994).

Emile Jaques-Dalcroze (1865–1950), a Swiss composer and harmony professor at the Geneva Conservatory at the

Figure 1-6   Instruments for Young Children

Triangles are suspended from a cord so they hang freely. Strike them gently with a metal striker. The triangle produces a lovely, bright sound.

Claves are thick, polished sticks made of hardwood. Place one clave in the palm of your hand, and strike it with the other clave.

Rhythm sticks are played in pairs. They can be smooth or serrated. Play them by holding one rhythm stick and striking it with the other, or rub one along the ridges of the other. Rhythm sticks are wonderful for keeping time or, when appropriate, helping children maintain a steady beat.

Wood blocks are small, hollow blocks of wood that produce a resonant sound. Strike the wood block lightly with a wooden or hard rubber mallet.

Maracas are made from gourds (or hard plastic) and are filled with seeds or pebbles. Shake them sharply, at intervals, to produce rhythm. Maintain steady shaking for continuous sound.

Drums produce many different sounds, depending on how they are played. Drums can be played with your fingers, hand, or knuckles or with a drumstick or mallet. Drums sound best when struck with a quick bouncy touch so that the drumhead can reverberate.

Sand blocks are small wooden blocks covered with coarse sandpaper or emery cloth. Hold them by the handle or knob and rub them together.

Jingle bells mounted on sticks can be shaken vigorously or tapped rhythmically against your palm. Other types of jingle bells are mounted on plastic or fabric and can be shaken by hand or attached to an ankle or wrist.

Tambourines are a favorite of young children. They are circular frames of wood or plastic with a plastic or skin drumhead and small sets of jingles fastened around the frame. You can strike the head with your hand or finger, shake the tambourine to hear the jingles, or combine both actions.

turn of the century, thought of movement as a way of using the body as a "musical instrument" and believed that body movement was a counterpart to musical expression. He further believed that early musical intelligence could be encouraged by using one's body in conjunction with musical responsiveness. This understanding can be facilitated by drawing on the "universal language" of classical music: "Music is significant for us as human beings principally because it embodies movement of a specifically human type that goes to the roots of our being and takes shape in the inner gestures which embody our deepest and most intimate responses" (Jaques- Dalcroze, 1921, p. 129).

Classical music can be naturally infused into the early childhood classroom in a variety of ways, from playing Bach's Preludes during quiet activities to marching around the room to the "March of the Toys" from Herbert's *Babes in Toyland.* Figure 1-7 is an overview of classical music selections that seem to naturally invite children to move their bodies in certain rhythmic patterns.

Classical music comes in all forms, shapes, and sizes, and a few of the different styles available to you and your children are mentioned here. In addition to the symphony, there are sonatas, string quartets, concertos, concertinas, trios, and dances—and let's not forget opera. Opera has

Finger cymbals produce delightfully delicate sounds. Put one on a finger of each hand and bring them together to lightly chime the finger cymbals. You can also put one finger cymbal on your thumb and another on your middle finger of the same hand and strike them together.

Cymbals are usually made of brass and have handles or straps. Cymbals produce their best tone when they are struck while being moved in a vertical motion. Hold one cymbal slightly higher than the other, bring it down, and let it strike the lower one. You may want to practice playing cymbals and master the technique of producing a pleasant-sounding ring before you introduce cymbals to children. If your children can hear the lovely tone cymbals can make, they may be more inclined to respect them as a real musical instrument.

Resonator bells are played with a mallet and can provide children with experiences in pitch, melody, and harmony. Because resonator bells are tuned, children can experiment with an accurately pitched instrument while working out patterns and melodies.

Orff instruments were originally designed by German composer Carl Orff. Although these high-quality instruments are expensive, they are a wonderful addition to an early childhood environment. They produce beautiful, pure tones. The lowest pitched instrument, the metallophone, produces rich alto and bass tones. The bars are made of thick metal. The bars of the xylophone are made of hardwood. They are removable and can be taken apart and changed for different tonal patterns. The glockenspiel is the highest pitched instrument. The metal bars are also removable, and they produce a bright, soprano tone. Very young children may have difficulty playing the glockenspiel because of the small size, but 4- and 5-year-olds, as well as older children, will enjoy striking the bars and hearing the crisp, clear tones.

Autoharps can be valuable if you consider yourself to be a nonmusical teacher. You don't need special musical training to play an autoharp. It is a stringed instrument that can be played either by holding it flat on your lap or in an upright position. You strum the autoharp while pressing the buttons. Each button has a letter, or musical notation, that corresponds to the chords you are playing. Most music includes chord notation in the form of letters above the music bar. Follow the letter notation as you press the corresponding button while strumming the autoharp. Your children can learn to play the autoharp, too, so don't be afraid to let them explore all the chords, sounds, and sensory impressions the autoharp provides.

increased in popularity through the years, probably because the combination of music, movement, and speech are inseparably presented in ways that seem to touch our humanity. When opera is mentioned to students, they are often unexcited about studying opera because of lack of exposure or unpleasant experience. No one expects you to become an opera fan or that you introduce opera to your children in any formal kind of way. However, give yourself a gentle nudge and do not discount the idea of playing opera as quiet background music in your classroom. Children may not even notice that you have included a different type of music into your musical selections, but nevertheless you will have broadened their exposure to yet another classical form. Many years ago, after hearing selections from *Madame Butterfly* on several occasions during quiet time, a 5-year-old went up to the teacher and said that the lady's voice made her sleepy! What more could a kindergarten teacher ask for during quiet time?

Figure 1-8 lists some favorite instrumental classical music recordings that may be useful as you begin to build your own musical library, both for your personal enjoyment and for the listening pleasure of your children. These

Figure 1-7   Classical Music and Movement Exploration

Walking	Kabalevsky: "Pantomime" from *The Comedians*
	Prokofiev: "Departure" from *Winter Holiday*
Marching	Vaughan Williams: "March Past of the Kitchen Utensils" from *The Wasps*
	Grieg: "Norwegian Rustic March" from *Lyric Suite*
Hopping	Moussorgsky: "Ballet of the Unhatched Chicks" from *Pictures at an Exhibition*
	Bach: "Gigue" from *Suite No. 3*
Swaying, Rocking	Offenbach: "Barcarolle" from *The Tales of Hoffman*
	Saint-Saens: "The Swan" from *Carnival of the Animals*
Sliding, Gliding	Khachaturian: "Waltz" from *Masquerade Suite*
	Tschaikovsky: "Waltz" from *Sleeping Beauty*

can be found on inexpensive compact discs, and the sound quality is exceptionally good. These are not listed in any particular priority, so when you approach the classical section of your local music store, select the titles that suggest your own sensitivity to the possibilities these recordings may hold for you.

Classical music must be played in early childhood classrooms right along with Hap Palmer and Ella Jenkins. As McGirr tells us, "Too often, early childhood programs use only children's music, nursery rhymes, fingerplays and light, short humorous pieces, all played mainly on popular instruments. Young children are capable of much more sophisticated listening" (1995, p. 75). Exposure to classical music affords children unique opportunities to enjoy a whole complement of musical experiences and puts them in touch with a wide range of musical expression. "Even the youngest child, when given a proper chance, will respond sensitively to the music of great composers—Palestrina, Beethoven, Strauss, or Prokofiev—and should never be limited solely to a musical diet of fingerplays and one-line songs" (Franks, 1983, p. 54). Without exposure to the great classical composers and their

Figure 1-8   Your Classical Music Collection: Suggested Recordings

Wolfgang Amadeus Mozart. *Symphony no. 39 in E-flat* and *Symphony no. 41 in C. no. 39 in E-flat,* the first of Mozart's greatest trilogy, is dated June 26, 1788. Within the space of only six weeks, Mozart composed his last three symphonies, and *no. 39* is the only one of the three to take full advantage of clarinets. It is composed of an "Adagio," "Allegro," "Andante," "Menuetto," and "Finale." *No. 41 in C* is dated August 10, 1788. It is believed that Mozart knew this was to be his last symphony. The last movement seems to express with absolute finality all that Mozart could wish to say through the medium of the full orchestra.

Frederic Chopin. *Sonata no. 3, op. 58.* This sonata is for those of us who love piano music. Robert Schumann wrote this about Chopin's *Sonata no. 3, op. 58:* "The idea of calling it a sonata is a caprice, if not a jest, for he has simply bound together four of his most reckless children" (Van Cliburn, 1992). However, George Sand said, "The self-sufficing coherence he achieved in this work marks him as a master who knew precisely what he was doing" (Van Cliburn, 1992). There is intense beauty and power in this piece that accumulates fantastic momentum and rushes to the crowning point with immense boldness and brilliance. The coda fulfills the work with a fiery conclusion!

Ludwig van Beethoven. *String Quartet no. 3 in D Major* and *String Quartet no. 4 in C Minor.* The string quartet has four parts so a composer has enough lines to fashion a full musical form; there is not much to spare for "padding." Beethoven was a long-term planner and follower-through of highly organized musical composition, and his string quartets, as his sketchbooks show, are filled with almost superhuman laboriousness. In the life work that came from four decades of compositional toil, he completed sixteen string quartets.

Johann Sebastian Bach. *Brandenburg Concertos nos. 1–6.* Bach was a composer of the Baroque period. At the head of an orchestra, he was a dominating figure and score reader. His hearing was so fine that he was able to detect even the slightest error in a large orchestra: "While conducting, he would sing, play his own part, keep the rhythm steady, and cue everybody in, the one with a nod, another by tapping with his feet, the third with a warning finger, holding everybody together, taking precautions everywhere and repairing any unsteadiness, full of rhythm in every part of his body." His vision was the greatest, his technique unparalleled, his harmonic sense frightening in its power, expression, and ingenuity. The *Brandenburg Concertos* are pronounced in the qualities of who Bach was as a person. They are filled with mysticism, exuberance, complexity, decoration, allegory, distortion, and exploitation of the grandiose (Schonberg, 1981). If you don't already own a recording of the *Brandenburg Concertos,* you must discover how all these qualities are represented in his music.

music, we cannot expect children to develop an appreciation for *all* music. Furthermore, without this opportunity, some children may not find out that classical music exists until they are young adults and find themselves in a college-level music appreciation class. We must encourage even the youngest children to listen to a variety of music, including classical, if we want them to develop musical appreciation in the broadest context.

PROCESSES FOR MUSIC AND MOVEMENT

One of your primary responsibilities as a teacher of children is to establish a warm and safe environment of trust, freedom, and communication where positive and pleasurable music and movement experiences happen. Enjoyment of expression is the prime value of music and movement. We must be very careful that we don't demand perfection of form as children move through space or experiment with time and force. "Children move because movement gives them a tremendous lift, a sense of freedom, exhilaration akin to flying high above the waters, above the clouds, above the earth, and into the sky" (Logan & Logan, 1967, p. 39). Our job is to create an atmosphere that welcomes this freedom.

How will you structure this atmosphere? How will music and movement thrive in your classroom? Involvement is more likely in an atmosphere in which children feel and are assured of the following conditions:

- It is safe to try.
- I can deal with events.
- My teacher encourages me to make the attempt.
- I am fulfilled for having done so.

When children find themselves in a safe, supportive, and encouraging environment, they are free to explore, experiment, and respond with unlimited creative expression. Once you have established an environment in which children feel safe to try out new and different ways of expressing themselves, you may wonder how to begin. Good teachers always begin with a plan, and the following sections can be translated into lesson plans as you prepare to begin this journey with your children.

Introducing Movement and Dance

Ensure that your children know that they have their own space and that their space belongs to them and only them. You can help your children identify their personal space by guiding them through an imagery process of finding their own imaginary space bubble.

1. Walk among the children, and point out all the space in the room. Show them the empty spaces between tables and chairs and wave your hand in the space between children. Ask the children to look up and see the space between them and the ceiling.
2. Have children find a space on the floor where they can stand, sit, or lie down without touching anyone else. Ask the children to move their hands and arms around, filling up as much space as they can.
3. Encourage children to move their legs and stretch them as far as they can, seeing how much space they can fill with just their legs.
4. Tell children to stand and move their arms through their own space, reaching as far as they can without moving their feet. Ask them to explore their own space with their feet and legs.
5. Ask your children to imagine that they are inside a big space bubble that is theirs alone. Tell them that no one else can come into their bubble or into their space unless they are invited. They can move inside their imaginary space bubble in many different ways. They can also carry their space bubble with them as they move around the room.

Materials for Creative Movement

The use of materials and props can also encourage and stimulate children to express themselves through movement. Materials that are especially enjoyable to young children include these:

Scarves
Give your children lightweight, colorful scarves, and encourage them to let each scarf flow up and down and all around as they move through space. Scarves can be magically transformed into capes for flying, wings for soaring, or umbrellas for dancing in the rain.

Streamers
Children can use long streamers to make interesting, flowing designs as they move and sway in a group movement activity. When placed on the floor, streamers can define a space or become a bridge for little billy goats to tramp across.

Hoops
You can place several hoops on the floor and let the children explore different ways of moving inside the hoop, in and out of the hoop, and outside the hoop. Encourage your children to experiment with putting some parts of their body inside the hoop and other body parts outside. For example, ask the children, "Can you put both feet in the hoop and let your hands walk around the outside of the hoop?" They also can use the hoops as they would a single jump rope to practice jumping skills.

When you get a new parachute, you must cut off the sewn-in handles.

Beanbags

Play the beanbag game. Give each child a beanbag (have a variety of colors available). The leader (either the teacher or another child) suggests movements for the other children to follow: Put your beanbag on your head, and walk around the room without letting it fall off. Put the beanbag on your shoulder, your arm, your elbow, your foot. Put it on your back, and crawl around the room. Put it on the floor, and jump over it. Sit on your beanbag. Roll over your beanbag. Toss it into the air, and catch it with both hands. Combine the beanbag activities with the hoops or streamers.

Parachutes

Parachutes with sewn-in fabric handles should *not* be used with young children. Children have a tendency to put their little wrists through the handles, and this makes it difficult for them to free themselves when the parachute is filled with air. If your parachute does have these sewn-in fabric handles, cut them off. When the force of an air-filled parachute gets too strong for children to hold on, they must be able to let go easily so that they are not pulled in any uncomfortable position. Encourage your children to move the parachute up and down. Help them move it in a circular pattern, or put a lightweight ball in the middle and let them bounce the ball around. You and your children (with the help of a few extra adults) can make a momentary tent out of your parachute. Viewed from underneath, the colors are beautiful. It is an easy process: Position your children and several adults at close intervals around the parachute. Raise it high in the air until it is full of air, run under it, and quickly sit on the edges. The parachute will balloon, and you and your children will delight in the magical quality it creates!

The music and movement experiences in all of these activities can be changed and modified into developmentally appropriate practice for your children. Once you have had the personal experience of exploring the wonderful world of your own musical potential, you should also have a broader understanding of how you, as a professional, can bring similar yet age-appropriate activities to children. Your role as an early childhood teacher is to provide music and movement encounters that will bring satisfaction and enjoyment to your children. Mastery of pitch, rhythm, or melody is not the goal, and you certainly don't have to be a musical genius yourself. The goal is for young children to find pleasure and joy in the process of singing, moving, dancing, and playing instruments. Your job is to plan for these experiences, to be open and flexible in your planning, and to know the developmental levels of your children. You must search for new ideas and techniques. Even though young children love repetition, they will soon get tired of songs and fingerplays if you have only three or four in your repertoire. Finally, you must enjoy and find pleasure in the creative self-expression that flows naturally and spontaneously from the child's own wellspring of creative potential.

> *Music is your own experience, your thoughts,*
> *your wisdom. If you don't live it, it won't come out your horn.*
> *They teach you there's a boundary line to music.*
> *But, man, there's no boundary line to art.*
>
> Charlie Parker

REFERENCES

Barrett, K. (1977). Education dances. In B. Logsdon, M. Broer, R. McGee, M. Ammens, L. H. Alverson, & M. A. Robertson (Eds.), *Physical education for children: A focus on the teaching success* (pp. 328–333). Philadelphia: Lea and Febiger.

Bredekamp, S. (Ed.). (1987). *Developmentally appropriate practice in early childhood programs serving children from birth through eight.* Washington, DC: National Association for the Education of Young Children.

Bredekamp, S., & Copple, C. (Eds.). (1997). *Developmentally appropriate practice in early childhood programs* (Rev. ed.). Washington, DC: National Association for the Education of Young Children.

Brown, J. M. (Ed.). (1979). *Graham 1937: The vision of modern dance.* Princeton, NJ: Princeton University Press.

Cecil, N., & Lauritzen, P. (1994). *Literacy and the arts for the integrated classroom: Alternative ways of knowing.* New York: Longman.

Chenfeld, M. (1978). *Teaching language arts creatively.* New York: Harcourt Brace Jovanovich.

Cohen, M. A., & Gross, P. J. (1982, March). Let's make music. *Parents,* pp. 53–57.

Dimondstein, G. (1971). *Children dance in the classroom.* New York: Macmillan.

Dixon, G. T., & Chalmers, F. G. (1990). The expressive arts in education. *Childhood Education, 67*(1), 12–17.

Downey, V. (1995). Expressing ideas through gesture, time, and space. *Journal of Physical Education, Recreation, and Dance, 66*(9), 18.

Edwards, L. E., & Nabors, M. (1993). The creative arts process: What it is and what it is not. *Young Children, 48*(3), 77–81.

Franks, O. P. (1983). Teaching reading through music: Literacy with a plus. In J. Cohen (Ed.), *Teaching reading through the arts* (pp. 52–54). Newark, DE: International Reading Association.

Gee, S. (1997). Connected by music: Music in special schools. *Times Educational Supplement, 4235, A34*(1).

Gensemer, R. E. (1985). Body movement and learning. In F. B. Tuttle, Jr. (Ed.), *Final arts in the curriculum* (p. 39). Washington, DC: National Education Association.

Hymes, J. L. (1981). *Teaching the child under six.* Columbus, OH: Merrill.

Jaques-Dalcroze, E. (1921). *Rhythm, music, and education.* New York: G. P. Putnam's Sons.

Laban, R. (1948). *Modern education dance.* London: MacDonald and Evans.

Logan, W. M., & Logan, V. G. (1967). *A dynamic approach to the language arts.* Toronto, Canada: McGraw-Hill.

Mazo, J. (1991). Martha remembered. *Dance, 65*(7), 34.

McGirr, P. I. (1995). Verdi invades the kindergarten. *Childhood Education, 71,* 74–79.

Metz, E. (1989). Music and movement environments in preschool settings. In B. Andress (Ed.), *Promising practices in prekindergarten music* (pp. 89–96). Reston, VA: Music Educators National Conference.

Moomaw, S. (1984). *Discovering music in early childhood.* Boston: Allyn & Bacon.

Van der Linde, C. H. (1999). The relationship between play and music in early childhood: Educational insights. *Genetic, Social, and General Psychology Monographs, 119,* 2–8.

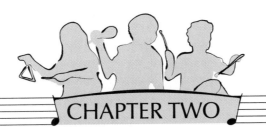

CHAPTER TWO

Infancy

*The first cry of the newborn is the generator
not only of the spoken language and of musicality
but also of movement and of musical rhythm.*

Ruth Fridman, 1973

THE YOUNG CHILD'S MUSICAL DEVELOPMENT

Today, music permeates children's lives through more avenues than ever before due to stereos, radio, television, and videos. Music in the early years contributes to healthy development for all children.

The child's whole world is filled with sound and music. It is everywhere. Children all over the world have an ability to make and respond to music. They like to explore its many possibilities, like to create it, and are highly motivated by its fascinating sounds and rhythms.

Children's musical growth is similar to the rest of their development. As children grow, they are constantly gathering all sorts of sounds and movement impressions. Children who have ample opportunities to experiment with sound and movement will acquire a rich background for later musical growth and understanding.

MUSIC MAKING IN INFANCY

From the moment of birth and even before, children adapt to the sounds within their environment, relating them to their own abilities to create and explore the rhythms and tonal patterns of sound. It has been determined that in the fifth month of pregnancy, the fetus responds to sounds of all kinds. It is not unusual to hear a mother-to-be announce that her unborn baby is much more active when she strums and plays a guitar or Autoharp® held close to her body.

The unborn baby's sense of hearing is activated when music is played at the same time each day. Being careful to adjust the volume, some expectant mothers place the headphones of a tape player or CD player on their stomachs and play classical music to the fetus. As cited by Shetler (1985), "Infants who received systematic prenatal stimulation exhibit remarkable attention behaviors, accurately imitate sounds made by adults and appear to structure vocalization much earlier than infants who did not have prenatal musical stimulation" (p. 27).

Soon after birth, infants begin to use their resources for exploring the world around them. They search for the sound when voices are heard. From the fourth week, babies can detect who is near them by the timbre (characteristic quality) of the voice. Around 3 months of age, they are often awakened or comforted by the sound of the parent's or caregiver's voice. Typically, babies will turn their eyes and heads in the direction from which the sound is coming. Even though they cannot grasp the object, babies will become excited, wiggle, and smile at the sound of a bell attached to a familiar toy.

At approximately 4 months, babies may use their feet or hands to strike a favorite toy that produces a pleasant sound when it is struck. At first, this action is reflexive and accidental in nature, but if the sound is interesting, pleasing, or perhaps amusing, infants will tend to repeat the action time and again. At around 4 months, they also enjoy the sound of their own laughter and repeat it.

There are two basic stages of music making during the child's first year and a half. The first stage is approximately from birth to 3 or 4 months. Crying is the baby's first sound. It does not take long for the baby to manipulate the cry by "opening and closing the mouth, thus varying the pitch, rhythm patterns, and dynamics" (Brand, 1985, p. 30). Babies will coo, gurgle, squeal, and babble during this stage. During the first year, babies will experiment in making sounds that are pleasing.

The second stage of music extends from approximately 4 months to 18 months (Greenberg, 1979). Babbling will increase. Often the vocalizations of babies will be motivated upon hearing their parents sing or talk to them. "Between six and nine months of age, musical babbling, defined as making speech sounds on various pitches, begins and often is produced when the baby moves to music. It is frequently produced when someone sings to the infant" (Greenberg, 1979, p. 60).

From 6 to 9 months, as babies continue to grow and experiment with their voices, their sounds often take on the form of singing. At this stage of a baby's development, they are in almost constant motion and will frequently make sounds to accompany their play and movement. These

Capture babies' attention by playing pat-a-cake.

sounds are often produced as babies interact with objects in their play. Around 11 months of age, jabbering begins, and by 18 months, a child is speaking and ready to sing. In their own way, babies constantly communicate with those around them. Very rarely are these beginnings of musical sound and bodily movement absent from the young child.

THE IMPORTANCE OF LULLABIES

Since response to sound is one of the most highly developed abilities in the newborn infant, children need to be musically nurtured from birth. Staincliffe Maternity Hospital in England soothes new infants by playing recorded music of such composers as Brahms, Handel, and Mozart. The effect on the infants works wonders, hospital attendants say. In some hospitals, a program of lullaby music is piped into rooms where mothers are feeding their babies.

Lullabies from the greatest composers and spontaneous melodies sung and hummed by loving caregivers have brought comfort and sleep to countless babies. For generations, people throughout the world have sung lullabies to their babies as they cuddled them in their arms and gently rocked them to sleep. Modern research is only beginning to discover the full importance of lullabies. Hearing soft, rhythmic songs brings a sense of calmness and security to the sensitive infant. Besides soothing an infant, rocking and singing help the infant become accustomed to the "feelings" of sound motion. Without this type of gentle introduction to music, many infants will continue to react with a startle to sudden movement and loud sounds and noises.

Another benefit of singing lullabies is the communication that occurs between the caregiver and the baby. An infant often seems to respond directly to the singer by cooing and babbling, thus encouraging the development of speech and singing.

In today's technological world, people are accustomed to hearing music produced by top professionals. It's understandable that when comparing themselves to the professional, some people feel inadequate in making music on their own. It is not unusual for parents and teachers to become unduly concerned about the quality of their singing voices. Some will not attempt to sing to or with children. Dr. John Lind, professor emeritus at Karolinska Institute in Stockholm, Sweden, discovered that children who have parents with rather poor singing voices still grow up to love to sing and are able to sing on key (Fletcher, 1981, p. 26). It is more important that parents sing to their babies than that they sing well. Authorities like Lind and Hardgrove (1978) remind us, "It is not the quality of the voice that matters, it is the connection. . . . It is not the on-key, smooth mechanical perfection that brings joy to infants as well as adults. The joy comes in

Figure 2-1   Suggestions for Singing Lullabies to Infants

1. Build a repertoire of favorite lullabies. If possible, memorize them. This is important, as many of today's young parents have no memories of being lullabied and are not familiar with the most beautiful lullabies from around the world. There are excellent lullaby books on the market. There is also a wide variety of good lullaby compact discs (CDs) and cassette tapes available. *Note:* Tapes and CDs should be used only as accompaniment or as an aid when learning new songs. The parent's or teacher's voice should always be present.
2. Some infants prefer one lullaby over another; however, don't limit your singing to only music labeled *lullabies.* Try singing contemporary songs and show tunes. Infants often enjoy variety and a change of pace.
3. As you securely hold and gently rock an infant, smile warmly and look directly into the infant's face and eyes. This kind of "bonding" brings contentment and security to the infant.

the rendition, and the example of this intimate parent-to-infant message encourages the child to sing" (p. 10).

Although singing lullabies comes naturally to many people, some may need a few tips on sharing them with infants. Figure 2-1 provides some tips for singing lullabies.

Infants' interest in a world of sound can be enhanced in different ways and through different qualities of tones and pitches, rhythmical movement, and songs.

AUDITORY STIMULATION OF INFANTS

Between birth and 1 year, most infants begin to refine their ability to listen to different sounds in their environment. It is during the early years that infants need to hear a variety of sounds and learn to focus their attention on them. It is very important for parents and caregivers to provide very young children with many listening experiences in which the children can actively participate. Music experiences are invaluable as children learn listening skills. Very young children will often combine listening with active participation as they move their bodies to the music. The next section suggests ways to increase auditory stimulation.

Birth to One Year

A well-developed sense of hearing is important to all future learning. Parents and others caring for infants should provide sound-stimulation toys and experiences that will promote auditory development. One such toy is a weighted apple that will reproduce a series of "ting-a-ling" sounds when it is shaken or struck. When an infant

Figure 2-2   Promoting Auditory Development, Birth to Six Months

1. Talk, hum, chant, or sing to the baby when you diaper, bathe, dress, and feed the baby. Poems and nursery rhymes are good choices.
2. Soothe and calm a restless infant by singing or playing a quiet song like "Hush Little Baby" or "Sleep Baby Sleep." Hold the baby in your arms. Sing or hum the song softly, and use a gentle rocking motion.
3. If the baby seems upset or unhappy, sing a livelier tune to catch the baby's attention. Then change to a quieter, soothing lullaby type of song to quiet the child. To make a baby more attentive, begin by singing a soothing lullaby and then change to a more active and rhythmic one.
4. Let the baby hear the ticking of a clock, as long as the ticking sound is not harsh. As infants and toddlers grow older, they are fascinated by the different sounds of clocks.
5. When talking to the baby, vary the tone of your voice. A baby likes to hear sounds that keep changing. Use inflection in your voice.
6. Occasionally play selections from a good-quality music box.

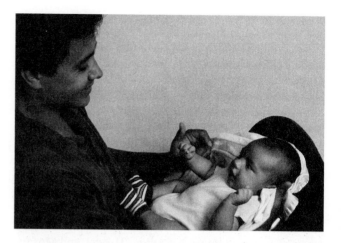

Music educators recommend that we find time every day to sing and play with babies.

is a few weeks old, the parent can shake the musical toy so it can be heard. Later, when the infant is being changed or is lying awake in bed, the musical toy should be placed close enough so that the infant can produce the same sound by striking the toy. The infant will probably continue to repeat this behavior because it is pleasing. Parents should be close by to enjoy and guide this experience with their child. Between 3 and 6 months, the infant will respond to sound stimulation or speech by vocalizing. Around 5 months, infants will react and vocalize to their own names.

Those caring for infants younger than 6 months will find the suggestions in Figure 2-2 helpful in promoting auditory development.

Babies need singing models so they can learn to sing, just as they need good speaking models to imitate for talking. When they hear others sing, they discover that there is another way of expressing themselves that is different from talking. It is important to do lots of singing to the baby, at a close range, so that the baby can see the shape and movement of the lips as the sounds are produced. Forrai (1996) reminds us that "music greatly influences the development of young children, especially with regard to their speech, movement, social, and emotional development" (p. 18).

One of the best ways parents and caregivers can model singing is to sing about what is going on. Make up little

musical phrases. It doesn't matter what notes you sing; make up the tune and rhythm spontaneously to fit the words. After a few attempts, you will be surprised at how easy it is to make up these little musical episodes.

Songs and rhythms that actively involve babies are usually liked the best by both parties. Babies will generally smile and squeal with delight when someone helps them clap their hands or move their legs up and down to a favorite nursery rhyme or lilting rhythmic tune. A baby's face will light up as she opens and closes the lid of a music box; she will delight in being in control of starting and stopping those beautiful sounds.

The staff of the Parent-Infant-Toddler Program at the Child Development Center at Kent State University has used music and auditory discrimination extensively in the program. Soon after the program was implemented, the staff quickly became aware that they had underestimated the enjoyment and importance to the children of the role of auditory discrimination and stimulation. They observed that infants showed continuous preferences for the auditory play materials. Some of these materials included Ticking Clock (Fisher-Price), Happy Apple (Childcraft), musical instruments (such as bells and drums), pots, pans, spoons, toys that squeak, and action-response toys (for example, a push-pull musical cylinder). They also observed the immediate impact of the sound of a recording playing in the classroom. When a staff member would begin playing a recording, virtually all of the infants in the 3- to 11-month class would stop interacting and turn toward the sound of the music.

Those caring for infants older than 6 months will find the additional suggestions in Figure 2-3 helpful in promoting auditory development.

Figure 2-3 Promoting Auditory Development, Six to Twelve Months

1. Talk, hum, and sing to the baby. Talk about toys, and play games like pat-a-cake and peek-a-boo. Infants enjoy songs even more if their names are mentioned.
2. Attach a mobile near the baby's crib. Many mobiles revolve and have music boxes that play delightful nursery-rhyme tunes. Other mobiles contain objects that make different sounds when struck with the hand or foot.
3. Tie a bell to the baby's bootie or shoestring. Older infants like to shake a bell.
4. Provide lightweight, colorful rattles that produce different sounds. Choose rattles with pleasing, musical sounds. Many rattles are just noisemakers.
5. Shake a set of keys.
6. At times, hold the telephone receiver up to the baby's ear so the voice on the other end can be heard. Babies are usually fascinated by this.
7. Clap your hands. Go from loud clapping to soft clapping. Take hold of the baby's hands. Clap them together. Sing in time to the clapping.
8. When reading books containing pictures of animals or other objects that make sounds, try to imitate the sounds with your voice.
9. Give the baby a pan and lid or a pan and a wooden spoon. Some babies prefer these sound makers over musical toys.
10. Hold the baby in your arms, and dance to music. Change your movements according to the tempo and mood of the music.

Babies learn very early how to shake toys to make noises.

Musical Learning Activities

Infants are attentive to musical sounds and games in their environment and move gradually from receiving to participating. Parents and infant caregivers can do much to nurture the attention and response infants give to music. Honig (2001) recommends that parents and caregivers find time every day to sing with babies during routine activities: "Sing about what you are doing—diapering, rocking, settling the baby on a play mat" (p. 24). Using music in this manner will attract attention and help build positive emotional bonds. The following activities have been used successfully in the Parent-Infant-Toddler Program at Kent State University.

Fancy Footwork

Participants
A 3- to 8-month-old infant and an adult

Materials
Velcro strip ankle bells

Explanation
Gently shake the ankle bells in front of your baby to focus the baby's attention. Allow time for examining. Now place the bells on your baby's ankles. Observe how your baby responds. If the baby becomes frustrated, remove the bells. Perhaps your baby simply wants to see or touch them at first.

Purpose
This activity is one way of offering leg exercise to your baby in preparation for creeping and crawling. It offers opportunities to flex and extend the legs. It is also an action-response activity: "When I move my legs, the bells ring!"

Variation
Take a stuffed animal, hang a few bells on it, and tie it with heavy string to the crib rails so that it hangs just above baby's feet. This tempting toy is out of hands' reach, so feet become the next best thing to make the sound. Baby may kick vigorously. The bell sound will be a motivating factor in getting the baby to stretch and kick.

Mirrors with Infants

Participants
A 6- to 8-month-old infant and an adult

Materials
Hand mirror

Explanation
Place the baby comfortably on your lap, and have the baby look into a hand mirror to see the reflection.

"Look, here's ___. Where's ___?" Have the baby point to the image in the mirror. The question and response may be sung. Do this at various times, and you will notice that babies will begin to recognize themselves. About a year from now, they will playact in front of a mirror, striking poses and making faces.

In time, you can add to this activity by pointing to parts of the body and naming them after you're sure that the baby recognizes the total as him- or herself. Parts of the body may be sung as you point to them.

Caution

It takes two to play this game. If the mirror is breakable, do not leave it unattended.

Touch and Name

Parents are encouraged to try a "Touch and Sing" adaptation as they play the game with baby.

Participants

A 6- to 12-month-old baby and an adult

Explanation

Touch different parts of your baby's body, and name them. For example, "This is ___ 's nose. Here is ___ 's foot. Where is ___ 's arm? Here it is. Here is your arm!" Now, touch your own body parts, and do the same thing. "Here is Mommy's nose." If others are close by, touch their noses; for example, "Here is Daddy's nose."

Purpose

To develop in babies an awareness of themselves and their body image and to help babies understand the difference between themselves and others. In addition, the activity shows connections between objects or actions and words, including names and pronouns. Even though it will be a while before babies use these words,

they will learn (through this type of experience) to recognize words and their meanings.

Variation

Once the child begins, through practice, to learn the names of some of the parts of the body, try turning the game around. Ask, "Where is ___ 's arm? Where is Mommy's arm?"

Give and Take

Participants

A 9- to 12-month-old baby and an adult. Some babies will continue to enjoy this game or a variation of it after their first year.

Materials

A block, small ball, or some other object like a rattle or small musical toy that can be easily held in the baby's hand.

Explanation

Having developed the ability to grasp, most babies now are learning to let go. This is an example of a game that many babies initiate independently. Be enthusiastic as you play the game. Give the object to the baby and say, "Here's the ball" (or whatever the object is). Then put your hand out as if to receive it back. When the baby places the object in your hand, take it and say, "Thank you." If the baby imitates your "thank you," respond, "You're welcome." The responses may be sung. Continue this give and take for as long as the baby enjoys it.

Purpose

To give babies practice in letting go and using their hand muscles in a controlled way. This activity also serves as a form of social interchange. It is a good way to teach the use of appropriate language to accompany social interchange.

FAVORITE SONGS AND RHYTHMS

PEEK-A-BOO

Words and music by K. BAYLESS

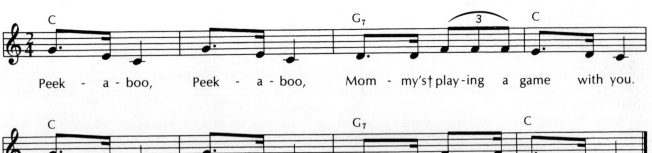

Peek - a - boo, Peek - a - boo, Mom - my's† play-ing a game with you.

Peek - a - boo, Peek - a - boo, See if you can play it, too.

*Use appropriate actions.
†May substitute other names.

PAT-A-CAKE, PAT-A-CAKE

Adapted by K. BAYLESS

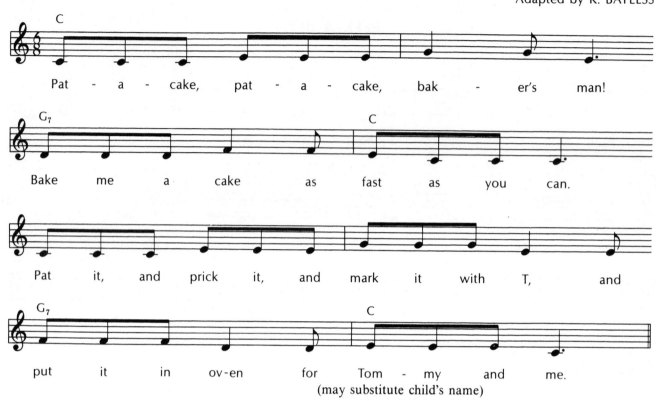

Short, rhythmic singing games also please the young child. Around 6 months of age, babies begin to enjoy playing peek-a-boo. Peek-a-boo and pat-a-cake, longtime favorites, have been set to music so that the family can sing and play these games with baby.

ALL THE FISH

Adapted by
"Miss Jackie" Weissman

Reprinted by permission of "Miss Jackie" Weissman.

"All the Fish" is a favorite of children around 6 months of age and older. Put your hands together (palms flat touching each other), and move them around like fish swimming in the water. During the "splash" part, push them apart and pretend you are splashing someone. Make up new verses, such as "All the frogs are hopping in the water" and "All the ducks are quacking in the water."

BABY'S FACE

Words and music by
"Miss Jackie" Weissman

Here are ba-by's eyes to look a - round,

Here are ba-by's ears to lis-ten to the sound, Here is ba-by's nose to

smell some-thing sweet, Here is ba-by's mouth that likes to eat.

© 1983 Jackie Weissman

This song will help your baby identify body parts. There are many ways to play the game when you sing the song. Sing the song to the baby and touch each body part as you name it in the song. At the end of the song when you sing the words "likes to eat," pretend you are eating and say, "yum, yum, yum." Another way to sing the song is to take the baby's hands and put them on his eyes, ears, etc. A third way to sing the song is to use a doll or stuffed animal to touch as you sing.

The following lullabies are favorites of parents, teachers, and children.

ROCK-A-BYE BABY

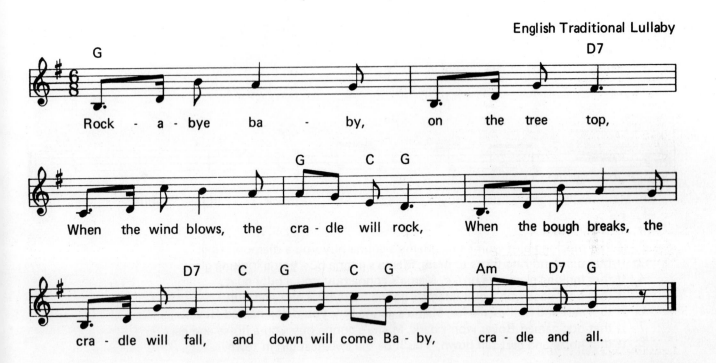

English Traditional Lullaby

Rock - a - bye ba - by, on the tree top,

When the wind blows, the cra - dle will rock, When the bough breaks, the

cra - dle will fall, and down will come Ba - by, cra - dle and all.

HUSH LITTLE BABY

Alabama Folk Song

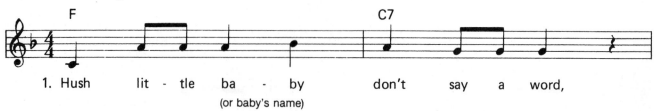

1. Hush   lit - tle ba - by   don't   say   a   word,
(or baby's name)

Ma - ma's gon - na buy   you   a   mock - ing   bird.

2. If that mocking bird won't sing, Mama's gonna buy you a diamond ring.
3. If that diamond ring turns to brass, Mama's gonna buy you a looking glass.
4. If that looking glass gets broke, Mama's gonna buy you a billy goat.
5. If that billy goat won't pull, Mama's gonna buy you a cart and bull.
6. If that cart and bull turn over, Mama's gonna buy you a dog named Rover.
7. If that dog named Rover won't bark, Mama's gonna buy you a horse and cart.
8. If that horse and cart fall down, You'll be the sweetest girl in town.

*The word *babe, boy,* or *children* may be substituted for *girl.*

This beloved folk song appeals to children and persons of all ages. As part of our cultural heritage, it should be passed on from one generation to the next. It is often sung as a lullaby.

SLEEP, BABY, SLEEP

German lullaby

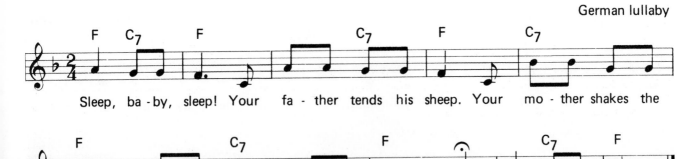

Sleep, ba - by, sleep! Your fa - ther tends his sheep. Your mo - ther shakes the

dream - land tree. Down falls a lit - tle dream for thee. Sleep, ba - by, sleep.

HUSH! BE STILL

Source unknown
Lullaby as sung by GRANDMA THOMAS

1. Hush! be still as an - y mouse, There's a ba - by in the house,

Not a dol - ly, not a toy, But a laugh - ing, cry - ing boy.

2
Hush! be still as any mouse,
There's a baby in the house,
Not a dolly, with a curl,
But a laughing, crying girl.

SELECTIVE SKILLS FOR CHILDREN

A reference list of selected skills for children from birth to 36 months is shown in Figure 2-4. It describes cognitive and expressive language and gives parents and caregivers approximate ranges during which young children will begin to respond to sound and music.

Figure 2-4   Selected Skills Reference List for Children Birth to 36 Months

Cognitive	Responds to sounds birth–1 month
	Responds to voice birth–2½ months
	Listens to voice for 30 seconds 1–3 months
	Begins to play with rattle 2½–4 months
	Awakens or quiets to mother's voice 3–6 months
	Localizes sound with eyes 3½–5 months
	Shows interest in sounds of objects 5½–8 months
	Plays peek-a-boo 6–10 months
	Moves to rhythms 11–12 months
	Matches sounds to animals 18–22 months
	Enjoys nursery rhymes, nonsense rhymes, fingerplays, poetry 18–30 months
	Matches sounds to pictures of animals 22–24 months
Expressive Language	Cry varies in pitch, length, and volume to indicate needs like hunger and pain 1–5 months
	Coos open vowels (*aah*), diphthongs (*oy* as in *boy*) 2–7 months
	Disassociates, vocalizations from bodily movement 2–3 months
	Cries more rhythmically with mouth opening and closing 2½–4½ months
	Responds to sound stimulation or speech by vocalizing 3–6 months
	Reacts to music by cooing 5–6 months
	Looks and vocalizes to own name 5–7 months
	Babbles to people 5½–6½ months
	Babbles with inflection similar to adult speech 7½–12 months
	Babbles in response to human voice 11–15 months
	Babbles monologue when left alone 11–12 months
	Attempts to sing sounds to music 13–16 months
	Jabbers tunefully at play 17–19 months
	Imitates environmental sounds 18–21 months
	Attempts to sing with words 18–23 months
	Sings phrases of songs 23–27 months
	Recites a few nursery rhymes 30–36 months

Source: Selected from *Hawaii Early Learning Profile (HELP) Activity Guide* by the Enrichment Project for Handicapped Infants, by Setsu Furuno, Katherine A. O'Reilly, Carol M. Hosaka, Takayo T. Inatsuka, Toney L. Allman, and Barbara Zeisloft. Available from VORT Corporation, Palo Alto, CA 94306.

> *If you can walk, you can dance.*
> *If you can talk, you can sing.*
> —Zimbabwean proverb

KEY IDEAS

1. Children's musical growth is similar to the rest of their development.
2. In homes where musical expression is encouraged, children's responses to music are better and of a higher quality as they grow older than the responses of children from other homes.
3. Music making should begin in infancy.
4. A well-developed sense of hearing is important to all future learning.
5. Babies usually favor songs and rhythms that actively involve them.

SUMMARY

Music is basic for all people, from infancy through adulthood. Those caring for the very young can provide a good beginning for music enjoyment and appreciation by singing and sharing music, such as lullabies, chants, and rhymes. Begin to explore music with children when they are infants; share the variety and richness of our musical heritage. In addition to nurturing through food and love, add the nurturing quality of music. Infancy is a good time for beginning with simple activities and music experiences. When you, as a caregiver, become involved, so will the very young child in terms of alertness, awareness, and enjoyment.

QUESTIONS TO CONSIDER

1. Begin an informal two-week log of an infant you observe. Record short, precise details of the infant's activities. Are any of the activities influenced by music or rhythm?
2. Visit a day care center. How is music used as a learning experience or as an activity integrated throughout the day?
3. Try at least four of the activities suggested in this chapter. Record your observations and how you modified the activities to suit your purpose or the infant's reactions.

REFERENCES

Brand, M. (1985, March). Lullabies that awaken musicality in infants. *Music Educators Journal*, pp. 28–31.

Fletcher, S. K. (1981, September). The importance of being lullabied. *Baby Talk*, p. 26.

Forrai, K. (1996). The influence of music on the development of young children: Music research with children between 6 and 40 months. *Early Childhood Connections, Journal of Music and Movement-Based Learning, 2*(4), 14–18.

Fridman, R. (1973, Fall). The first cry of the newborn: Basis for the child's future musical development. *Journal of Research in Music Education, 21*(3), 265.

Greenberg, M. (1979). *Your children need music.* Upper Saddle River, NJ: Prentice Hall.

Honig, A. S. (2001) Building relationships through music. *Scholastic Early Childhood Today, 15*(4), 24–25.

Lind, J., & Hardgrove, C. (1978, July–August). Lullabies. *Children Today*, p. 10.

Shetler, D. J. (1985, March). Prenatal music experiences. *Music Educators Journal*, p. 27.

SONG COLLECTIONS

Let's Sing and Play to Grow, 2nd ed., 1998
Karen Jorgenson and Marty Richardson
Retono Books
1721 Wendy
Edinburg, TX 78539
> *A play-and-learn recording. Includes lullabies and learning songs for movement.*

Rock-a-bye Baby Book 1990
Committee for UNICEF
> *Lullabies of many lands and peoples. A music book with original words and translations.*

RECORDINGS

Quiet Time (CD)
Harrel C. Lucky
Melody House
> *Music for resting, relaxing, or enjoyable listening.*

Songs for Sleepyheads and Out-of-Beds! (CD)
Pat Carfra
A & M Records of Canada Ltd.
> *Forty-one easy-to-sing lullabies and play songs for very young children.*

Tickly Toddle: Songs for Very Young Children (CD, video, book)
Hap Palmer
Children's Book and Music Center
> *For use with small groups of children in day care and nursery school settings or for use at home. The activities are simple and afford opportunities for interaction between adult and child.*

CHAPTER THREE

Music for the Ones and Twos

Without music,
life is a journey through a desert.

Pat Conroy

NEW OPPORTUNITIES FOR ENJOYMENT AND LEARNING

As children continue to grow and to become more interested in their world, music can offer new opportunities for moving, listening, creating, singing, and playing instruments. Besides imparting to children the enjoyment and pleasure of music activities, adult guides can also teach children skills and competencies by choosing *appropriate* activities. The selection of activities should be based on what can reasonably be expected of children at certain stages of their development. Caregivers, teachers, and specialists—such as music and physical education teachers—need to work closely to plan music experiences that are suitable for young children of different ages. As Howle (1989) reminds us, a child's environment can have a profound impact on the very young. Parents and teachers who want to instill a love of music within young children must lay the groundwork during a child's earliest years.

Creating the Environment

Teachers who make music a natural and ever-present part of the classroom environment teach their children to be curious about music and to listen to many styles of music. Teachers should encourage the development of aural and vocal music skills throughout the early years when the child is developing expressive language skills (Scott, 1989). Fox (1991) notes, "Reinforcement and valuing of music by significant others most probably indicates to children the importance of music and its role in our lives" (p. 45). It is vital that the selection of music activities and experiences be based on sound principles of child growth and development.

Wide variations exist in children's maturation and experience. Figure 3-1 gives an overview of the characteristics of 1- and 2-year-olds, which should prove helpful to caregivers who wish to provide musical experiences that are appropriate for young children.

NURSERY RHYMES

Adults who love poetry and music will find themselves reciting poetry and nursery rhymes and singing those unforgettable nursery songs to the very young. Children's interest in a world of sound can be enhanced through different qualities of tone, varying pitches, and rhythmic movements. Adults working with young children should share with them the many delightful Mother Goose rhymes and the chants of early childhood.

Figure 3-1   Selected Characteristics of One- to Two-Year-Olds

- Enjoy listening to certain sounds, such as the fluttering of the tongue, and enjoy imitating them
- Answer questions like "What does the cow say?" by making the appropriate sound
- Can point to or put hands on body parts on request
- Rock or sway hips to a familiar tune, although not necessarily in time with the music
- Like to play peek-a-boo and hiding games
- Continue to reproduce sounds or combinations of sounds to explain wants and needs (for example, may half-sing, half-say, "Bye-bye," when they want to go for a ride in the car)
- Generally enjoy being held and sung to
- May "mouth" the words of a song or whisper them while others sing
- May choose to join a group socially but not to sing
- Will often refrain from singing any of the words to songs like "Twinkle, Twinkle, Little Star" because they are concentrating so intently on doing the actions

Using Nursery Rhymes with Infants

It is quite natural for infants to move their bodies to the rhythm of nursery rhymes and chants. Howle (1989) reminds us that rocking frequently accompanies singing experiences, and lullabies are certainly no exception. She suggests that sensory stimuli, such as touching, rubbing, smiling, warmth, and cuddling, aid in mental development while promoting a loving relationship between parent and child. Howle also believes that these early music experiences prepare the child for later development in music, speech, and movement. Additional benefits include the development of communication skills. Young children respond directly to the adult who is singing, and this attention can prompt the adult to begin talking to the child. This encourages speech development, listening skills, and the ability to hear rhyming words (Howle, 1989). As children grow older, the appeal of rhymes seems to increase. Young children care little about the origin and meaning of nursery rhymes; their value lies in their delightful rhythms, repetition, good humor, nonsensical words, and imagination. Children receive much pleasure from listening to and attempting, in their own inimitable ways, to repeat the chants and rhymes while moving their bodies to their interesting rhythmic patterns.

It is desirable to say and to sing these rhymes over and over again and to include the family in this sharing process. If children are provided with these experiences,

Toddlers can use instruments to produce sounds and they can use their voices to sing songs.

they will soon spontaneously participate in these fun episodes. This activity establishes a good foundation for children's lifetime reading and musical tastes.

The nursery rhymes in Figure 3–2 are considered classics in children's literature and have been loved by generations of young children. If you are unfamiliar with any of these rhymes, now is a good time to learn them, especially if you plan to work with very young children.

CHANTING

Children love the sound of their own voices. Parents and teachers should encourage young children to improvise and should themselves serve as models. Buchoff (1994) recommends that parents and teachers model chants for children by reading them aloud dramatically and with enthusiasm many times. Buchoff also suggests that teachers snap their fingers while chanting to emphasize the rhythm of the chants and to encourage children to lis-

ten for the beat. Bring the chant to life by modifying the volume and pace of the chant to fit the message or mood. Present the chant in full form, complete from beginning to end, and avoid dividing the chants into lines or phrases. Remember that chanting should be for fun and pleasure. It is inappropriate to expect very young children to memorize chants. The goal must be to give children the opportunity to share the joy of rhyming words and language play.

The Link Between Speech and Rhythm

Some authorities call the half-speaking, half-singing sounds children make as they go about their play "chanting." Whether children are pounding with a hammer, pushing a toy, or running with a balloon, one can hear melodic fragments. Anderson and Lapp (1996) describe a chant as any group of words that is recited with a lively beat. Through chanting, all children speak together in unison. They learn the importance of clear and expressive pronunciation as their voices combine to make the message of the chant come alive.

Children often half-speak, half-sing names of people, animals, and the like, using the tones of the minor third:

Songs or little melodies using the pentatonic scale often make use of the minor third. The scale has five tones to an octave. Found in the diatonic scale, the five-tone scale is do, re, mi, sol, la. The scale can originate in any tone. It is often found in songs children make up themselves:

_____

(*Note:* This little melody makes use of only the black keys.)

Figure 3-2   Nursery Rhymes

Five Little Pigs

This little pig went to market;
This little pig stayed at home;
This little pig had roast beef;
And this little pig had none;
This little pig said, "Wee, wee, wee!"
All the way home.
[One line for each of the child's toes]

To Market, To Market

To market, to market, to buy a fat pig,
Home again, home again, jiggity jig;
To market, to market, to buy a fat hog,
Home again, home again, jiggity jog;
To market, to market, to buy a plum bun,
Home again, home again, market is done.

Baa, Baa, Black Sheep

Baa, baa black sheep
Have you any wool?
Yes, sir, yes, sir, three bags full.
One for my master, one for the dame,
One for the little boy that lives in the lane.

Humpty Dumpty

Humpty Dumpty sat on a wall,
Humpty Dumpty had a great fall;
All the king's horses and all the king's men
Couldn't put Humpty Dumpty together again.

Little Jack Horner

Little Jack Horner
Sat in a corner,
Eating his Christmas pie.
He put in his thumb
And pulled out a plum
And said, "What a good boy am I!"

Pussy Cat, Pussy Cat

Pussy cat, pussy cat, where have you been?
I've been to London to visit the queen.
Pussy cat, pussy cat, what did you do there?
I frightened a little mouse under the chair.

Jack and Jill

Jack and Jill went up the hill
To fetch a pail of water;
Jack fell down and broke his crown,
And Jill came tumbling after.

Roses Are Red

Roses are red,
Violets are blue;
Sugar is sweet,
And so are you!

One Potato

One potato, two potato,
Three potato, four;
Five potato, six potato
Seven potato, more.

Rain, Rain, Go Away

Rain, rain, go away,
Come again another day,
Little Johnny wants to play.

To develop further the tie-in between speaking and singing, it is advisable to sing requests and the like to children:

Cin-dy, roll the ball to Dad-dy. Thank you!

Mat-thew, would you like a cook-ie?

San-dy, give your cup to Mom-my.

Observe that the minor third chants just introduced comprise a two-note pattern. This is a very natural and easy way to improvise a little tune to sing to a child. We want to stress the importance and value of making up these short, fun melodies, in which one sings about the everyday things the child or people around the child are doing. Babies and toddlers who have had such rich and plentiful experiences, who have been talked to, played with, and sung to, will be able to join in quite accurately with words and "snatches" of melodies of familiar songs, chants, or nursery rhymes when they are starting to talk.

The chants in Figure 3–3 are fun for very young children because the actions are easy to imitate and the words and rhythms are repetitive.

Too often, teachers and caregivers have narrow ideas about what constitutes music when they work with young children. They need to listen to children and observe them carefully. Children can respond to music that is brought to them. It is up to parents and teachers to provide meaningful music experiences for these active, persistent music makers. Songs from all cultures and countries offer a wonderful source for teachers and parents alike.

Music from Around the World

One legendary woman has worked with children from all over the world and has written songs in many languages,

Figure 3-3 Spoken Chants

Clap Your Hands

Clap your hands just like me,
Clap as slowly as can be.
Now clap fast and you will see,
What great fun clapping can be.

[Add your own verses, and let the children make up their own verses using different body parts. For example: "Snap your fingers," "Tap your toes," and "Blink your eyes."]

I Have Hands

I have hands that clap, clap, clap.
I have feet that tap, tap, tap.
I have eyes to see you too,
Peter Talbert, I see you.

[Point to the child named, and continue the chant until all the children have heard their names.]

Children can sing "Hola, hola, hola" as a greeting in Spanish.

including Spanish, Chinese, Hebrew, Korean, Maori, and Swahili. Ella Jenkins has brought a treasury of songs to children of the world. She has appeared on several television programs, including *The Today Show, Showbiz Today, Barney and Friends, Mister Rogers' Neighborhood,* and *Sesame Street.* She is the quintessential authority on multicultural music for children. She has received the American Society of Composers, Authors and Publishers (ASCAP) Foundation Lifetime Achievement Award in the area of children's music. In fact, she was the first woman to receive an ASCAP Lifetime Achievement Award. Her albums and videotapes have received the

Parents' Choice Award, and her latest album was nominated for a Grammy Award.

Ella Jenkins, Educator

In a 1995 article, Jenkins discusses her role as an educator. She says, in part, "As an educator, it's important to me to share my excitement about cultures with children. When I do—and you do, too—we help them appreciate the varied peoples, places, songs, words, dances, rhythms, and rhymes in their own communities and around the world" (p. 40). In an interview with Reninger (2000), Jenkins talks about chants. "Children in most countries like chants, even if they have to be translated. I use little chants that have a verse and a lot of rhythm and a lot of rhyming. Children are fascinated by rhyme. Sometimes, if they're singing and they forget the words, they try to make up their own rhymes" (p. 41). Jenkins recommends that one way of introducing children to chants and rhymes in languages different from their own is to teach them how to extend a greeting to someone who lives in a different place. In the previous section, we talked about toddlers "snatching" parts of a chant just as they are beginning to talk. Even 2-year-olds can chant "Hola, hola, hola" as a greeting in Spanish. Jenkins's classic album, "You'll Sing a Song and I'll Sing a Song," introduces many of her songs and chants. This recording and many others are available through Jenkins's website, www.ellajenkins.com. In the meantime, teachers and children whose first language is English can chant this old favorite:

Peas Porridge

> Peas porridge hot
> Peas porridge cold
> Peas porridge in the pot
> Nine days old!

Teachers can also make up chants based on themes, the children's interests, the weather, and other relevant subject matter. Teachers should begin with simple chants in the children's native language to help them get used to the rhyme and rhythm before introducing chants in other languages.

ELEMENTS OF MUSICAL BEGINNINGS

All growth, musical or otherwise, is an active process. For optimum musical development to occur, children must be actively involved in making music from their birth. Some learning does take place through watching and listening to others, but the best learning takes place through trying for oneself. Before you begin thinking about ways to plan and implement music experiences for young children, it is important to understand the basic stages of early musical development. The following description of musical devel-

Young children enjoy acting out the song "Sometimes I Am Tall"

opment for 2-year-olds includes suggested music and movement activities for young children.

Two-Year-Olds

The 2-year-old enjoys rocking, swaying, moving up and down, clapping games, fingerplays, and action songs. For example, "Sometimes I Am Tall" encourages young children to reach up high and bend down low. Here are the words and directions:

Sometimes I Am Tall

Sometimes I am tall.
[Stand at full height]
Sometimes I am small.
[Bend down close to the floor]
Sometimes I am very, very tall.
[Stretch on tiptoe]
Sometimes I am very, very small.
[Bend down as close to the floor as possible]
Sometimes tall, sometimes small.
(Stretch high and bend low)
See how I am now.
[Stand normally]

Fingerplays

A favorite fingerplay of 2-year-olds is the traditional "Eency Weency Spider." Children should be allowed to make their own spider any way they want to make it. Too many times, well-meaning teachers show just how to make a "proper" spider and distract children from the fun of the fingerplay. All spiders created from children's fingers are correct and perfect!

Eency Weency Spider

The eency weency spider climbed up the waterspout.
[Children transform their fingers into their own climbing spider]
Down came the rain and washed the spider out.
[Wiggle fingers in downward motion]
Out came the sun and dried up all the rain.
[Arms in circle over head]
And the eency weency spider climbed up the spout again.
[Fingers repeat climbing motion]

Movement

Two-year-olds also enjoy experimenting with imitating rhymes and rhythms and responding to music through body movements. "Teddy Bear, Teddy Bear Turn Around" is a wonderful prelude to nap time.

"Teddy Bear, Teddy Bear" is a wonderful song for helping active children calm down.

Teddy Bear, Teddy Bear

Teddy Bear, Teddy Bear, turn around.
Teddy Bear, Teddy Bear, touch the ground.
Teddy Bear, Teddy Bear, show your shoe,
Teddy Bear, Teddy Bear, that will do!
Teddy Bear, Teddy Bear, go upstairs,
Teddy Bear, Teddy Bear, say your prayers,
Teddy Bear, Teddy Bear, turn off the light,
Teddy Bear, Teddy Bear, say "Good night!"

Simple Songs and Instruments

Two-year-olds can learn short, simple songs and enjoy experimenting with instruments and sounds. Rhythm sticks are wooden sticks with both a smooth surface and a ribbed surface. They are small enough in diameter to fit nicely into the hands of 2-year-olds. Children hold one stick in each hand and strike them together or scrape one stick over the ribbed surface of the other. Rhythm sticks can be used to strike other objects, such as the floor, sleeping mats, and other things in the classroom. Two-year-olds love to "march" around the room, striking their rhythm sticks. Teachers can use a tambourine to help keep the beat.

Children at this age can respond to songs with simple patterns. The traditional pattern song "Put Your Finger on Your Nose" is very appropriate for 2-year-olds because it repeats the same phrases over and over and introduces only two different movements. For teachers who want to sing, rather than chant, this little verse, the melody to "If You're Happy and You Know It" is a perfect fit.

Put Your Finger on Your Nose

Put your finger on your nose, then your toes.
Put your finger on your nose, then your toes.
Put your finger on your nose. Put your finger on your nose.
Put your finger on your nose, then your toes.

Exploring Space
Young children are eager to explore space as they move forward and backward, up and down. They also enjoy moving low to the floor and walking on tiptoe. The "imaginary space bubble" described in chapter 1 is a good activity to help children define their own personal space. They can move inside their imaginary space bubble in many different ways. They can also carry their space bubble with them as they move around the room. It is important to remember, however, that 2-year-olds are still very egocentric in that their thinking does not take into account the viewpoint of others. Because of this very special trait, they may move in and out of other children's bubbles. When this happens, be gentle, and remember that the whole idea is to have fun while learning new patterns of movement and new ways to explore the space in the classroom.

Adults in the classroom provide many experiences and opportunities to extend children's language and musical abilities. We introduce children to nursery rhymes and fingerplays, encourage children to sing songs and listen to recordings, and facilitate children's play of movement games and action songs. Always be aware of the role you play in providing musical experiences that match your children's developmental needs.

FAVORITE SONGS AND RHYTHMS

When not asleep, babies and toddlers are in almost constant motion. The following songs lend themselves to such movement, which is an important element in the life of a growing child. Suggestions for different kinds of actions and movements are given with each song.

A jazz musician is a juggler who uses harmonies instead of oranges.

—Benny Green

LAZY MARY

Traditional

La - zy Mar - y will you get up, Will you get up, Will you get up,

La - zy Mar - y will you get up this cold and fros - ty morn - ing.

This traditional song has long been a favorite of young children. As you sing to awaken the baby, replace the word *lazy* with the word *baby* or other words like *happy* or *blue-eyed*. The baby's name can also be substituted for "Mary." For variety, change "cold and frosty morning" to the appropriate weather conditions, such as "bright and sunny morning" or "cloudy, rainy morning."

CLAPPING SONG

Traditional

Clap,   clap,   clap your hands,   clap your hands to - geth - er.

Between 12 and 18 months, babies experience great physical growth, and many of them will begin to move their body parts to music quite spontaneously. At this time, episodes and rhythmic games can be created between adults and children for both enjoyment and learning. The repeat of rhythmic patterns could be initiated at this time. The patterns to be repeated should be given at a slow, simple pace.

Place the baby in a high chair or sit in front of her. Sing and clap the above song to the baby. (Repeat several times.) If the baby doesn't respond, gently take the baby's hands in yours, and clap the beats to the song again. (Repeat.)

Children older than 24 months will be able to recognize familiar songs and many times will start clapping without much encouragement. As much as possible, adults should encourage children to tap their thighs to the beat of the music. This is an easier way of keeping the beat.

DEEDLE, DEEDLE, DUMPLING

Mother Goose

Dee-dle, dee-dle, dump-ling, my son John, Went to bed with his trou-sers on.

One shoe off, the oth-er shoe on, Dee-dle, dee-dle, dump-ling, my son John.

"Deedle, Deedle, Dumpling," an age-old Mother Goose favorite, lends itself to bouncing movements. Hold the child on your lap, and bounce him or her up and down to each "deedle, deedle, dumpling."

TWINKLE, TWINKLE, LITTLE STAR

Traditional

Twin - kle, twin - kle, lit - tle star; How I won - der what you are,

Up a - bove the world so high, Like a dia - mond in the sky!

Twin - kle, twin - kle, lit - tle star; How I won - der what you are.

The moon and the stars are wonders to be enjoyed at an early age. Young children are particularly fascinated to look out of a window and see the yellow moon and shining stars. This is a delightful rhyme to sing at nighttime.

Show the child how to wiggle the fingers as the song is sung. In time, the child will imitate the movement. On the words "Up above the world so high," point a finger to the stars in the sky.

HEY, DIDDLE, DIDDLE

Mother Goose

J. W. ELLIOTT

Hey, did-dle, did-dle, The cat and the fid-dle, The cow jump'd o-ver the moon;   The

lit-tle dog laughed   to see   such sport, And the dish ran   a-way with the spoon.

The Mother Goose rhyme is full of good humor. Hold the child, and gently sway back and forth while singing the rhyme. On the word *jump'd,* take one jump. On the phrase "And the dish ran away with the spoon," take running steps in time to the music.

KEY IDEAS

1. Music activities should be based on reasonable expectations of children's abilities and sound growth and development principles.
2. The value of nursery rhymes lies in their rhythms, repetition, good humor, nonsensical words, and imagination.
3. Musical awareness should be built on a gradual introduction to songs, nursery rhymes, chants, and instruments.

SUMMARY

Sights and sounds surround us in our everyday lives. Artists are tuned in to the environment and depend on their acute awareness to express their ideas to others through their paintings. This is also the case with music. Children need to be made aware of the sounds in their environment and of music. All of us can help children learn to appreciate the beauty of sound so that music can become an enjoyable, lifelong experience.

QUESTIONS TO CONSIDER

1. What evidence can you cite from your personal experience showing that children love the sound of their own voices? How can chanting encourage such behavior? Give examples.
2. Devise several activities that involve young children in chanting, fingerplays, nursery rhymes, or instrumentation. Use the activities with one or two children, and record your results.
3. Describe your immediate environment. What elements could be used to promote musical awareness?

REFERENCES

Anderson, P. S., & Lapp, D. (1996). *Language skills in elementary education*. New York: Macmillan.

Buchoff, R. (1994). Joyful voices: Facilitating language growth through the rhythmic response to chants. *Young Children, 49*(4), 26–30.

Fox, D. B. (1991). Music, development, and the young child. *Music Educators Journal, 77*(5), 42–46.

Howle, M. J. (1989). Twinkle, twinkle, little star: It's more than just a nursery song. *Children Today, 18*(4), 18–22.

Jenkins, E. (1995). Music is culture. *Scholastic Early Childhood Today, 9,* 40–42.

Reninger, R. D. (2000). Ella Jenkins: The perennial music maker. *Teaching Music, 8*(1), 40–44.

Scott, C. R. (1989). How children grow—musically. *Music Educators Journal, 76*(2), 28–31.

SONG COLLECTIONS

The Raffi Singable Songbook (1984)
Chappell
14 Birch Ave.
Toronto, Ontario, Canada
  A collection of 51 songs from Raffi's first three records for young children.

Nursery Songs (1980)
Joseph Moorat
The Metropolitan Museum of Art/Thames and Hudson, New York, NY.
  Thirty old-time nursery songs.

RECORDINGS

Golden Slumbers (Cassette)
Children's Book and Music Center
  Twenty-four lullabies from around the world, sung by eight folk singers.
Music for Ones and Twos (Cassette)
Tom Glazer
Children's Book and Music Center
  Songs for the very young. A favorite recording of many.
My Teddy Bear and Me (Cassette)
Children's Book and Music Center
  Musical play activities for infants and toddlers. Familiar melodies and simple actions structured to help the very young become aware of objects and spatial relationships and develop coordination and listening skills.

Songs to Grow On, **Vol. 1** (CD)
Woody Guthrie
Children's Book and Music Center
  Woody Guthrie sings his famous chants and folksy songs, including his popular "Put Your Finger in the Air."

CHAPTER FOUR

Music for the Twos and Threes

Music is a more potent instrument than any other for education.

Plato

MUSICAL EXPERIENCES FOR TWO- AND THREE-YEAR-OLDS

Music activities for young children must include a variety of opportunities to explore music through singing, moving, listening, and playing instruments. These activities must also include experiences through which children can verbalize and visualize musical ideas.

Early childhood educators know that play is the primary means through which children grow, and appropriate music experiences for young children should always occur in child-initiated, child-directed, teacher-supported play environments. The teacher's role is to provide a musically stimulating environment and to facilitate children's involvement with music activities. Young children also need time to share and make music with others in a small group.

CHARACTERISTICS OF TWO- AND THREE-YEAR-OLDS

Where live music is being played that has a marked rhythm, most 2- to 3-year-old children will be seen bouncing up and down and swaying and twirling their bodies to the music. When working with children of this delightful age, we find that sound and movement are almost inseparable. Since children are so sensitive to sound and movement, we will present and discuss some of the activities that they might enjoy if given the opportunity, and, at the same time, we will indicate how conceptual development can take place with these activities. Knowledge of the characteristics of 2- and 3-year-olds helps us plan meaningful experiences for them. Selected characteristics are listed in Figure 4–1.

TODDLERS' RESPONSE TO SOUND AND MOVEMENT

Music often elicits a particular response from toddlers. They can be seen swaying or stepping in time to an appropriate rhythm. One has only to watch young children as a band plays a lively march or dance to observe their response to music. If they are in a setting in which they can move, most of them will invariably begin to clap their hands and move their feet in time to the music. Their faces will light up with pleasure and delight.

Toddlers enjoy banging. Any percussion instrument can instantly become a rhythm instrument. Tambourines are lightweight and can be carried and tapped by children as they move around the room. Teachers can use tam-

Figure 4-1   Selected Characteristics of Two- to Three-Year-Olds

- Are very active and like music to which they can respond
- Like music having marked rhythm, such as band music, nursery rhymes, or catchy TV jingles
- May gallop like a pony
- Often clap hands or tap hips to rhythm when hearing music
- Attempt to dance to music by bending knees in a bouncing motion, turning circles, swinging arms, and nodding the head
- Are able to sing phrases of songs
- Can lie or sit down quietly and listen for longer periods of time
- Enjoy making sounds to accompany play
- Like imaginative, dramatic play
- Begin to show interest in listening to and playing real musical instruments like drums, rhythm sticks, and tambourines

bourines to encourage children to change from a slow movement to a fast movement (Strickland, 2001). Select music that children can listen to and play along with. Be sure to include different styles of music, such as jazz, country-western, classical, gospel, and lively multicultural music. It is very important that children have the opportunity to play their instruments along with many different kinds of music. It is through these experiences that toddlers learn the feeling of rhythm, learn how to establish a beat, are exposed to music from different cultures, and have fun (Smith, 2000).

Music making at this age is usually an individual activity. During a play period, for example, Sara may use a wooden spoon to tap on a pan; Andrew might push his fire truck across the floor as he makes an authentic siren sound with his voice; Jennifer might stand on tiptoe to reach and play the white keys on the piano. On occasion, children will form a musical group of their own and play their sound-producing instruments as they stand beside one another. It is from these spontaneous activities that we should take our cues in helping children enjoy these playful, musical experiences.

Music for young children facilitates discovering sounds both inside and outside the home and school. As adults, we need to observe young children closely, particularly in their play, and learn more about the many ways in which they deal with sound and movement. Children ages 2 and older are always on the move and involved in sound-making experimentation.

Developing Listening Skills

As children grow and develop, one of the most important things that we can do is help them build good listening skills. Children have little motivation on their own to listen carefully unless parents and teachers encourage it. This does not imply that we must impose drill-like, structured procedures to accomplish this purpose. We need to assist children in helping them make sense out of the myriad kinds of sounds in their environment. As Carleton (2000) reminds us, "Listening is necessary to hear same and different letters of our alphabet, words, sounds in our environment, and musical pitches. There will be a lifetime of sounds our children will need to identify. The sooner we encourage listening skills, the more opportunities children will have to develop them" (p. 54).

Music in Context

For children to make sense and meaning out of the sounds they hear, sounds need to be put in context. Adults can do this quite easily by helping children relate sounds closely to everyday objects and events. It is easier to do this for children around the age of 2, since children at this age are becoming more mobile and have increased ability to talk about the things they are doing. Children need to acquire language so they can talk and think about sound. With the help of understanding adults, conversations about sound can be initiated through a variety of ways. For example, the adult might say to the child, "Listen, do you hear the siren? Is that the fire truck?" (Use your own judgment when talking about any type of siren to young children. Always use them to make children feel safe rather than afraid.) Here are some other examples you might use:

"Listen to that barking dog. He sounds like he is very happy!" "That's the doorbell ringing! I wonder who's at the door. Do you have any idea?" "I hear the telephone ringing. Do you hear it, too?" "Hmmm, do you smell the popcorn? Listen and see if you can hear it popping."

One of our challenges as teachers is to provide quality music and listening experiences with respect to the collective needs of all the children. Because children's intuitive responses to music and listening activities may vary, be sure to remember that all responses have value. It would be a boring classroom indeed if all the children responded the same way at the same time.

BUILDING ON CHILDREN'S NATURAL MOVEMENTS

It is important to remember that children of this age need many opportunities to move—to walk, run, climb, bounce, and jump—not only to aid their muscular development, but also for the sake of pure enjoyment. At first, movements will be uncoordinated, but with plenty of opportunity to move and express themselves, the children will eventually gain control of their bodies, and their movements will become refined.

Children around the age of 2 like to bounce up and down on a bed or a sofa. As they do this, it is not uncommon to hear them singing words to accompany their movement. For example, children might be heard singing "bouncy-bounce, bouncy-bounce," keeping time with their bouncing. Some adults will scold or reprimand a child for such actions without redirecting this natural behavior. Why not provide some type of cushiony material, such as an old mattress or a gym pad, for this type of activity?

When accompanying children's movements or singing, teachers should synchronize the accompaniment to the tempo of the children's movements.

Have you ever noticed how many children run in complete abandon, waving their arms like birds? Have you ever watched and listened as youngsters keep perfect time while walking around the playground, dragging sticks behind them? Have you watched as they teeter back and forth from one foot to another, humming in rhythm to their teetering movements? An appropriate recording can be played, a song hummed or sung, or clapping provided to accompany these kinds of body movements. Join in with the children. Make it a game. Show your approval.

Music as a Support to Movement

Music should support movement. Children sometimes ask for musical accompaniment as they move about. A sensitive adult can encourage a child's movements by clapping or tapping on a drum or some similar instrument. When accompanying children's movements, synchronize the accompaniment to the tempo of the movements. When working with preschoolers, teachers need to accommodate the child's own rhythm rather than have the child conform to the beat. This can be done by first watching and listening to children as they clap, tap, walk, tiptoe, and the like, then providing accompaniment that matches the child's own body rhythm.

Traditional songs for young children are popular because they encourage movement. "Patty Cake, Patty Cake" encourages children and adults to play a movement game together. "London Bridge" fosters cooperation and communication because you can't fall down or "lock 'er up" by yourself. "The Farmer in the Dell" encourages children to understand and focus on relation-

ships as children take a wife, a dog, a cat, and a mouse (Moore, 2000).

SINGING AND MUSICAL AWARENESS

Researchers have found that during the preschool and primary years, children demonstrate very positive attitudes toward many kinds of music (Wilcox, 1999, p. 31). Feierabend (1999) says, "We see a very large difference in the singing capacity and musical awareness between children five years old and younger who have been exposed to music and those who have not" (p. 19). Current research makes it very clear that children use music as meaningful communication in their earliest years of development. Parents and teachers must be involved in early music experiences with children and must continue to offer opportunities for shared music making in their homes and classrooms (Fox, 2000).

Elements of Musical Beginnings

The following basic stages of early musical development are important to consider when planning music and movement activities for 3-year-olds.

Three-year-olds can sing along with familiar songs and can establish and maintain a regular beat. For example, the 3-year-olds at the Early Childhood Development Center at the College of Charleston recently learned "Tony Chestnut," which they sang to the Board of Trustees during a special recognition awards program. They delighted in the movements, familiar phrases, and regular beat that "Tony Chestnut" provides.

TONY CHESTNUT

Traditional **Arranged by LINDA EDWARDS**

To - ny Chest - nut knows I love you, To - ny knows,

To - ny knows, To - ny Chest - nut knows I love you,

That's what To - ny knows.

(Children point to body parts as they follow the motions of an adult.)

Toe	knee	chest	head	nose	eye	hug	point
To-	ny	Chest-	nut	knows	I	love	you.

Three-year-olds also enjoy singing songs with repetitive words and often talk and sing during their daily activities. Two all-time favorites of children this age are "Row, Row, Row Your Boat" and "Old MacDonald Had a Farm." Three-year-olds can successfully make the rowing movements and sing at the same time and have been known to roll on the floor giggling when singing "E – I – E – I – O"

ROW, ROW, ROW YOUR BOAT

Traditional   **Arranged by LINDA EDWARDS**

Row,   row,   row   your boat   gent - ly down   the   stream.

Mer - ri - ly,   mer - ri - ly,   mer - ri - ly,   mer - ri - ly

Life   is   but   a   dream.

"Row, Row, Row Your Boat" can also be sung as a three-part round, but singing rounds is inappropriate for very young children. Stick to the melody and have fun rowing!

OLD MACDONALD HAD A FARM

Traditional

Old Mac - Don - ald had a farm, Ee - i, ee - i - o.

And on this farm he had some chicks,*

Ee - i, ee - i - o. With a chick, chick, here, and a

chick, chick, there, Here a chick, there a chick, ev - ry - where a chick, chick.

Most children like to sing the traditional song "Old MacDonald Had a Farm." It is usually one of the first ones they like to memorize. They are "tickled" and excited as they hear their own voices produce the animal sounds in strict adherence to the interesting rhythmic pattern ("with a chick, chick, here, and a chick, chick, there," etc.). Throughout the years, this song has been adapted for many purposes. One of the ways it has been used is to help children learn their short and long vowel sounds. It is an enjoyable way for them to memorize the sounds. Once they learn it in the song, the children can easily recall a sound by associating it with the animal. The vowels are substituted for the animal sounds. For example:

Short Vowel Version

(Sing the following to the tune of "Old MacDonald")

Old MacDonald had a farm,
    Ee-i, ee-i-o.
And on this farm he had a cat,
    Ee-i, ee-i-o
With a ă-ă here, And a ă-ă there, Here
    a ă, There a ă,
    Everywhere a ă-ă .
Old MacDonald had a cat, Ee-i, ee-i-o.
Other verses: a hen—ĕ
           a pig—ĭ
           an ox—ŏ
           a duck—ŭ

Long Vowel Version

(Sing the song as above, but substitute animals having the long vowel sounds)

For example: a tapir—ā
            a sheep—ē
            some mice—ī
            a goat—ō
            a mule—ū

Note: Zoo animals could be used instead of farm animals.

Children of this age enjoy listening to recorded music and responding to or imitating the motions of others. Teachers and parents should build their own libraries of recorded music, including classical, folk, jazz, gospel, country-western, and other popular genres. College students should be encouraged to begin building their music libraries while still in school. Recorded music makes great gifts for birthdays and holidays. Most school librarians will have copies of the *Schwann Spectrum* catalog of compact discs (CDs) and tapes for reference. Listings in this catalog include available commercial recordings of musical selections by composer. You might consider organizing your musical library according to composer, country, or genre (classical, rock, pop, folk) and labeling these on the cassette or CD boxes. Follow these general guidelines when purchasing and organizing CDs and tapes:

- Choose a recording by a well-known and well-respected performing ensemble, conductor, or solo artist.
- Be sure the recording was properly engineered from an excellent master source and was well crafted.
- Purchase a recording that falls within your budget.

Keep in mind that when you download bootlegged music from the Internet, neither the composer, the performer, or the record label receive any payment. It is a matter of professional ethics to avoid involvement with pirated music from the Internet.

Three-year-olds often suggest new words for songs or add additional verses. They are also interested in rhythm instruments and enjoy playing with adults who provide simple rhythmic patterns to imitate. For example, "Four Little Monkeys" includes the frequent use of rhythmic speech with a simple pattern that is easy to imitate.

FOUR LITTLE MONKEYS

Traditional

Arranged by LINDA EDWARDS

Four lit – tle mon – keys jump – ing on the bed.

One fell off and bumped his head.

Mom – ma called the doc – tor, the doc – tor said:

"Get those mon – keys off that bed!"

Opportunities for practicing simple patterns that are easy to imitate abound in "The People on the Bus."

THE PEOPLE ON THE BUS

American Traditional   **Arranged by LINDA EDWARDS**

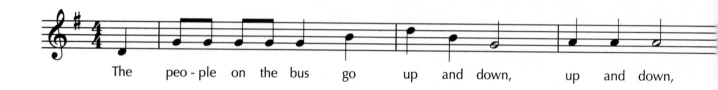

The peo-ple on the bus go up and down, up and down,

up and down, The peo-ple on the bus go

up and down, All round the town.

The wipers on the bus go swish, swish, swish.
The wheels on the bus go round and round.
The horn on the bus goes beep, beep, beep.

"The Bus" song, p. 153, from *Singing on Our Way* of OUR SINGING WORLD series. Copyright 1959, 1957, 1949. Adapted by permission of Pearson Education, Inc.

Children create their own motions to represent the words. They can also make up new verses such as "The children in the room move forward and back."

THIS LITTLE LIGHT OF MINE

Spiritual

This lit-tle light of mine, I'm gon-na let it shine.

This lit-tle light of mine, I'm gon-na let it shine.

This lit-tle light of mine, I'm gon-na let it shine, let it

shine, let it shine, let it shine.

This big world of ours, I'm gonna help it shine,
This big world of ours, I'm gonna help it shine,
This big world of ours, I'm gonna help it shine,
Help it shine, help it shine, help it shine.

THERE'S A LITTLE WHEEL

Spiritual

Arranged by K. BAYLESS

Other verses that can be added to "There's a Little Wheel":

2. Oh, I feel so very happy in my heart,
3. There's a little drum a-beating in my heart,
4. There's a little harp a-strumming in my heart,
5. There's a little bell a-ringing in my heart,
6. There's a little bit of kindness in my heart,
7. There's a little song a-singing in my heart,

*If the A is too low, sing middle C instead.

FAVORITE SONGS AND RHYTHMS

TURN AROUND

K. BAYLESS

1. Can you turn a - round with me? It's as eas - y as can be.
2. Round and round a - bout just so, Then "ker - flop," we're bound to go.

Little children like to turn around in circles. This short song makes a game of it.

Hold the child's hands. Move slowly to avoid dizziness. On the word "ker-flop," fall to the floor.

Movement concepts: turning in a circle and falling

JUMP, JUMP, JUMP

K. BAYLESS

1. You can jump, jump, jump like a lit - tle kang - a - roo.
2. When you jump, jump, jump we will sing a tune or two.

Sing the song several times until the child gets the "feel" of it.

Movement concept: jumping

SALLY, GO 'ROUND THE MOON

English Folk-Tune
Adapted by K. BAYLESS

Sal - ly, go 'round the moon, Sal - ly, go 'round the stars,

Sal - ly, go 'round the chim - ney pots, Ev - 'ry af - ter - noon. Bump!

This is a very popular singing game for children of this age. A circle is formed, and the children walk around it. (Hands may be held or dropped at sides. A circle can be made for the children to follow by using masking tape. They could also walk around the backs of a circle of chairs to keep the circle intact.) At the word *bump,* the children fall down. They get up, form the circle, and play the game again.

Tonal and rhythmic concepts: exact repetition of melody and rhythmic pattern

Music concept: staccato—note sung or played abruptly

SWING, SWING

K. BAYLESS

Swing, swing, swing, swing, See how high I go.

Up, down, up, down, to and fro.

As children swing arms back and forth, up and down, you may find this short tune appropriate. Remember, do not hesitate to make up your own musical phrases to match the movement of the child. Begin with arms swinging upwards.

Movement concept: swinging

Directional concepts: up and down

ROCKING YO HO

K. BAYLESS

Rock - ing and rock - ing, yo, ho, ho, ho. Fast - er and fast - er a -

way you go. Rock - ing and rock - ing, yo, ho, ho, ho.

Is - n't it fun to rock_____ just so!

Rocking is one of the favorite movements of most 2- to 3-year-olds.

I composed this song while watching my grandson Matthew rock back and forth on his trusty red rocking horse, a horse that has been used by three generations. The rhythm was exactly "matched" to Matthew's rocking. Matthew was 2½ years old when this song was composed.

Movement concept: rocking

I'M LIKE A BOUNCING BALL

K. BAYLESS

Steadily

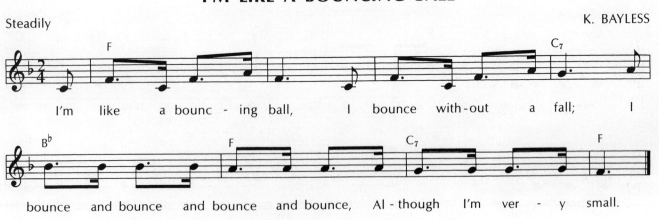

I'm like a bounc - ing ball, I bounce with-out a fall; I

bounce and bounce and bounce and bounce, Al - though I'm ver - y small.

This is a short song involving bouncing, another favorite movement of small children.

Bounce a rubber ball on the floor for the children to see. Encourage the children to bounce their bodies like the bouncing balls. Provide plenty of space for the children to move.

Movement concept: bouncing

TWO LITTLE BLACKBIRDS

Traditional   Arranged by K. BAYLESS

Two lit-tle black-birds sit-ting on a hill, One named Jack, And one named Jill.

Fly a - way Jack! Fly a - way Jill! Come back Jack! Come back! Jill.

Actions for "Two Little Blackbirds":

Two little blackbirds	(Hold up both hands,
Sitting on a hill,	thumbs erect, fingers bent)
One named Jack,	(Wiggle one thumb)
And one named Jill.	(Wiggle other thumb)
Fly away, Jack!	(Bend down one thumb)
Fly away, Jill!	(Bend down other thumb)
Come back, Jack!	(Raise one thumb erect)
Come back, Jill!	(Raise other thumb erect)

Tonal and rhythmic concepts: exact repetition of melody and rhythmic pattern

TWO LITTLE APPLES

Chant and Song   Traditional

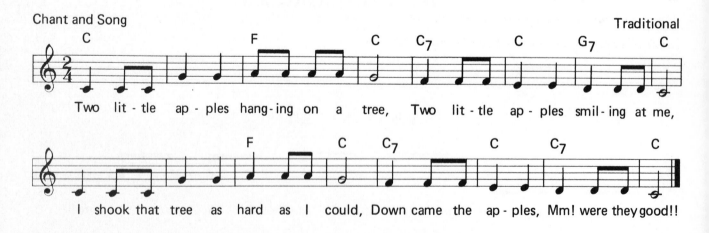

Two lit-tle ap-ples hang-ing on a tree, Two lit-tle ap-ples smil-ing at me,

I shook that tree as hard as I could, Down came the ap-ples, Mm! were they good!!

Chant the words of the verse, and add appropriate movements.

This can also be used as a song. Extend the arms to each side. Pretend to be holding two apples, one in each hand. Shake the body (tree). Squat down, and rub the tummy.

Concept: coordination of movements and words

WHERE IS THUMBKIN?

Traditional

Musical fingerplay

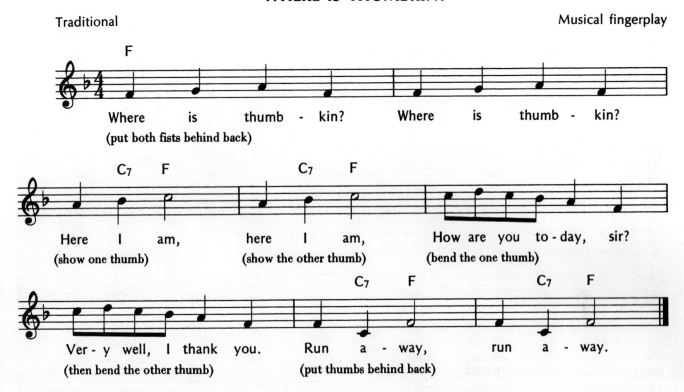

Where is thumb - kin? Where is thumb - kin?
(put both fists behind back)

Here I am, here I am, How are you to - day, sir?
(show one thumb) (show the other thumb) (bend the one thumb)

Ver - y well, I thank you. Run a - way, run a - way.
(then bend the other thumb) (put thumbs behind back)

2. Where is pointer? (forefinger)
3. Where is tall man? (middle finger)
4. Where is ring man? (ring finger)
5. Where is pinkie? (little finger)

Movement concept: development of small muscles

Musical concept: matching measures that sound the same

THE OLD GRAY CAT

Traditional American song

Accompaniment by K. BAYLESS

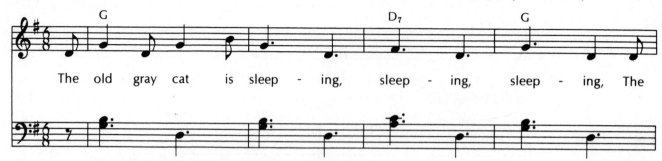

The old gray cat is sleep - ing, sleep - ing, sleep - ing, The

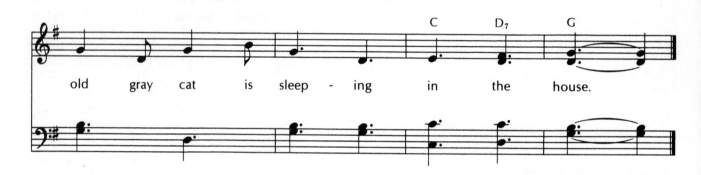

old gray cat is sleep - ing in the house.

2. The little mice are creeping, creeping, creeping,
   The little mice are creeping through the house.
3. The little mice are nibbling . . . in the house.
4. The little mice are sleeping . . . in the house.

5. The old gray cat comes creeping . . . through the house.
6. The little mice all scamper . . . through the house.
7. The little mice are hiding . . . in the house.

Pets are always a favorite topic of conversation with children. "The Old Gray Cat" is a song-game that young children like to dramatize. As the song is sung, listen to the words. They tell you what to do.

Suggestions
On verses 1, 2, 3, 4, 5, and 7, soft voices should be used. In verse 6, use louder voices.

Rhythmic concept: *adapting rhythmic movements to word meanings*

Dynamic concepts: *soft and loud*

PLANNING MUSIC ACTIVITIES FOR YOUNG CHILDREN

Giving children both opportunities and encouragement with musical experiences can lead to a lifetime of enjoyment. It is extremely important that children be given a variety of musical experiences. Some of these may be through listening, others through exploration of what their bodies can do, such as singing, movement, and playing instruments. At various ages and stages, children will discover new and different ways in which music can enrich their lives.

Since most children naturally love to sing, allow them to pursue this activity as much as possible. Don't limit singing to nursery rhymes. Present "folk tunes, camp songs, songs from musicals, or songs you've learned from other sources. Children have an endless hunger to hear new songs and to repeat old favorites" (Gorka, 1989, p. 93). The benefits of singing for the toddler are many. "Singing improves vocabulary and language skills as well as auditory memory and introduces him in a very pleasant way to the dynamics of cooperative group activity" (Gorka, 1989, p. 93).

During this age, movement activities should be given high priority. Andress (1989, p. 30) reminds us that "in the area of movement, research supports the long-held belief that preschool children move at a faster overall tempo than adults and that effective teaching in terms of beat coordination involves matching the tempo of the child." This finding is often forgotten. Smith (2000) recommends four essential elements that should always be included in music activities for young children: singing, listening, playing instruments, and moving (p. 47). She identifies these as the core activities in music and movement development. This chapter introduced a variety of ways to involve young children in these core activities. Just remember that when you plan music and movement experiences for young children, it is imperative to keep in mind their growth and development patterns. Too often, children are asked to engage in activities that are beyond their abilities. As you continue to think about the importance of children's developmental patterns and stages of growth, you should consider the Music Educators National Conference standards for music education. The following section reviews these standards and provides guidelines to keep in mind when planning music activities for young children.

National Standards for Music Education

The Music Educators National Conference (MENC) established standards (1994) that reflect that organization's beliefs concerning the musical learning of young children. These standards provide a framework for teachers who work with young children and should assist teachers in planning a music curriculum that is developmentally appropriate. In a position statement (available at www.menc.org), the MENC reports that effective music teaching in the preschool classroom should

1. Support the child's total development—physical, emotional, social, and cognitive
2. Recognize the wide range of normal development in preschoolers and the need to differentiate their instruction
3. Facilitate learning through active interaction with adults and other children, as well as with music materials
4. Consist of learning activities and materials that are real, concrete, and relevant to the lives of young children
5. Provide opportunities for children to choose from among a variety of music activities, materials, and equipment of varying degrees of difficulty
6. Allow children time to explore music through active involvement

The national standards for 2- and 3-year-old children are more general in nature than those for older children. The younger children should be exposed to a variety of sound sources and recorded music. They should be given opportunities to freely improvise songs and to build a selected repertoire. Children at this age should have a variety of individual musical experiences, with little or no emphasis on activities that require them to perform.

All of the activities and experiences presented in this edition are built on these standards and can be adapted to individual children, different classroom settings, and the regular classroom teacher's ability to explore these ideas with young children.

The truest expression of a people is in its dance and music.

—Agnes de Mille

KEY IDEAS

1. For 2- and 3-year-olds, music making is often an individual activity.
2. Children learn by listening and experimenting.
3. Caregivers should capitalize on the child's environment and responses as cues.

SUMMARY

Observation and participation will provide the teacher or caregiver with ample direction for music making with the twos and threes. Observation means seeing, asking questions, listening, and looking—wherever young children are. Participation means playing, singing, chanting, eating, and moving with young children. Spontaneity and creativity should mark much of the activity at these age levels. The environment should be uncomplicated and uncluttered to promote freedom of expression. Above all, keep in mind that for the twos and threes, music is predominantly individual; music is for enjoyment and delight; music is for sharing.

QUESTIONS TO CONSIDER

1. Select four or five unusual objects that could be used to build good listening habits. Describe an activity with each.
2. Find and record on tape several catchy, action-oriented rhythms appropriate for twos and threes. How might your tape enhance listening skills?
3. Interview the mother of a toddler, and determine how the home environment is used to develop the child's perceptual awareness.
4. Revisit the day care center. Select three songs from this chapter to present to the children. Summarize the results.

REFERENCES

Andress, B.(1989). Music for every stage. *Music Educators Journal, 76*(2), 22–27.

Boutte, G. (2000). Multiculturalism: Moral and educational implications. *Dimensions of Early Childhood, 28*(3), 9–16.

Campbell, P. S. (1995). Mellonee Burnim on African American music. *Music Educators Journal, 82*(1), 41–48.

Carleton, E. B. (2000). Learning through music: The support of brain research. *Childcare Information Exchange, 133*, 53–56.

Feierabend, J. M. (1999). Make music, America! At MENC's national conference. *Teaching Music, 7* (3), 19–27.

Fox, D. B. (2000). Music and the baby's brain: Early experiences. *Music Educators Journal, 87*(2), 23–27.

Gorka, J. (1989, March). The gift of music. *Parents*, pp. 88–93.

Moore, T. (2000). Music: The great connector. *Childcare Information Exchange, 133*, 50–52.

Music Educators National Conference. (1994). *National standards for music education*. Retrieved March 19, 2002 from http://www.menc.org/publication/books/standards.htm.

Puckett, M., & Diffily, D. (1999). *Teaching young children*. New York: Harcourt Brace College.

Saul, J. D., & Saul, B. (2001). Multicultural activities throughout the year. *Multicultural Education, 8* (4), 38–40.

Smith, C. (2000). For the love of music—and children. *Childcare Information Exchange, 133*, 45–60.

Strickland, E. (2001). Move to the music. *Scholastic Early Childhood Today, 15*(4), 36–37.

Wilcox, E. (1999). Straight talk about music and brain research. *Teaching Music, 7* (3), 29–33.

SONG COLLECTIONS

Once a Lullaby. (1983)
B. P. Nichol
Greenwillow Books, New York, NY

120 Singing Games and Dances for Elementary School (1996)
Lois Choksy and David Brummit
Prentice Hall, Upper Saddle River, NJ

RECORDINGS

All About Me (**I Like to Sing, Vol. I**) (Cassette)
Millie Burnett
Alfred, Van Nuys, CA (1990)
Baby Face (Cassette and CD)
Georgiana Stewart Kimbo
> *Activities for infants and toddlers. Ways of turning baby's playtime into fun and meaningful learning experiences.*

The Baby Record (Cassette and CD)
Bob McGrath and Katherine Smithrim
Children's Book and Music Center
> *Rhymes, fingerplays, action songs, and lullabies for babies.*

Come on Everybody, Let's Sing (CD)
Lewis Birkenshaw-Fleming
Gordon V. Thompson Music Pub., Toronto
Music for Very Little People: 50 Playful Activities for Infants and Toddlers (Cassette)
John Feierabend and Ernst Krenek
Boosey and Hawkes, Farmingdale, NY (1987)
Musictivity: Sing Me a Story (CD and book)
Hap Palmer
Hal Leonard, Milwaukee, WI (1993)

CHAPTER FIVE

Music for the Threes and Fours

*Knowledge is tied to action. It is through children's
exploration and discovery among their actions that the first
structures of mind are formed.*

Jean Piaget

Around 3 years of age, children are beginning to take a real interest in music and movement of all kinds. As physical development progresses from large to small muscle control, the random movements of the infant progress to the point at which the child gains control over specific parts of the body and refines their use. Early childhood developmental specialists describe movement in terms of locomotor skills, such as walking, running, jumping, hopping, galloping, and skipping. Manipulative development includes movements such as reaching, grasping, releasing, throwing, catching, and striking. "In the cognitive realm, movement activities can help preschoolers learn body parts and understand abstract, spatial concepts such as up and down, backward, forward, and sideways, and over and under" (Paglin, 2000, p. 28).

Movement is fun for young children, and movement for movement's sake is significant. Children learn to use their bodies and move with confidence. They feel more self-assured and enjoy themselves while developing a physical awareness that enhances their ability to explore on their own.

Laban's (1963) classic theory on young children and movement includes two areas of awareness that young children develop through movement. Laban suggests that children develop body awareness and space awareness. Pica (1995) expands on Laban's theory by suggesting three different approaches for early childhood teachers when planning music and movement activities for young children. The direct approach is teacher directed and taught through demonstration, modeling, and imitation. For example, hand clapping can be demonstrated and imitated by young children who have not been introduced to clapping. The guided discovery method allows children to experiment while a teacher guides them through a process. For example, the children are asked to move like a rabbit, hopping and leaping. Or a teacher might ask children questions such as "How do rabbits move?" The third approach, exploration, encourages children to respond to open-ended suggestions that can produce a variety of responses. For example, if children are asked to pretend to grow from a seed into a tall tree, numerous combinations of movement are possible. When combined with music, more experimentation is encouraged and more possibilities are available to the children.

GARDNER'S THEORY OF MULTIPLE INTELLIGENCES

Harvard University psychologist Howard Gardner, author of *Multiple Intelligences,* believes that human beings possess nine intelligences, including the "musical intelligence," "bodily kinesthetic intelligence," and "logical-mathematical intelligence." Children possess a natural awareness and sensitivity to musical sounds. They explore music with more spontaneity than any other age group,

and they venture forward into music and movement activities with their voices, their bodies, and their emotions. The whole child is involved. The child's affective, cognitive, and psychomotor responses to a musical encounter are the hallmark of creativity. Gardner (1973) provides us with a very perceptive observation that paints a lovely picture of children and their music:

> The child attending to a piece of music or a story listens with his whole body. He may be at rapt attention and totally engrossed; or he may be swaying from side to side, marching, keeping time, or alternating between such moods. But in any case, his reaction to such art objects is a bodily one, presumably permeated by physical sensations (pp. 152–153)

Musical Intelligence

This intelligence involves the ability to perceive, produce, and appreciate pitch (or melody) and rhythm and to appreciate the forms of musical expressiveness. Composers, performers, musicians, conductors, and "the child attending to a piece of music" all possess a great deal of musical intelligence. Conductor and composer Leonard Bernstein, composer and performer Ray Charles, classical composer Igor Stravinsky, conductor Zubin Mehta, the world's "First Lady of Song" Ella Fitzgerald, renowned 20-century pianist Arthur Rubinstein, and guitarists and songwriters James Taylor and Eric Clapton are all examples of individuals with immense musical intelligence.

Bodily-Kinesthetic Intelligence

The ability to control one's body movements and to handle objects skillfully are the core components of bodily-kinesthetic intelligence. Gardner specifies that bodily intelligence is used by dancers, choreographers, athletes, mimes, surgeons, craftspeople, and others who use their hands and bodies in a problem-solving kind of way. Classic examples of individuals whose skills are embodied in this form of intelligence include American dancer and choreographer Alvin Ailey; Isadora Duncan, the pioneer dancer of this century; Katherine Dunham, the first choreographer and dancer to bring African dance to the American stage; Charlie Chaplin and Buster Keaton, the great silent clowns of the past; and contemporary masters of humorous characterizations, such as Robin Williams and Bill Cosby. Athletes like Venus and Serena Williams and Michelle Kwan also excel in grace, power, and accuracy.

Logical-Mathematical Intelligence

Mathematicians, scientists, and composers certainly have this form of intelligence, which involves a sensitivity to and a capacity to discern logical or numerical patterns (including rhythm, meter, time signature, and note value) and the ability to handle long chains of reasoning. Some examples of people who demonstrate highly developed logical-mathematical intelligence include Johann Sebastian Bach, scientists Albert Einstein and Madame Curie, biologist Ernest Everett Just, and botanist George Washington Carver. The capacity to explore patterns, categories, and relationships can be heard in the four-part harmony and counterpoint music from the baroque period.

An example of logical-mathematical intelligence in composers is revealed in Bach's colossal work, *The Art of Fugue,* often referred to as a transmission of a purely abstract theory. In any case, *The Art of Fugue* is an excellent example of logical-mathematical intelligence, carrying pure counterpoint to its height. Read the following description of *The Art of Fugue,* and you may agree that Bach's work is as complex as any mathematical problem you have ever tried to solve.

> It starts with four fugues, two of which present the theme, the others presenting the theme in contrary motion (that is, back to front). Then there are counter fugues, in which the original subject is inverted (turned upside down) and combined with the original. There are double and triple fugues, several canons, three pairs of mirror fugues. To make the mirror reflection doubly realistic, the treble of the first fugue becomes the bass of the second fugue, the alto changes into a tenor, the tenor into an alto, and the bass into a treble, with the result that No. 12:2 appears like 12:1 standing on its head. (Schonberg, 1981, p. 43)

Certainly, few readers will understand what all of that means, but it does make a good case for including logical-mathematical intelligence in this chapter on music and movement!

The concept of musical, bodily-kinesthetic, and logical-mathematical intelligences suggests that our ability to produce and appreciate rhythm, pitch, and timbre while appreciating the many forms of musical expression and our ability to use our bodies and to handle objects skillfully deserve to be nourished so that we can function at our fullest potential as human beings. According to Gardner, our success as adults in musical, bodily-kinesthetic, and logical-mathematical competency may have been helped or hindered by experiences during our early childhood years. Gardner challenges educators to recognize these separate intelligences and to nurture them as universal intelligences that serve important functions in children's cognitive, affective, social, and physical development.

SUPPORTING CHILDREN'S INTELLIGENCES

As you prepare to guide young children in these areas of intelligence, remember to plan for a broad range of hands-on learning activities. Introduce your children to Marcel Marceau and the great tradition of mime. Show them how the artistic form of mime integrates body movement and

"Miss Polly" is a wonderful song that encourages children to integrate play and music.

the ability to use the body in expressive, nonverbal ways. Give your children crayons and paper, and encourage them to "draw" Pachelbel's *Canon in D*. Provide opportunities for children to use their bodies as a medium of expression. Let them dramatize or role-play stories or different outcomes to traditional folktales. Introduce physical awareness exercises, and use kinesthetic imagery to increase body awareness. Videotape the dances of your children, and allow them to watch and reflect on the dances they have created.

Gardner's Message to Teachers

If we, as teachers, are to be committed to the development of all of a child's intelligences, we must provide music and movement activities as a means of fostering these important areas of human potential. To do anything less is to deny children an opportunity to function at their fullest. In a 1991 interview, Daniel Gursky (1991) quotes Gardner as saying, "To get teachers to think deeply about their strengths, their students' strengths, and how to achieve curricular goals while taking those strengths and different profiles seriously is a huge job. Teachers can't be expected to become 'multiple intelligence mavens' but they should know where to send students for help in, say, music or dance" (p. 42). Gardner's statement does not give us permission to assign musical and bodily-kinesthetic development solely to the music, dance, or physical education specialist. Music, movement, dance, physical awareness, and physical activities deserve the same natural assimilation in the early childhood curriculum as do storytelling and nap time.

At 3 and 4 years of age, children are almost continually in motion: walking, jumping, running, rocking, swinging, galloping, stomping, and tapping. In many instances, these movements can be channeled into the dramatization of action songs or simple, musical episodes or stories. The selected characteristics of 3- to 4-year-olds, shown in Figure 5-1, will be helpful when selecting and planning appropriate music activities for this age group.

NATIONAL STANDARDS FOR MUSIC EDUCATION FOR FOUR-YEAR-OLDS

The standards in this section are intended for 4-year-old children. It is important to remember that the skills of young children develop along a continuum, and developmentally appropriate activities can be used with younger children (Music Educators National Conference, 1994).

Singing and Playing Instruments

Young children enjoy singing and playing instruments. Four-year-olds are able to differentiate between their singing and speaking voices. They are also able to express themselves by playing instruments. The following standards identify the type of singing and instruments that are most suitable for 4-year-olds.

- Children use their voices as they speak, chant, and sing.
- Children sing a variety of simple songs in various keys, meters, and genres, alone and in groups, becoming increasingly accurate in rhythm and pitch.
- Children experiment with a variety of instruments and other sound sources.
- Children play simple melodies and accompaniments on instruments.

Creating Music

Four-year-olds are quite capable of creating sound patterns with their bodies, their voices, and instruments. They often create simple melodies while at play. They also create musical sounds to express an idea. The following standards focus on a child's ability to create music.

- Children improvise songs to accompany their play activities.
- Children improvise instrumental accompaniments to songs, recorded selections, stories, and poems.
- Children create short pieces of music, using voices, instruments, and other sound sources.
- Children invent and use original graphic or symbolic systems to represent vocal and instrumental sounds and musical ideas.

Responding to Music

Four-year-olds are able to recognize musical phrases and show an awareness of simple cadences. They can identify the speed of music (fast/slow, getting faster/slower) and can describe the volume of music in their own words. The standards listed below focus on responding to music.

- Children identify the sources of a wide variety of sounds.
- Children respond through movement to music of various tempos, meters, dynamics, modes, genres, and

Children respond through movement to various tempos and styles. They also enjoy the attention they get when dancing with their teacher.

Figure 5-1 Selected Characteristics of Three- to Four-Year-Olds

- Like to gallop, jump, walk, or run in time to music
- Are much more fluent with language, like to talk and chatter, want adults to listen and to give their undivided attention
- Have more interest in detail and direction (for example, can usually find a favorite book or CD from a shelf upon request)
- Enjoy simple versions of imaginative, dramatic play
- Enjoy singing games and rhythm instruments (they still need to explore, experiment, and manipulate instruments)
- Are beginning to dramatize songs
- Spontaneously make up their own songs, often with repetitive words and tunes that resemble familiar ones

Consider the following when planning musical activities for a child this age:
- Encourage informal singing throughout the day.
- Continue to improvise short action songs based on what the child is doing.
- Provide plenty of opportunities for the child to dramatize songs and to "act out" song-stories.
- Provide simple props like scarves, puppets, and instruments for the child to use with musical activities.
- Introduce humorous, active songs, which hold high appeal.
- Continue to introduce rhythm and melody instruments to enhance musical activities.
- Provide increased opportunities for movement with music, such as performing locomotor movements (walking, running, jumping), nonlocomotor movements (swinging, pushing, bending), and clapping or tapping the beat of a steady rhythm.
- Encourage children to move and dance to music using their own creative ideas.

styles to express what they hear and feel in works of music.
- Children participate freely in music activities.

Understanding Music

Four-year-olds will listen attentively to a selected repertoire of music. They are also capable of using musical terms and concepts to express thoughts about music. They are good at practicing basic audience and performance etiquette. This last set of standards addresses understanding music.

- Children use their own vocabulary and standard music vocabulary to describe voices, instruments, music notation, and music of various genres, styles, and periods from diverse cultures.
- Children sing, play instruments, move, or verbalize to demonstrate awareness of the elements of music and changes in their usage.
- Children demonstrate an awareness of music as a part of daily life.

CONCEPTUAL LEARNING THROUGH MUSIC AND MOVEMENT

The American Academy of Pediatrics reports that movement is essential to the physical and cognitive development of preschoolers. Children at this age master basic movement skills, such as running and skipping, as they explore their world. When using movement activities with these young children, we should remember that there is much individual variation in development. Movement experiences are a critical part of early childhood education (Paglin, 2000).

Music as Communication

Movement, as a form of expression, is fundamental to conceptual development. For young children especially, movement is among the earliest forms of communication through which children explore and learn about their world because movement allows for the expression of ideas and imagination without words (Koff, 2000). Movement also helps children with their overall gross motor development. When children move, they explore their bodies in relation to space, which is valuable in developing body awareness. When combined with music, movement helps children acquire a feel for the rhythm and mood of the music. Children will use their whole body to explore changes in tempo or rhythm, and these kinesthetic actions facilitate muscle development and heighten awareness of the kinesthetic senses.

Movement is also a great source of joy and pleasure to children. They are eager to be physically free to move, to be spontaneous in their physical responses to music, and to show joy in movement simply for its own sake.

As all early childhood educators know, movement to music begins very early. Émile Jaques-Dalcroze (1865–1950), a Swiss composer, believed that movement was the best way to help children learn to love and appreciate music (1921). He believed that it was important to focus on the *process* of movement during the early years, rather than on the *product* (Brewer, 1995). Movement experiences for young children should include both creative and structured movements. When children move in creative ways, they are interpreting the music and movement in their own ways; their movements may or may not match the beat of the music. For example, when children move in response to a teacher's suggestion—such as to move fast or slow or to move high or low—all of the children will not move the same way all of the time.

Music and Play

Much movement for children this age takes place during free playtime. "From a developmental perspective, a child's interest in play and physical exploration continues throughout childhood" (Koff, 2000, p. 28). It is also important to provide unstructured activity, such as recess, so that young children can have the freedom to move their bodies. Unstructured time can foster physical development, aid self-exploration through nonverbal communication with others, and provide exciting reinforcement to more traditional movement activities. When inside the classroom, music often accompanies indoor free play. If a recording with an inviting rhythm is played, one or more children may spontaneously decide that they would like to dance. Two children may take each other's hands and dance to the music.

Musical Concepts

Preschoolers can be challenged to explore the relationships between types of movement and kinds of sounds. For example, Strickland (2001) suggests that "a triangle produces a high-pitched sound that may encourage tiptoeing or prancing. A drumbeat produces a low-pitched sound that might encourage plodding movements or stomping" (p. 36). Teachers might collect a variety of animal pictures and match these to the sounds produced by rhythm instruments. Show the children the picture of an animal, play the corresponding instrument, and ask the children to move like that animal might move. Or play an instrument, and ask the children to look at several animal pictures and identify the animal that matches the sound.

Musical concepts can be taught quite easily. They are not taught in a highly structured manner during one session but are learned gradually over a period of time. For example, songs and singing games involving movement are very appropriate to use with children at this age. Initially, some children will not want to join in these sessions, but with time they will want to become a part of the group. *Remember to keep the group small.*

Music from Around the World

The early childhood classroom should reflect a variety of cultures integrated into all curriculum topics every day. The National Association for the Education of Young Children (NAEYC) recommends that "staff provide books, dolls, toys, wall decorations, and recordings that reflect diverse images children may not likely see elsewhere" (National Association for the Education of Young Children, 1991).

With the current emphasis on multiculturalism in education, it is critical that we provide young children the opportunity to learn the music of cultures other than their own. When we do this, we help young children better understand these other cultures. This must be a high priority for all early childhood teachers. The following section presents a delightful song and dance from the Carribean Islands—"Brown Girl in the Ring"—that can be used to promote just such understanding and sensitivity.

Caribbean Ring Dances

The rhymes and songs of the Caribbean Islands can often be traced to their French, English, and African roots. The song "Brown Girl in the Ring" is sung as a circle game. One child stands in the middle of the ring and makes a motion that the other children mimic. The source for this song is a collection of Afro-Caribbean rhymes, games, and songs for children compiled by Grace Hallworth and illustrated by Caroline Binch (1996).

Brown Girl in the Ring

There's a brown girl in the ring
Tra la-la-la-la.
There's a brown girl in the ring
Tra la-la-la-la.
A brown girl in the ring,
Tra la-la-la-la.
For she's sweet like a sugar
And a plum, plum, plum.
Now show me your motion,
Tra la-la-la-la.
Now show me your motion,
Tra la-la-la-la.
For she's sweet like a sugar
And a plum, plum, plum.
Now hug and kiss your partner,
Tra la-la-la-la.
Now hug and kiss your partner,
Tra la-la-la-la.
Now hug and kiss your partner,
Tra la-la-la-la.
For she's sweet like a sugar
And a plum, plum, plum.

In addition, you might consider purchasing a recording by Marley and Booker of reggae and calypso songs for children. I highly recommend their *Smilin' Island of Songs: Reggae and Calypso Music for Children* (Redway, CA: Little People Music, 1992).

Figure 5-2 Dramatizing Movement

- Move in a happy way.
- Move in an angry way.
- Move as if you were sad.
- See how gently (roughly) you can move.
- Dance like a rag doll.
- Pretend that you are a tree and that the wind is blowing you around.
- Gallop around the room like a horse.
- Hop around the room like a rabbit.
- Move as if you were carrying something very heavy.
- Swing and sway your body and arms like a monkey.
- Pretend you are swimming. How would your body, arms, and legs move?
- Pretend that you are a jack-in-the-box.
- Make yourself into a flat balloon, and slowly blow yourself up.
- Pretend that you are a puppet with strings and that someone else is making you move.
- How would you move if you were looking for something you have lost?
- Move as if you were walking in very deep snow, through a deep river, in hot sand, on cold ice.

Young children often combine elements of space, time, and force into spontaneous dance.

Creative Movement

Early childhood teachers recognize that movement involves the use of space, energy, and time. We also know that young children often combine elements of space, energy, and time into dance. They love to walk, run, jump, and clap to music freely or as directed. Young children can express themselves through a variety of body movements. The ideas presented in Figure 5-2 provide open-ended experiences for children. The activities are designed to allow freedom of expression, which will differ from child to child. As children become involved in these movement activities, they may begin to add drama and their own creative interpretation and imagination to their movements. For example, you might ask your children to move as if they were pushing a heavy wagon. Some of your children may have some knowledge of how to move a heavy wagon, while others may

represent their understanding of wagons from what they have seen on television. As another example, you might ask children to pretend they are popping popcorn. How would they move as the kernels start to sizzle and then explode into fluffy, delicious popcorn? Whatever the case, when children express what they know about walking in the rain or how a jack-in-the-box actually pops forward, their interpretation must be honored. Most significantly, your children are moving their bodies in ways that represent what they know (or don't know) about the workings of their world.

FAVORITE SONGS AND RHYTHMS

Have you observed how often children chant and sing about what they are doing? You will often hear them sing their own words to a familiar tune like "Here We Go Round the Mulberry Bush." This kind of spontaneous play with words and music should be encouraged. The following songs make use of this idea.

People don't sing because they are happy, they're happy because they sing.

—Goethe

THIS IS THE WAY

Adapted by K. BAYLESS
Here We Go Round the Mulberry Bush

Traditional English nursery rhyme tune

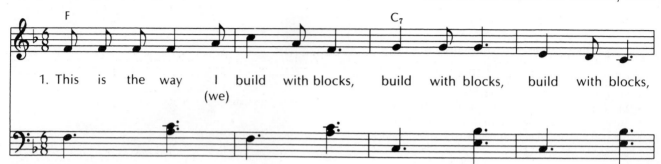

1. This is the way I build with blocks, build with blocks, build with blocks,
   (we)

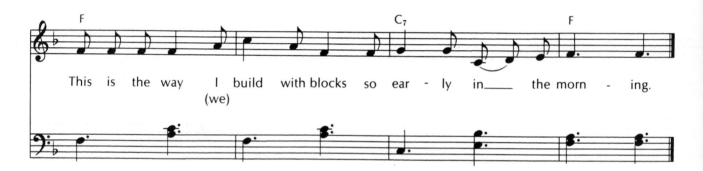

This is the way I build with blocks so ear - ly in___ the morn - ing.
(we)

Additional suggested verses:

2. This is the way we clean our room.

3. This is the way I water the plants.

4. Tammie is wiping the tables clean.

5. Tommy is putting the trucks away.

I'M A LITTLE TEAPOT

Traditional

Words and music by CLARENCE KELLEY and GEORGE H. SANDERS
Adapted by K. BAYLESS

Suggestions

This is one of the favorite songs of young children. They love to act it out and will usually learn the words and melody quickly. When they know the song well, try the following. Sing to the children the musical phrase "I'm a little teapot, short and stout." Then ask them to listen carefully while you sing "When I get all steamed up then I shout." Tell them that the words are different but that the music sounds alike. Then sing it again in the same manner. This method will help sharpen children's awareness that some phrases in music are exactly alike. If they have this concept pointed out to them as they sing different songs, some children will soon be able to hear these similarities. *Caution:* Do not drill this. The ability to detect these similarities and differences will come with practice. Always keep the spirit of enjoyment as the foremost concern.

Tonal and rhythmic concepts: *repeated melody and rhythmic pattern*

Movement concepts: *sweeping and bending*

LOOK AND SEE

Adapted by K. BAYLESS

1. Look and see, Look and see, Look and see what I can do!

2
Try with me,
Try with me,
Try and see what we can do!

3
Tap with me,
Tap with me,
Tap and see what we can do!

This song encourages children to participate. Choose one child to be the leader and act out a movement. The group follows the action of the leader. Children take turns suggesting other actions, such as jumping and twisting. Until the children get used to this type of game activity, the teacher may need to make suggestions.

"Open, Shut Them" is one of the favorite musical fingerplays of children. It is an excellent song to help improve children's enunciation of words, to help them stabilize each tone as it is sung, and to help them build better listening skills. Children need to listen intently so they can follow the directions indicated by the words. The song is also used as an effective transition song in settling children for another activity.

OPEN, SHUT THEM

LAURA PENDLETON MACCARTENEY

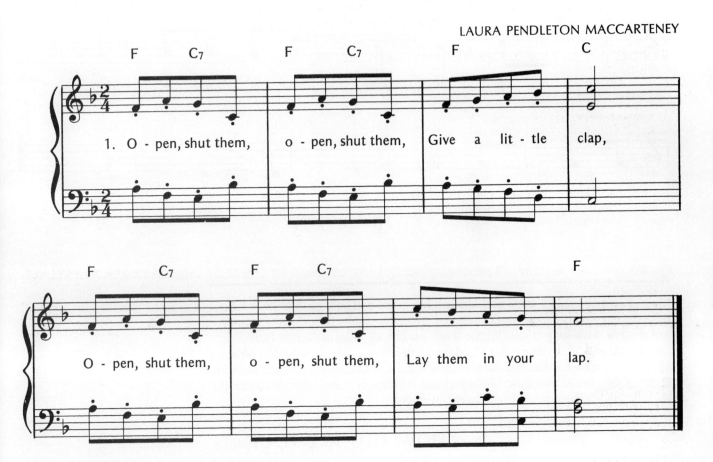

2
Creep them, creep them, creep them, creep them,
Right up to your chin,
Open wide your little mouth,
But do not let them in.

From MacCarteney, Laura Pendleton. *Songs for the Nursery School.* Florence, Ky.: Willis Music Co., 1937.

Expression concepts*: staccato singing and playing*

Children will differ in their responses to types of music, rhyme, and suggested activities. Short, easy-to-sing songs like "Dance in a Circle" often motivate young children to participate, thus freeing them to initiate their own creative responses.

DANCE IN A CIRCLE

Source unknown
Adapted by K. BAYLESS

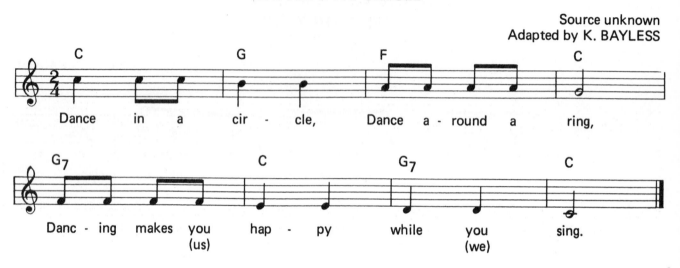

Most children like to be asked how old they are. Some will hold up their fingers for the number of years and then will smile and answer correctly. Note that the melody and rhythm in the song "How Old Are You?" are exactly alike in the first two measures. Sing "How old are you?" and then pause before singing it the second time. Help the children discover that the two measures sound exactly alike. It will not take children long to discover these similarities and differences in melodies and rhythms if they are guided in a developmental, sequential way.

HOW OLD ARE YOU?

K. BAYLESS

Musical concepts: repetition of melody and rhythmic pattern

"The Peanut Song" and "Miss Polly" are two favorite songs of young children that have been handed down through the years. Children love the fun-filled words in "The Peanut Song" and the definite rhythmic quality and rhyming words of "Miss Polly." When singing "Miss Polly," most children begin immediately to act out the words of the song. Often, when singing an action-type song with other children, the shy child begins to feel more comfortable in joining in with the others.

THE PEANUT SONG

Traditional

1. Oh, the pea - nut sat on the rail-road track, His heart was all a - flut - ter. The choo-choo train came down the track, Toot, toot, pea - nut but - ter.

2
Oh, the bullfrog sat on a lily pad,
A-looking up at the sky.
The lily pad broke, and the frog fell in
And got water in his eye.

MISS POLLY

Unknown

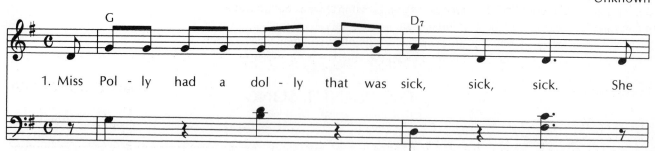

1. Miss Pol - ly had a dol - ly that was sick, sick, sick. She

phon'd for the doc - tor to come quick, quick, quick.

2
The doctor came with his cane and hat.
He knocked on the door with a rat, tat, tat.

3
He looked at the dolly and he shook his head.
He said, "Miss Polly, put her straight to bed."

4
He wrote on the paper for a pill, pill, pill.
"I'll be back in the morning with a bill, bill, bill!"

Children are very proud when they can tell others their names and addresses. The words to "Name Your Street" have been set to the familiar tune "London Bridge Is Falling Down." Children find it much easier to sing new songs that have familiar melodies.

NAME YOUR STREET

Traditional tune

Adapted by K. BAYLESS

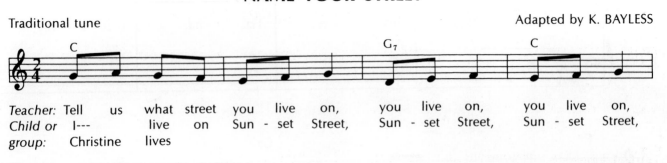

Teacher: Tell us what street you live on, you live on, you live on,
Child or I--- live on Sun - set Street, Sun - set Street, Sun - set Street,
group: Christine lives

Tell us what street you live on, (Chris - tine), please.
I--- live on Sun - set Street, Yes, I do.
Christine lives Yes, she does.

HA, HA, THIS-A-WAY

American folk song

Arranged by K. BAYLESS

KEY IDEAS

1. Around 3 years of age, children are beginning to take a real interest in music activities.
2. At this age, children are almost continually in motion. This motion can often be channeled into productive ways of using music.
3. Children frequently chant and sing about what they are doing. This kind of play with words and music should be encouraged.
4. Teachers and parents can begin to help children understand that music has structure.

SUMMARY

When music is presented within a cognitive framework that is appropriate for young children, meaning and understanding take place. Concepts should not be taught in a highly structured manner, but introduced gradually over a period of time. Since children of this age are almost continually in motion, they should be given opportunities to act out stories, play singing games, and use movement in meaningful ways.

QUESTIONS TO CONSIDER

1. Select four humorous songs appropriate for 3- and 4-year-olds. Develop activities for each song to promote conceptual awareness.
2. Select three everyday experiences common to this age level, and adapt each to a familiar melody. Present the songs to a child.
3. Develop a lesson plan for presentation using three songs from the chapter. Include activities, materials, and questions you wish to raise.

REFERENCES

Brewer, J. (1995). *Introduction to early childhood education: Preschool through primary grades.* Needham Heights, MA: Allyn & Bacon.

Gardner, H. (1973). *The arts and human development.* New York: Wiley.

Gursky, D. (1991, November–December). The unschooled mind. *Teacher,* 38–44.

Hallworth, G. (Ed.). (1996). *Down by the River: Afro-Caribbean Rhymes, Games, and Songs for Children* (C. Binch, Illus.). New York: Scholastic.

Jaques-Dalcroze, É. (1921). *Rhythm, music, and education* (L. F. Rubenstein, Trans.). London: Hazell Watson and Viney for the Dalcroze Society.

Koff, S. R. (2000). Toward a definition of dance education. *Childhood Education, 77*(1), 27–31.

Laban, R. (1963). *Modern educational dance.* London: MacDonald and Evans.

Music Educators National Conference. (1994). *National standards for music education.* Retrieved March 19, 2002, from http://www.menc.org/publication/books/standards.htm.

National Academy of Early Childhood Programs. (1998). *Accreditation criteria and procedures of the National Academy of Early Childhood Programs.* Washington, DC: National Association for the Education of Young Children.

Paglin, C. (2000). Dance like a caterpillar: Movement is a big part of learning for little kids. *Northwest Education, 6*(1), 26–35.

Pica, R. (1995). *Experiences in movement: With music activities.* Clifton Park, NY: Delmar Learning.

Schonberg, H. C. (1981). *The lives of the great composers* (Rev. ed.). New York: Norton.

Strickland, E. (2001). Move to the music. *Scholastic Early Childhood Today, 15*(4), 36–37.

SONG COLLECTIONS

Songs to Sing with Babies (1983)
"Miss Jackie" Weissman
10001 El Monte, Overland Park, KS 66207
   Sixty-four pages of songs and activities to do with babies. Categories include songs for rocking and nursing, riding in the car, taking a bath, cuddling, and more. Chords for piano, guitar, and Autoharp® included with the songs.

The Lullaby Songbook (1986)
Jane Yolen
Harcourt Brace Jovanovich, New York, NY

RECORDINGS

Baby Songs (VHS and DVD)
Hap and Martha Palmer
Educational Activities, Inc.
  Songs about baby's world and daily experiences.

Golden Slumbers (Cassette)
Children's Book and Music Center
  Twenty-four lullabies from around the world, sung by eight folk singers.

It's Toddler Time (Cassette and CD)
Children's Book and Music Center
  Activities designed for toddlers' fitness and development.

Lullabies from 'Round the World (Cassette)
Children's Book and Music Center
  Fourteen lovely international melodies for quiet time.

Lullabies and Laughter (Cassette)
Pat Carfra (A & M Records of Canada, Ltd.)
Children's Book and Music Center
  For babies and small children, 33 lullabies and play songs that make it easy to sing to the young child.

CHAPTER SIX

Music for the Fours and Fives

The most perfect expression of human behavior is a string quartet.

Jeffrey Tate

Music activities have traditionally been a part of preschool and kindergarten programs. Friedrich Froebel (1878), "father of the kindergarten," believed in the value of musical experiences for young children. His book, *Mother Play and Nursery Songs,* brought this point to the attention of those who worked with children of this age. He believed that children should be given ample opportunity to sing songs and to play singing games. This thought has prevailed, and now it is considered important to make music as integral a part of a child's day as eating or sleeping.

BUILDING A MEANINGFUL MUSIC CURRICULUM

Today's socioeconomic conditions demand that many parents work outside the home while their children are still young. Increasing numbers of children are being enrolled in day care centers, preschools, kindergartens, corporate child care centers, and latchkey programs throughout the country. The time spent in these programs is extending the children's day away from home. Because so many 4- and 5-year-old children are spending much of their day in these group settings, there is a great need to plan and develop optimal learning environments and programs for them.

Wolf (2000) reminds us that young children probably benefit most from early exposure to music: "Educators at all levels tout the benefit of singing and playing musically with young children" (p. 29). Music is valued not only for its potential intellectual benefits, but for the enjoyment that it gives children. Music is one facet in the total education of the child that must be nurtured and experienced. It is important to remember that music should not be limited to just singing songs; music is everything from crooning a lullaby to creatively interpreting the swans or the toy soldiers in "The Nutcracker Suite" by Tchaikovsky.

Keep these facts in mind, capitalize on them, and recognize that the early years are critical ones in forming favorable attitudes toward music. We suggest that you review the Statement of Beliefs at the beginning of this book. A music curriculum built on these beliefs can provide a solid base for establishing and carrying out the goals of a well-developed, sequential music program.

The Teacher's Role

The orientation and abilities of early childhood classroom teachers differ considerably. The teacher does not have to be classically trained in music or any of the other performing arts. The most important thing for teachers to consider is their willingness to open their classroom to musical experiences for their children and to be willing to try,

along with their children, new ways of exploring the many elements that music has to offer. With this in mind, Moravcik (2000) offers suggestions for teachers to consider when providing music activities for children. She suggests that it might be useful for teachers to reflect on the role of music in their own lives. Specifically, Moravcik recommends that you reflect on what you feel and do when you hear

- A lively piece of dance music
- A song you loved in school
- A slow processional
- A song your mother sang to you when you were a child
- A carol, hymn, or spiritual
- A song you listened to with a special friend (p. 27)

Thomas Moore, in an interview with *Early Childhood Today* (2000), says that children need to see adults who are open to music and music experiences in general. As we sing to children and with children, we open ourselves to each child's way of experiencing music. As Moore says, "It's a way of acknowledging that we are human" (p. 43).

National Standards for Music Education for Five-Year-Olds

The Music Educators National Conference (MENC) identifies age-specific standards for 2-, 3-, and 4-year-old children (http://www.menc.org/publication/books/standards.htm). These were discussed in previous chapters. The standards for 5-year-old children are included in the K–4 section of the national standards. The standards for K–4 describe the cumulative skills and knowledge expected of all students upon exiting Grade 4. Children in the earlier grades should engage in developmentally appropriate learning experiences designed to prepare them to meet these standards at Grade 4. Determining the curriculum and the specific instructional activities necessary to achieve the standards is the responsibility of states, local school districts, and individual teachers. It is important for early childhood teachers to contact their state board of education to request a copy of specific state standards.

Although the national standards for music education for 5-year-olds are grouped with Grades 1, 2, 3, and 4, it is possible to identify key standards that are appropriate for 5-year-olds. The Music Education Curriculum Standards for South Carolina, for example, are based on the national standards but have been grouped into categories for Grades K–2, Grades 3–5, Grades 6–8/7–9, and Grades 9–12. The standards listed below for K–2 are gleaned from the national standards and can be found at http://www.state.sc.us/sde/educator/standard/vparts/music.htm.

Singing

Children use their voices expressively as they speak and sing. They also enjoy singing a variety of simple songs alone and with a group. The standards listed below identify the content and skills for singing.

- Children sing in tune.
- Children use clear free tone and correct breath support.
- Children sing alone or with others.
- Children sing a variety of simple songs in various keys.

Performing on Instruments

Children perform music using a variety of sound sources. The following standards address instrumentation.

- Children play unpitched and pitched instruments.
- Children improvise simple rhythmic accompaniments.
- Children improvise simple rhythmic variations.

Movement

Children demonstrate an understanding of creative movement through self-expression.

- Children demonstrate pulse and pitch direction of music with locomotor and nonlocomotor movements.
- Children demonstrate elements of space, time, and force through expressive movement.

Listening

Children identify instruments and basic vocal types.

- Children describe musical selections.
- Children use listening skills to describe elements of music.
- Children respond appropriately with correct etiquette in a variety of concert situations.

Understanding Music in Relation to History and Culture

Children describe in simple terms how elements of music are used in music examples from various cultures of the world.

- Children explain how music is a part of and a reflection of many cultures and ethnic groups.
- Children sing, play, and listen to music from a variety of periods and musical styles and from different geographic areas.
- Children recognize that music can be associated with other art forms.

The Children's Role

The following three conditions can make or break your success as a facilitator of musical experiences for your children:

Children need to know that their classroom is a safe place to try new things when experimenting with dances or movement activities.

- *Psychological safety.* It is safe to try. Make sure your children know that your classroom is a safe place to try out new behaviors, to share ideas, and to make mistakes when learning new songs, dances, or movements or when playing instruments.
- *Comfort zone.* Assure your children that the songs they are learning, the movements they are doing, and the instruments they are playing are easy and fun.
- *Encouragement.* All children should be encouraged to participate in musical activities. However, you should never force children to participate, even if you think they should. Shy children, especially, will enter into the musical activity when they feel comfortable and not a minute before. Remember that the musical activities are for the children's enjoyment, not to complete your lesson plan.

By the time children are 4 or 5, they are ready for more planned experiences. These activities should include a good balance of listening and appreciation, singing, playing instruments and sound makers, creating songs and melodies, and moving about extensively. Consider the information in Figures 6-1 and 6-2 when planning musical activities for 4-year-olds. Figures 6-3 and 6-4 will help when planning musical activities for 5-year-olds.

LISTENING TO MUSIC

Listening (aural perception) is embodied in every phase of every activity that contributes to musical understanding and growth. It is considered to be the foundation for all

Figure 6-1 Selected Characteristics of Four-Year-Olds

- Are very active and can run up and down steps
- Can throw a ball overhand
- Like to do things their own way and resist too many directions
- Are very curious and ask many questions concerning why and how
- Talk a great deal. They like nonsense words, silly language, rhymes, and words that are repeated in poems or songs
- Love to listen to stories, will often listen to two or more stories at one sitting, and have favorites
- Are becoming more creative and imaginative
- Are beginning to understand seasons of the year, including when they occur and what takes place during each season
- Are socializing more easily and are ready for more group experiences
- On command, can place an object on, under, in front of, and in back of some other object
- Like to dramatize songs and poems as well as stories and parts of stories
- Should be able to carry out two simple directions in sequence

Figure 6-2 Characteristics to Consider When Planning Musical Activities for Four-Year-Olds

- Are beginning to enjoy group singing more
- Show increased desire to listen to music
- Take pride in their ability to identify familiar songs
- May enjoy taking a turn singing alone
- Show increased voice control and a closer approximation of pitch and rhythm
- May be able to sing an entire song accurately
- Are beginning to create songs during play
- Can talk about what a piece of music suggests
- Like to try out instruments and play along on instrumental songs
- Can improvise simple melodies
- Can identify certain sounds made by different instruments

Figure 6-3 Selected Characteristics of Five-Year-Olds

- Are generally conforming in nature, like to please, thrive on positive feedback, and are sensitive to praise and blame
- Like to jump and climb and still need plenty of big muscle activity. Muscle coordination is improving
- Are described as "wigglers" and "bundles of endless energy"
- Can sometimes skip on alternate feet and do quite well at galloping
- Like to talk a great deal and are interested in words and their meanings
- Know how old they are and can generally tell how old they will be in another year
- Like to remain close to familiar surroundings; are primarily interested in their home and community, not distant places; are interested in different cities and states if they know someone who lives there, such as grandparents or previous playmates
- Understand and can carry out actions involving words like *forward* and *backward*
- Are learning the meaning of *small, smaller,* and *smallest*
- Are often very adept at rhyming words
- Are relatively independent and self-reliant, dependable, and protective toward younger playmates and siblings

Figure 6-4 Characteristics to Consider When Planning Musical Activities for Five-Year-Olds

- Are refining and exploring musical skills previously learned
- May be able to read words to songs
- Can generally play instruments accurately
- May begin to show an interest in piano and dance lessons
- Can better synchronize body movements with the rhythm of the music

musical experiences. Listening requires skills that focus on the sound source, remembering sound sources, and responding (Anderson & Lawrence, 2001).

The ability to listen involves more than just hearing. It requires children to focus their minds on the sounds perceived. Haines and Gerber (2000) state, "This ability to pay attention is not innate but it is a learned skill, and the young child needs training and help to acquire it" (p. 9).

Earlier in this book, we urged parents and teachers to help young children become more sensitive to the sounds around them and to help them translate these sounds into meaningful experiences. These efforts should continue, since sound discrimination is vital to the musical development of the child. Unless someone has really made a point of helping a child sharpen his or her listening skills, the myriad sounds that must be confronted will often cause poor listening habits to be established prior to school.

Music activities provide an excellent means for increasing children's listening skills. Four- and five-year-olds can develop listening skills that will help them sing in tune, create melodies, accompany themselves on instruments, and move to music. They can be taught to listen to the expressive elements of music, such as melody, rhythm, and dynamics. "In one way or another, music at all levels is focused on listening. The purposes and outcomes of listening may vary with the age of the listener and the musical setting, but there is perhaps no other music behavior so widely valued as good listening" (Flowers, 1990, p. 21).

Headphones can help children focus on listening to music.

A very important principle to keep in mind is that children cannot develop a high level of listening skill unless attentive listening is stressed. Listening is perceiving and requires thought and reasoning. Children's minds must be "filled" with musical images in order to build on what is new and unfamiliar to them musically. This takes time and can only be developed gradually through children's active participation in diverse and varied musical experiences.

Conditions That Promote Good Listening

It is relatively easy to encourage children to listen to a variety of music. Children may need guidance in what to listen for, such as phrases, melody, and rhythm, but listening experiences are most effective if they include music that is pleasurable to the child's ear. Figure 6-5 explains how to create conditions that promote good listening.

It is very important for early childhood teachers to understand the relationship between music, music education, and the development of the whole child. Neelly (2001) cites current research that supports this idea. She cites David Elliott, a prominent music educator, who reports that "whenever there is music, all kinds and levels of appraisals are going on at the same time" (p. 35). Neelly also notes that listening to music involves children in "problem solving, decision making, and other complex processes that energize neuronal patterns similar to those exercised when playing chess or working complex math problems" (p. 35). Since listening is involved in all the musical skills, attention must be given to activities that improve the children's ability to listen. Thinking and reasoning should be enhanced.

Figure 6-5   Promoting Good Listening

During the early years, children need many opportunities to hear sounds and focus their attention on them. Listening and actively participating in musical experiences can enhance this ability.

1. Establish a happy, friendly atmosphere.
2. Make sure the children are physically comfortable. Rooms with acoustical tile ceilings and "soft" areas like carpet, pillows, and drapes tend to absorb sound and make for easier and more comfortable listening.
3. Put away any articles that might distract the children.
4. Provide a good variety of listening activities. These activities should require different comprehension levels and different interests.
5. Give children a reason for listening. That is, they should understand what to listen for.
6. Serve as a model. It is well recognized that the example the teacher sets is by far the single most important and influential factor in conditioning children to sensitive and discriminating listening. If you show enjoyment of music and actively participate, your children will generally feel the stimulation and will respond heartily and creatively.
7. Plan listening activities according to the maturity levels, abilities, and interests of your children. Gradually plan activities that encourage children to reach for the next level of understanding.
8. Provide an atmosphere in which your children can think creatively. For example, ask, "What instrument would you choose to make the sound of a ticking clock?"
9. Keep the experience short enough so that discipline problems will not intrude.

SINGING

Singing brings much joy to children. We know that most young children love to sing and to be sung to. If one listens carefully as children go about their work and play, one will find them singing short created songs that fit the rhythm of their movements. One might hear them chanting, "Swing, swing, swing, swing, watch me go up and down." Recently, a group of 5-year-olds was observed coloring with purple crayons. As one child rhythmically made dots on her paper with her crayon, she started to sing over and over, "Purple-durple, purple-durple, purple-purple-durple." Soon the entire group joined in the singing, picking up the little girl's rhythm and dotting their papers as she did. They had just heard the story of *Harold and the Purple Crayon*. Adults can sometimes sing back the chants and songs children improvise. These should occasionally be written down so children can see how songs are created and written.

At ages 4 and 5, some children are unable to carry a tune. Therefore, one must be careful not to place too much emphasis on singing in tune and building musical skills at this age. Singing should not be taught formally at this time.

When you sit down to sing, watch the reactions of children. Usually their faces will light up as they gather around to ask for their favorite songs. We believe that an enthusiastic teacher singing in the classroom provides children with a more rewarding experience than even the best singer on a recording or a film. All teachers, whether or not they are naturally talented in singing, should sing to their children.

Research and the Singing Voice

Research is beginning to help us better understand the child's singing voice and to choose songs that will aid its natural development. In general, 3- and 4-year-olds prefer singing in the range of middle C to A (a sixth above). McDonald and Simmons (1989) found that children learn songs in predictable patterns. Children first learn the words and then how to move to the rhythm of the song.

Anderson and Lawrence (2001) identify the vocal characteristics and the abilities of 4- and 5-year-old children:

- Young children's voices are small and light.
- Children are generally unable to sing in tune.
- Singing range for young children is D to A for most; D to D for some.
- Children can sing play chants and easy tonal patterns.
- Children can sing short melodies in major, minor, or pentatonic scales.
- Children can sing melodies with one note to a syllable.
- Children can sing with an awareness of a steady beat.
- Children can sing repeated rhythmic patterns accurately.
- Children can sing softly and loudly.
- Children can sing melodies with or without a simple accompaniment. (p. 81)

Suggested Singing Experiences

The following suggestions, based on research on vocal development, should help adults plan singing experiences for young children.

- Encourage your children to improvise and sing about their everyday activities at home or at school.
- Tape the children's voices. Play them back. It is essential to tape individual voices so that each child can hear his or her own. A word of caution here: Use a tape recorder that reproduces voices accurately and does not distort the quality of the child's voice. Do not tape the children if they seem afraid of the experience. This

Teachers do not have to be musically talented to enjoy singing with children.

could result in their withdrawing from singing. In most instances, youngsters thoroughly enjoy this activity.

- Provide many opportunities for children to make sounds using different pitches (e.g., the sound of a mewing kitten or a barking dog). These opportunities are essential in helping children learn to control their voices.
- Vary the beginning pitch of songs. All too often, adults find a comfortable starting pitch to fit their own voices and never change it for their children. This "sameness" could be a contributing factor in the limited singing ranges of children as they grow older.
- Recite or say poems, nursery rhymes, or songs. Encourage children to use different voice inflections to "match" the meaning and sound. The song "If You're Happy and You Know It" has unlimited possibilities. Have the children say the words using inflection in their voices—for example, "If you're happy and you know it, toot your horn, toot, toot!" or "If you're happy and you know it, hum out loud!" This approach helps children find yet another way to learn to control both their speaking and singing voices.
- Songs that make use of repeated words, musical phrases, or repeated rhythmic patterns are good choices. An example of a good song is "Do You Know the Muffin Man?"

Choosing Songs

It is extremely important to select song material that is appropriate for the age of the children. All too often, adults do not take age into consideration when they write or choose songs for their class. Careful thought should be given to what children are like, what they can do, and what their interests are at their particular stage of development. This should be done before writing, selecting, or presenting songs for them.

When choosing songs, one should consider more than appropriate pitch range, as indicated before. Difficult pitch leaps and the speed at which intervals are sung can contribute to singing problems. Keep in mind also that short songs will probably be most successful.

Choose songs where the subject matter and words are closely related to the child's understanding and interests. Four- and five-year-old children particularly enjoy action songs and singing games, contemporary and television-related songs, and songs about

- Nature and the seasons
- Their own names
- Fun and nonsense
- School activities
- Families and friends
- Their bodies, parts of their bodies, and clothing
- Feelings, such as happiness

- Animals and pets
- Mechanical things

Other types, such as question-and-answer songs, help develop critical thinking. Remember, folk songs are considered one of the best sources of song material for young children.

Haines and Gerber (2000) offer excellent criteria to use when selecting songs for young children:

1. The song must appeal to the children through:
   (a) its clear rhythm.
   (b) its pleasing, simple melody that is based on chord tones and stepwise progressions.
   (c) its singable range.
   (d) its content (good poetry, natural word order, and topics of interest to the children).
2. It must be well known and well liked by the teacher.
3. It must have a close relationship between words and the melody. The meaning of the words should be reflected in the style of the music. The phrasing of the words and the melody line should coincide. The words and the melody should fit together like a hand in a glove. (p. 132)

Presenting New Songs

New songs can be introduced spontaneously when the situation seems just right or at a planned group time. They may be introduced to a small group of children who are informally gathered together or to the entire class. It is important to keep the situation as natural as possible.

Almost all children are eager to learn new songs as well as to sing their favorite ones. Children like to repeat their favorites, but interest will begin to wane if songs are overworked. Variety is necessary, as the same song will not appeal to the entire group. To keep interest high, you need to have a number of songs at your fingertips that you know well. "When you first introduce songs to young children, they will probably not sing every word or follow every phrase," Edwards (2002) says. "If the song has repetition or a chorus, children will usually join in on the words or lines they hear most often. Do not be discouraged when you first introduce a song and your children sing just a word or two and do not match your pitch or sing with your tune. By the time you have sung it several times, your children will begin to pick up the lyrics and melody and will say, 'Let's sing it again!'" (p. 122).

Whenever possible, memorize the words and melody of a song so you can use the nonverbal cues and eye contact that are so necessary when sharing a song with children. If your voice is accurate and of good quality, it is best to introduce the song without any accompaniment. It is easier for children to match their tones with the human voice than it is for them to match the melody played on an instrument. If your voice is somewhat shaky, or for the sake of variety, an instrument like a piano, guitar, or Autoharp® can be used.

When teachers are unsure of the quality of their singing voice, they often use instruments to support their singing.

Some songs will need a short introduction; others will not. You might introduce a song by showing a picture or a diorama (a three-dimensional scene showing objects and figures representative of a particular song or situation), asking a leading question, sharing a related incident, or giving some helpful background information. When presenting songs, this introduction is extremely important and must not be overlooked. Such motivation promotes interest and helps the children understand the "message" of the song.

Teachers who are eager to share songs with young children but are unsure of their singing talent or the musical quality of their singing voice should not hesitate to offer singing opportunities to children. It is not essential that you have a good singing voice. If you are unsure, let go of your musical inhibitions and enjoy the activities with the children. See yourself as a participant and not as a performer. All that children require is a responsive, encouraging teacher who knows how to interact with them and how to stimulate them to learn songs and enjoy singing (Van Der Linde, 1999).

Reluctant Singers

Do not be disturbed if all the children do not join in the singing. Once in a while you will find a child who will not sing with the others. These children may sing freely at home or when they are alone but not in the school setting. Their reluctance to participate may be because they are totally absorbed in watching the other children sing or because they simply are not ready to join in. These cases are rather uncommon, since most children like to sing whether or not they can carry a tune accurately. Many children of this age are still trying to find their singing voices. In dealing with reluctant singers, encourage but do not force them to participate. Give them time to respond.

The length of time will depend on each child's personality and previous experiences.

In addition, emphasis should be placed on those music activities and experiences that will encourage the shy child and the "off-key" singer to join in the singing without fear and self-consciousness. Children can best improve the quality of their singing voices only after they have had many opportunities for singing in social groups that give meaning to their efforts. We must not forget that good attitudes about singing are as important as good singing voices.

Since children are highly motivated by action songs, reluctant singers will often become involved in songs that call for action by the hands, feet, or other parts of the body. As children become involved in the physical sense, the words of the song seem to emanate and become part of the activity. Soon these children begin to take part.

Props for a song can also lend much interest. For example, for the song "Two Little Blackbirds," two blackbirds made of construction paper and mounted on lightweight sticks can be the motivating factor in getting children involved. Children enjoy holding the blackbirds, carrying them around, and acting out the song. There is also a great sense of security that goes along with having something in one's hands.

Teaching a New Song

Knowing how to teach a song effectively to young children can influence whether the children will like the song. Smile as you sing. Rotate your head so you make facial contact with every child. Do not make the mistake of asking the children if they like the song. They may say, "No!" When they like a song, children will generally say, "Let's sing it again!" Remember that singing songs should be a joyful experience that provides opportunities for successful participation.

Sing the song slowly (but not *too* slowly) and distinctly at first, keeping in mind the rhythmic flow. Haines and Gerber (2000) recommend that teachers start a song and sing it all the way through, repeating it until the children begin to sing. If interest is high, it will not be long before the children begin to sing right along. This method, called the *whole method*, is encouraged. It gives children the opportunity to "chime in" with a word or a phrase that is easy for them to grasp and remember. The phrases become longer, and soon the entire song is learned in a relatively short time. Songs that get children involved quickly and naturally are songs that invite participation. An example is "Old MacDonald Had a Farm."

Teaching a song line by line is not good practice. This method, if used repeatedly, can destroy the entire effect of a song and can cause children to dread learning a new song. However, this does not mean that a teacher should never sing a line of a song or a certain word of a song and have the children repeat it. This practice is, indeed, sometimes necessary so that children learn the pronunciation of a word or how to fit the words and melody together correctly. When children are not matching the teacher's singing, Haines and Gerber (2000) suggest "echo singing" selected phrases until the children learn the song as a whole. The problem arises when teachers use the line-by-line method in teaching every new song.

Brewer (2001) reminds us that we do not have to teach a new song during one lesson. A new song may have to be taught over a period of days and maybe weeks before the children are comfortable with it. As new songs are repeated on successive days, it will not be long before you know if the children like the song. If, after a careful introduction, they do not seem to respond to a particular song, do not use it again for a while. Because there is so much good song material, do not feel upset if children do not seem to care for a particular song. Once in a while, after the children have learned a song well, sing along very softly or not at all so the children can hear themselves singing and strengthen their ability to carry the melody all by themselves.

Singing together can be a pleasant, happy experience for teachers and children. Above all else, keep in mind that the joy of singing should hold the highest priority.

INSTRUMENTS

Children are fascinated by devices and instruments that produce sound. Around one year of age, a child's attention is quickly drawn to the movement and sound of a musical toy. If one tries to divert the child's attention, almost in- variably the youngster will return to watch the movement and sounds of the toy.

Children are such natural inventors! As they move through the infant stage, one of their favorite activities is taking a wooden spoon and striking it against a pot or on a cup or cereal dish. We often hear parents say that their children prefer pots, pans, and spoons to commercial sound-making toys.

Have you ever watched older children jump mud puddles, landing on both feet? Have you watched them pound nails in rhythm or stomp their feet to band music? This is movement and body percussion combined. This is the "stuff" of which good rhythmic experiences are built.

Body Percussion

Children delight in using different parts of their bodies to produce sounds (body percussion). They soon discover, as they shuffle their feet back and forth in rhythm, that this kind of movement makes a very interesting sound. Experimentation of this kind often helps them express how a train starts up and slows down, for example. Encourage children to experiment in making other sounds with their bodies, such as snapping their fingers, thumping on their chests, and making hisses, clicks, and other sounds with their mouths. Ask them to make the softest body percussion sound they can make, then the loudest, the highest, the lowest, and the heaviest. As children explore sound making through body percussion, ask them how different things might sound. For instance, what sound would a very hot tea kettle make? A spacecraft taking off? Jet airplanes flying by? Rhythmic patterns should then become a part of the sound making. Children need time and guidance to help them explore and learn to control body percussion. It is important that instrumental patterns be reinforced in body percussion first and then extended to sound-making objects like instruments.

Percussion Through Sound-Making Devices

Percussion using objects logically follows experimentation with body percussion. At this point, adults and children can begin to bring together all sorts of interesting sound-making devices. Children, guided by the teacher, can begin to sort out and classify these devices according to the kinds of sounds they produce. Collecting and experimenting with sound-making things is a very important step in introducing instruments to children.

Introducing Instruments

You may remember the chaos associated with the traditional "rhythm band." Fortunately, there is a trend away from this approach to using instruments and toward a more relaxed and personally selected use of rhythm instruments. Under this approach, children can select an individual instrument and discover what tones it produces, what its dynamic range is, and what musical textures can be developed. They can experiment with different ways of playing the instrument and notice how differently a drum sounds when they play it with a mallet and tap it with their fingers. Children can compare the duration of the bell sound when they strike a triangle that is suspended from a string or held in their hands. They can discover the music hidden in the instrument and create rhythmic patterns of their own. The more children experiment with rhythm instruments, the more sensitive they will become to the delightful patterns, combinations, and possibilities these instruments hold for making music. Bringing a child and an instrument together with ample opportunity to explore can help eliminate the stereotypical "rhythm band" where all the instruments sound at once. Certainly, few things are more frustrating for a teacher and more confusing for a child than having to march to the beat of the drum as all the instruments crescendo to the maximum of their dynamic range (Edwards, 2002).

Brewer (2001), reviewing studies of children's use of musical instruments, recommends the following guidelines for teachers:

- Children should have many opportunities for free exploration with instruments before any structured activities are attempted.
- Teachers should attend to the child's interest and needs when providing any instruction on how to play an instrument.
- Children need to express rhythm through physical movement before instruments are introduced.
- Exploration with instruments can help children learn about pitch, timbre, rhythm, and melody. (pp. 398–399)

When children are old enough to respect instruments and to care for them, they should have the opportunity to use them. Both commercial and homemade instruments can be introduced. Children enjoy making some of these instruments. Adults can make others for use with children. Whole families and classes can become involved in making some of the instruments and will enjoy sharing the sound making together. When children go through the process of making instruments, they have a much better understanding of how the sound is produced, and problem solving and creative thinking are enhanced. It is extremely important to remember that the better the tone quality of the instrument, the more satisfying and more valuable the experience will be for the child. Instruments of genuine tone quality like resonator bells, wood and tone blocks, and xylophones are good instruments to use for sound exploration and discrimination.

Introduce one type of instrument at a time. As you introduce the instrument, explain it and then pass it around for the children to handle and explore. Some teachers prefer to introduce an instrument on one day and then reintroduce the same instrument on the next day before the children are permitted to explore and play it. It is important for the children to hear and see the instrument played enough times so that they can distinguish its sound and know its name and how to play it. Once this is accomplished, another instrument can be introduced, until children have had the opportunity to hear and explore many different instruments. This process takes time, and children need to be patient, but the results are rewarding. It is also wise at this point to establish a few rules for handling the instruments to prevent some of the problems that usually occur if expectations are not set. Keep the rules simple. Once children have explored different types of instruments, they can begin to use them creatively in different ways.

As children explore how to play different instruments, in addition to having fun, they are also developing important skills. As with singing, playing instruments allows children to be directly involved in making music. During this process, they are developing these musical concepts (Anderson & Lawrence, 2001):

- Steady beat
- Differences in dynamics
- Musical form
- Pitch and melody (p. 211)

ESTABLISHING A LISTENING MUSIC CENTER

A listening music center for children is a definite asset for any classroom if it is carefully prepared and regulated. Certain rules must be set up and expectations carefully explained to the children. A good listening/music center creates an environment where children are free to make choices. When children are playing in these centers, they are in charge of their own learning as they explore independently and make their own decisions about the activities in which they engage. Listening/music centers should give children the freedom to explore rhythm, melody, form, and expressive music qualities. The teacher creates the environment, and the children dictate the learning (Kenney, 1997).

A good center could include a piano, a CD player, a tape recorder, headsets, and melody and rhythm instruments like a xylophone (Orff-type), drums, resonator bells, wood blocks, and an Autoharp. When the budget permits, a double series of Montessori bells would be an excellent addition to the center. Montessori bells are used in training the ear to perceive differences between musical sounds. There are two sets of bells that look alike but produce successive tones of a chromatic scale. In using the bells, the task is for children to match the pair of bells that produce the same pitch. One set of bells in chromatic scale order remains stationary. The child strikes the first bell, which is "Do" of the stationary series, and then finds its match from the second, mixed set. When the correct bell is found, it is then placed beside its match. Each note of the scale is found in this manner. After much experimentation, children are then encouraged to place the bells in the order of the scale, guided only by the sound. This reinforcement aids children greatly in helping them sing the syllables of the scale, "Do," "Re," "Mi," etc. (McDonald, 1983).

Some of the instruments and listening activities within the center should be changed periodically to provide new interest and new challenges. Many teachers have found that the most profitable time to use the listening music center is during children's work and playtime activity periods.

Inviting Resource Visitors

As children's interest in instruments grows, it's a great idea to invite professional musicians to the classroom to demonstrate their instruments. In this way, children can learn firsthand what each instrument is like, how it is played, and how it sounds. The musician might encourage the children to touch the instrument and, in some cases, to play it. This needs to be done under careful supervision. With woodwind and brass instruments, it is good hygienic practice not to allow the children to blow into the instrument. Children will be pleased if the musician plays familiar melodies and songs they know. If the songs are familiar, the children will generally chime in with singing. It is also a good idea to have the visitor play a selection that is particularly well suited to the instrument being introduced.

MOVEMENT

Dancing

A hop, a skip, and off you go!
Happy heart and merry toe,
Up-and-down and in-and-out,
This way, that way, round about!
Bend like grasses in the breeze,
Wave your arms like wind-blown trees,
Dart like swallows, glide like fish,
Dance like anything you wish.

—Eleanor Farjeon

Movement for the Fours and Fives

Chenfeld (1976) reminds us that "movement is as natural to learning as breathing is to living. We have to be taught not to move as we grow up in our inhibited, uptight society" (p. 261). Movement is synonymous with the growing child. Today, more than ever, we realize the great amount of learning that takes place through psychomotor activities. As indicated in earlier chapters, young children should be free to explore and experiment with their own movements in response to stimuli. It is important that they experience these natural body movements before they are asked to respond to those initiated by adults.

With careful guidance, movement exploration gives children an opportunity to become aware of their own abilities and what their bodies can do. Through these experiences, they often lose their self-consciousness and inhibitions. Many times, movement exploration leads to creative movements and dance. This process helps children discover new ways of using their bodies. As children's muscle coordination improves, they can begin to coordinate the rhythmic movements of their body with such stimuli as the beat of a drum, a rhythmic poem, a song, and the like.

We strongly believe that as children learn to control their body movements, they build feelings of satisfaction, self-worth, and confidence, which will grow and carry over into mastery of other areas. Undoubtedly, children will become less fearful of trying out other activities. Have you ever seen the expression on a child who has just found the "right combination" for skipping or who has just walked across the balance beam for the first time without falling off? Success in mastery of movements like these helps the child grow psychologically as well as physically. The primary goals of movement programs are to help young children become more aware of what their bodies can do and to help them develop the balance and coordination needed to control all parts of their bodies. Children should have no fear of failure with experiences in movement exploration. Teachers should be constantly aware of this point as they provide guidance in this area.

Movement activities for the 4- and 5-year-old child vary greatly from one program to another. Ten to 15 minutes a day of marching and skipping to music or playing rhythm band instruments is not uncommon. We feel that children should have ample opportunity to move freely before they are required to respond to the steady beats of recorded or live music.

Imaginative Teachers

Young children move and respond naturally with an imaginative and sensitive teacher. Teachers who are willing to experiment can develop a vital, creative rhythmic program for their children. You can develop a good movement program by paying close attention to children as they move—as they skip down the hall, run with the wind, pound with their hammers, twirl around in circles, or stamp their feet in puddles. *There is no set way to begin.* One possible way to start would be to group children informally on the rug or gym floor. Have the children lie flat on their backs or stomachs. Can they wiggle their bodies without moving from their spaces? Can they wiggle their bodies away from their spaces? Can they move parts of their bodies that no one else can see? Can they move two or perhaps three parts of their bodies at the same time? Can they puff up their stomachs like a cake that is rising in the oven?

Keeping in mind that most children are very inventive, adults can encourage them to do all kinds of "tricks" with their bodies. It is not surprising that a child can roll up into a tiny ball, make himself so rigid that no part of his body wobbles or bends, push the clouds high into the sky, or crawl into a very, very tiny box. If they are motivated by a creative teacher, it won't be long before children's ideas begin to flow. Many times, the whole group picks up another child's idea and extends it. Trying out the movements of other children often encourages the more reticent youngster to try out movements of his own. Teachers can help with words of encouragement. For example, if the children are discovering different ways to move across the floor, the teacher might say, "Look! Tommy is moving sideways. Let's all try to move the same way as Tommy." After the children have tried Tommy's way, the teacher might say, "Who would like to show us another way to move across the room?" Once the children have begun to share their ideas freely, the teacher can play a very important part by expanding on the ideas that children begin.

Here is an example. A kindergarten boy eagerly told his teacher and classmates about a trip he had just taken with his family through Pennsylvania. He told them that at times his father had to turn on the headlights because it had suddenly become too dark to see. After considerable discussion as to what that dark place was called, a child sang out, "That dark place is called a tunnel." Other children agreed, "Yes, that's what you call it—a tunnel!" The children then asked their teacher if they could darken the room and pretend that they were going through a long, dark tunnel like the ones in Pennsylvania. The teacher asked, "What shall we use for a tunnel?" Some of the children suggested lining up a long line of tables and then crawling underneath them. Tables were quickly put together. The children pretended to be automobiles. They crawled through the tunnel, each in their own way. They had captured the mood of moving through a darkened space. More discussion followed. They began to tell what it was like to try to do things in dark places. The conversation and play lasted all morning.

We could cite many other examples in which a creative movement idea developed into a series of expanded learning experiences. If you observe your children in an environment that encourages movement and music activity, they will give you all the ideas you need!

Fundamentals of Movement

Movements can be divided into three categories: locomotor movements, axial movements (nonlocomotor), and a combination of movements. *Locomotor movements* are those movements that propel the body through space. They are classified as walking, hopping, jumping, running, and leaping. Movements like galloping, sliding, and skipping are variations or combinations of the locomotor movements. *Axial movements* are the nonlocomotor movements originating from a stationary position of the body. They include bending and twisting.

As you learned in chapter 1, movement can be further divided into three additional categories: space, time, and force. *Space* simply refers to the manner in which we use an area for movement, either "personal space" or "general space." *Time* is a quality of tempo or rhythm. A movement can be slow or fast. *Force* is involved when children experiment with light, heavy, sudden, or sustained qualities of movement requiring varying degrees of muscular tension.

Exploring Space, Time, and Force

As you continue exploring space, time, and force with your children, you can develop activities based on the suggestions presented in this section. Extend the experiences by adding recorded music or other rhythmic accompaniment. Both of these will add immensely to the movement and dance experience.

Do not initiate these activities all at one time or on a day that is designated as "movement day." If you think the traditional rhythm band creates chaos, you will certainly see your children transform themselves into an uncontrollable whirlwind should you decide to introduce all of these activities at once. Group the ideas as they fit into the natural progression of your plans, or select one each day to introduce your children to the creative and unique ways they can move their bodies.

Remember, there is no copyright on children's creative movements. As the teacher, you will provide children with "starter" ideas like those listed below, but the extension and stretching of those ideas is left up to the children and their own creativity.

Space

1. What is space? (Begin by describing space, or ask your children to tell you their definition of space.)
2. Can you find a space on the floor where you will not touch anyone and that will be your very own?
3. How tall can you make yourself?

4. How many different directions can you reach by stretching different parts of your body.
5. Can you make a long, low bridge using only two parts of your body?
6. Can you move forward in your space? Backward? Sideways? In a circle? Can you change your direction from upward to downward?
7. Lying on the floor, can you make a round shape in your space? Straight, crooked, twisted?

Time

1. How fast can you move about without bumping into anyone? How slowly?
2. Can you move about, changing your speed from fast to slow?
3. Can you move very fast without leaving your space?
4. Can you move one part of you very fast and another very slowly?
5. Can you combine a kick, a catch, and a throw in a smooth motion?

Force

1. How quietly can you walk? How heavily?
2. How would you walk against a strong wind?
3. Can you make your muscles feel very strong? Weak?
4. How would you lift a heavy object? A light object?

The ideas in Figure 6-6 will help you explore space, time, and force with your children. All of these ideas encourage children to create dramatic and creative movements to either imitate familiar things in their environment or to use their bodies to perform specific movements. Examine these movement ideas to determine which are developmentally appropriate for the age and skill of your children. When in doubt, refer to "Basic Stages of Early Musical Development in chapter 1.

Establishing the Beat

Once children have had plenty of opportunity for free movement and can move about without bumping into others, more locomotor and body movements like walking, running, and jumping can be used. You can strike up a steady beat on a drum, a tambourine, or a piano to accompany the children's movements. As children gain more experience, ask for a response to the steady beat being played. The ability to maintain a steady beat comes easily to some children but not to others. Research in young children's motor development and moving to music shows that the ability to maintain a steady beat by tapping develops with age and does not seem to change much after age 9.

After children have attained skill in walking, running, jumping, and leaping, they are ready to have more compli-

Figure 6-6 Ideas for Movement

- Make yourself as small as you can.
- See how much space you can fill by using different parts of your body.
- Make your body into a straight, long shape, and crawl like a snake or wiggle like a worm.
- Make your body as tall as you can, and move in and out of empty spaces.
- Try different ways of moving through space.
- Can you move straight?
- Can you move in a zigzag?
- Can you move forward and backward?
- Can you move sideways?
- Can you move upward, downward, or in a circle?
- Can you move very near to someone else without touching them?
- Move your arms and body as high as they can go and then as low as they can go.
- Lie on the floor on your back, and let your feet and legs fly in their space.
- Lie on your stomach and stretch your head back, kick your feet in the air, and wave your arms out to your sides.
- Move around the room as slowly as you can.
- Move around the room as fast as you can without touching or getting into anyone else's space.
- Without leaving your space, move as fast as you can. Without leaving your space, move as slowly as you can.
- Move as quietly as you can. Can you move as quietly as a mouse?
- Can you quietly creep and crawl like a spider?
- Can you dance through the air like a butterfly?
- How heavily can you move? Can you move like an elephant?
- Can you make your muscles very strong and swing and sway like a bear?

cated experiences, such as galloping and skipping. Around 3½ to 4 years of age, children begin to enjoy galloping. They are also attracted to horses at this age and often like to pretend that they are horses. For motivation, show pictures of horses, take a field trip to a farm, show a film, and so on. Children will be quick to respond to discussions about their own experiences of seeing horses. Have the children gallop at different tempos: some fast, some slow. You will need to use lots of "word pictures" to stimulate children as they try out new and different movements.

Skipping is much more difficult to do than galloping because it is a bilateral movement that combines the movements of walking and hopping. The song "Skip to My Lou" is good to sing when children are attempting to learn how to skip. The words to the song can be chanted slowly as the children try out the new movement. This song has helped many children get the "feel" of how to skip. We often find that the music used for skipping (once the movement is learned) is too slow, thus causing some children to have difficulty coordinating their skipping movements with the tempo of the music. Observe the children skipping. Then adjust the music's tempo to their movements. When children discover that they can make their bodies skip, it often becomes one of their favorite movements.

Folk songs and singing games also provide opportunities for children to move. These are particularly good for young children, since most of the songs are within their singing range. Pete Seeger's recording *American Folk, Game, and Activity Songs for Children* (2000) is perhaps the best-known collection of folk songs in America. Most of the songs invite participation and improvisation. Three-fourths of the tunes in this collection focus on action and are easy to dance, clap, and move to. As children listen to these folk songs, they will begin clapping on their own and performing other body movements, such as skipping, jumping, and kicking their feet. It is not uncommon for children at this age to make up new and inventive motions as the spirit of the music moves them (Seeger, 2000).

Using Recordings and Props

There are many fine recordings on the market that invite movement participation. These do not need to be recordings made especially for children. Some of the works of our finest composers, such as Grieg, Pierné, Saint-Saëns, Mendelssohn, Bartók, Debussy, and Stravinsky, are excellent for stimulating free movement. More contemporary selections like the bluegrass tune "Orange Blossom Special" and Copland's "Hoe-Down" from *Rodeo* are also good choices for encouraging children to move their bodies freely.

Homemade tapes and CDs have also been used with good results. If you record one piece of music several times on each tape or CD, the desired piece of music is always at the beginning and can be used as long as needed. You can stop or extend the music as desired. This technique saves time and helps with classroom control.

Props like scarves, fans, strips of crepe paper fastened onto cardboard tubes, balloons, and rhythm instruments, such as maracas, can be used to enhance movement. Props can aid in making children less inhibited. The opportunity to hold something in their hands often gives them balance and lends variety. Keep in mind, however, that overuse of props can become very distracting and may overshadow the purpose of the activity.

As children continue to move and to sharpen their listening skills, they can begin listening for special parts in the music. As music is played, you need to help children listen for changes of tempo, mood, and dynamics. Here again, word pictures help children interpret the many combinations of musical sounds.

Music from Around the World

Music is a universal language, and it brings excitement, joy, and satisfaction to children of all ages. Whether in the city or the country, China, the Caribbean, Dallas, or Rome, children are chanting, humming, and making up songs, as well as dancing, clapping, shaking, and moving to the rhythms of others and themselves. Culturally diverse music, dance, and expressive movement provide different lenses for conveying cultural traditions and ideas.

Many languages have no word that means "dance," while other languages have multiple words for different dances without having a single generic term (McCarthy, 1996). For example, the dance activity included in this section, the hula, has many referents—the dance, the dancers, and the song or chant used. Hanna (1987) notes that in Nigeria, the drum is an essential part of dance, so the word *dance* also refers to drumming.

The cultural traditions of Hawaii are reflected in the hula. From a global view music, movement, and dance are indeed a universal language, "an embodiment of culture, a way of knowing, a way of communicating, a kinetic human history" (Frosch-Schroder, 1991, p. 62).

The Hawaiian Hula

The children of Hawaii learn the hula at a very young age. The hula includes a variety of hand and body motions that tell a particular story. The basic steps are easy to learn and are introduced below. All you need is a recording of Hawaiian music or ukulele music. You might consider making and giving your children flower garlands called *leis* to wear while dancing. "Pearly Shells," introduced below, is a traditional hula known and loved around the world. The dance movements are simplified here to be appropriate for young children.

Basic Hula Steps

Hands on waist.
Step to the right and follow with the left.
(Hands and arms lift to the right.)
Repeat.
Step to the left and follow with the right.
(Hands and arms lift to the left.)
Repeat.

Shining in the sun: Bring both arms up above head to make a sun.

Love and heart: Touch chest with hands.

Pearly Shells

(Words can be sung or chanted)

Pearly shells (motion to pick up pearly shells from the sand)

From the ocean (ocean roll)

Shining in the sun (sun motion)

Covering the shores (extend arms and hands to touch sandy shore)

When I see them (hands to eyes)

My heart tells me (love and heart motion)

That I love you (love and heart motion)

More than all those little pearly shells (motion to pick up shells from the sand)

An excellent resource to share with your children is *Hula for Children*, a video recording that shows young Hawaiian children dancing the hula. If your library doesn't have a copy, you can purchase it through Taina Productions, Inc.

Taina Productions, Inc.
1127 11th Ave., Suite 204
Honolulu, HI 96816
(808)739–5774
http://www.galaxymall.com/hawaii/hula

FAVORITE SONGS AND RHYTHMS

Growing children need to keep moving. This is very much a part of the learning process, which continues throughout a lifetime. Keep in mind that movements expressed by children are often accompanied by their innermost feelings and ideas. Wise adults will do everything within their power to find a way to help children express their feelings and ideas.

The following selections are examples of songs that invite participation. Many of these songs motivate children to use different locomotor and nonlocomotor movements. Additional songs and singing games involving movement and rhythm can be found in other chapters of this book.

The hula is a traditional Hawaiian dance known around the world. The basic steps are easy to learn and appropriate for young children.

Bend knees with hands on knees and sway to the right and then to the left.

Repeat.

Hand Motions

Smile motion: Put hands on cheeks, and smile.

Coconut tree: Put one elbow on top of the other hand, and sway arms.

Ocean roll: Make a rolling motion with both arms in front of you.

Jazz tickles your muscles, symphonies stretch your soul.

Paul Whiteman

FOLLOW, FOLLOW

GLADYS ANDREWS
Adapted by K. BAYLESS

GLADYS ANDREWS

1. Fol - low, fol - low, fol - low me. Fol - low, fol - low, fol - low me.

Fol - low fol - low, fol - low me. See what I can do!

2
This is what I can do,
See if you can do it, too.
This is what I can do,
Now I'll pass it on to you.

"Follow, Follow" pp. 48–49 from *Creative Rhythmic Movement for Children* by Gladys Andrews. Copyright 1954 by Prentice-Hall, Inc. Reprinted by permission of Pearson Education, Inc.

This is one of the favorite songs of 4- and 5-year-olds. A child is chosen to think of an action while the class sings the first verse. The action might be nodding the head, for example. The child then leads the entire class "nodding heads" as verse 2 is sung. Another child is then chosen to think of the next action. The song should be sung to the tempo of the child's movements.

Rhythmic concepts: *creative rhythmic movements*

WHAT SHALL WE DO WHEN WE ALL GO OUT?

Traditional

After singing the first verse, children decide what they will do when they go out to play: "We will swing on the monkey bars," etc. Children do the actions as they sing each new verse. This is an excellent song for helping children understand the difference between a question and an answer.

Rhythmic concepts: *creative movements*

Language concepts: *children create their own verses*

SKIP SO MERRILY

Adapted and arranged
by K. BAYLESS

Children stand in a circle while one child skips around the inside. On the words
"choose a partner quick as a wink," the skipping child chooses a partner and the two
children skip around inside the circle. At the end of the song, the two skipping
children return to their original places in the outer circle. Another child is chosen,
and the song is repeated. (Skipping children do not sing, as it is too difficult to skip
and sing at the same time.)

Movement concept: skipping

STAMPING LAND

Folk song from Denmark
English words by LOUISE KESSLER

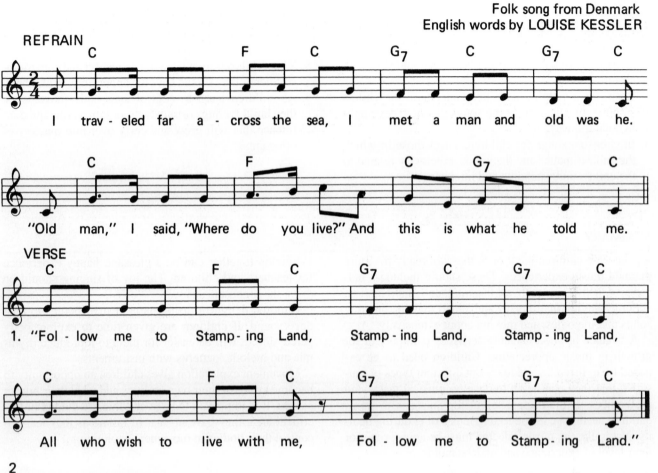

2
Follow me to Clapping Land. . .
3
Follow me to Tiptoe Land. . .

Rhythmic concepts: stamping to the beat, tapping to the beat, clapping to the beat, jogging to the beat

KEY IDEAS

1. Listening is considered the foundation of all music experiences.
2. Listening is perceiving and requires thought and reasoning.
3. Regardless of natural talent, teachers should sing with children.
4. Research is helping us better understand the child's singing voice and to choose songs that help develop it in a natural way.
5. In choosing songs for children, select those in which the subject matter and the words are closely related to the child's understanding and interests.
6. Knowing how to present a song effectively to the children can influence whether or not they will like the song.
7. Percussion using objects logically follows experimentation with body percussion.
8. When children are old enough to respect and care for instruments, they should have the opportunity to use them.
9. As children learn to control their body movements, they build feelings of satisfaction, self-worth, and confidence that will grow and carry over into mastery of other areas.

SUMMARY

By the time children are 4 or 5, they are ready for more planned music experiences. These should include a balance of activities, such as listening and appreciation, singing, playing instruments and sound makers, creating songs and melodies, and moving about extensively.

A balance of good listening activities is important for growth in music appreciation. Children need to be exposed to, to listen to, and to try out different types of music so that they can begin to develop musical tastes and preferences. If their appreciation for music is to grow, children need to be introduced to music of enduring quality. Naturally, the music selected must be appropriate for their level of experience and understanding.

Singing together can be a pleasant, happy experience for teachers and children. The joy of singing should be given the highest priority.

Children delight in using parts of their bodies to produce sound. If children are given time to explore body percussion, it will be easier for them to reproduce rhythmic and melodic patterns with instruments.

Movement exploration gives children an opportunity to become aware of their own abilities and what their bodies can do. It is important that, as children are guided in this critical area, they have no fear of failure as they learn to control their bodies in movement exploration.

QUESTIONS TO CONSIDER

1. As budgetary constraints in school systems create the need to eliminate programs, music instruction is often limited or curtailed. Develop a position statement on this issue.
2. Defend this contention: "Every teacher of young children should be a teacher of music."
3. Isolate yourself in an environment. In a 15-minute time span, record all of the sounds of which you are aware. Repeat this activity with a group of two or three children. Compare the results. What conclusions can you draw?
4. Select four favorite songs that could be used to enhance movement. Describe the activities that invite participation.

REFERENCES

Anderson, W. M., & Lawrence, J. E. (2001). *Integrating music into the elementary classroom,* (5th ed.). Belmont, CA: Wadsworth/Thomson Learning.

Brewer, J. A. (2001). *Introduction to early childhood education: Preschool through primary grades* (4th ed.) Boston, MA: Allyn & Bacon.

Chenfeld, M. (1976). Moving movements for wiggly kids. *Phi Delta Kappan, 58*(3), 261–263.

Edwards, L. C. (2002). *The creative arts: A process approach for teachers and children.* Upper Saddle River, NJ: Prentice Hall.

Flowers, P. J. (1990). Listening: The key to describing music. *Music Educators Journal, 77*(4), 21–23.

Froebel, F. (1878). *Mother play and nursery songs.* Boston: Lee & Shepard.

Frosch-Schroder, J. (1991). A global view: Dance appreciation for the 21st century. *Journal of Physical Education, Recreation, and Dance, 63*(7), 61–68.

Haines, B. J. E., & Gerber, L. L. (2000). *Leading young children to music.* Upper Saddle River, NJ: Merrill/Prentice Hall.

Hanna, J. L. (1987). *To dance is human: A theory of nonverbal communication* (Rev. ed.). Chicago: University of Chicago Press.

Kenney, S. (1997). *Music in developmentally appropriate integrated curriculum.* In C. H. Hart, D. C. Burts, & R. Charlesworth (Eds.), *Integrated curriculum and developmentally appropriate practice: Birth to eight.* Albany, NY: State University of New York Press.

McCarthy, M. (1996). Dance in the music curriculum. *Music Educators Journal, 82*(6), 17–21.

McDonald, D., & Simmons, G. (1989). *Musical growth and development: Birth through six.* New York: Schirmer.

McDonald, D. T. (1983). Montessori's music for young children. *Young Children, 39*(1), 58–62.

Moore, T. (2000). On music and young children. *Scholastic Early Childhood Today, 14*(8), 43–45.

Moravcik, E. (2000). Music all the livelong day. *Young Children, 55*(4), 27–29.

Neely, L. P. (2001). Developmentally appropriate music practice: Children learn what they live. *Young Children, 56*(3), 32–36.

Seeger, P. (2000). *American folk, game, and activity songs for children* [CD]. Washington, DC: Smithsonian Folkway Recordings.

Van Der Linde, C. (1999). The relationship between play and music in early childhood: Educational insights. *Education, 119*(4), 610–615.

Wolf, J. (2000). Sharing songs with children. *Young Children, 55*(2), 28–30.

SONG COLLECTIONS

More than Singing: Discovering Music in Preschool and Kindergarten (1997)
Sally Moomaw
Redleaf Press, St. Paul, MN
Musical activities for young children, including singing and movement.

Ninez: Spanish Songs, Games, and Stories of Childhood (1993)
Virginia Nylander Ebinger
Sunstone Press, Santa Fe, NM

RECORDINGS

Learning Basic Skills Through Music (Cassettes and CD)
Hap Palmer
Educational Activities, Freeport, NY
Dance-a-Story (Cassette and CD)
Ginn and Company, Rochester, NY

Respecting Myself, Respecting Each Other (Cassette)
Miss Jo Productions, Dallas, TX

CHAPTER SEVEN

Music Through the Day

The history of a people is found in its songs.

George Jellinek

Music is an integral part of contemporary American life. Think of your day. How often do you listen to music, hum a favorite melody, or observe children caught up in rhythms of popular TV programs or playground activities?

We do not need to be reminded of the joy of music or its importance to our mood or well-being. We have discussed the development of children in the early months and years, as well as the impact of parents and other adults on musical development. Attitude is important, as is opportunity. Music learning is inseparable from other learning; it is interwoven into the fabric of the child's day. We delight in singing; we sway, we clap, we tap our toes, we sing along with a companion. We sing in many places, often in the shower or as we drive. No matter what our age, music lightens the spirit.

- Music is basic.
- Music is a part of our being.
- Music is a part of our total education.
- Music is a part of romance.
- Music is a part of diplomacy.
- Music adds to our understanding of the cultures of the world.
- Music is a part of our family traditions.

Think of the many ways music can be added to the day. Young children are interested in

- Other children
- The family
- Home and pets
- Seasons
- Travel
- Holidays
- Themselves
- Food
- Shopping

There is music to match each of these interests: humorous songs, personal songs, action songs, singing games, chants, rhymes, and holiday songs. Remember that music has an integrity of its own. Children recognize what is false, what is artificial, what does not "fit." Select only music that enhances enjoyment and appreciation. A child's natural rhythm or perhaps an inner music will be revealed.

Music can be interwoven into the pattern of daily living for children. Consider the possibilities for the integration of music using the boundless enthusiasm and spontaneity of children. Encourage imagination, creativity, and the action art of music rather than assigning children to be spectators at a performance.

MUSIC AND LANGUAGE

For most young children, language unfolds naturally as part of the growth process. Maximum development comes only through careful nurturing of language opportunity by adults.

Music and Communication

Music and language are avenues of communication. Through each, children express delight, anger, and resentment. They quickly sense love, rejection, and concern as they listen to a voice. The arts are unsurpassed as an emotional release for young children. Fears, discomfort, and anxiety can find outlets in song and rhythm. How much healthier than aggressive acts are the expressive arts of music and language for the young! Children delight in language play and language games and respond intuitively to the fascination of music. Even a 15-month-old claps and burbles on hearing the tune released from a tiny musical lamb! Infants, too, are consistent and spontaneous music makers and sound explorers. Lullabies will produce cooing and gurgling, the precursors of language.

Language Development

Language development is very important in the child's total development. Singing is an excellent aid in promoting good language patterns. Many songs contain repetitive sounds that can help children with speech problems. Pronunciation of the words helps distinguish initial, medial, and final consonant sounds. The child can more easily understand sentence structure by singing musical phrases. McGirr (1994–1995) reports that young children can complement all areas of their language learning with music and can enhance their musical activities with language. Music provides a wonderful way for young children to extend their language. When "emergent readers hear, sing, discuss, play with, and write songs, they are building important background knowledge that they will draw upon during later reading and writing experiences. With each new song, students learn concepts and word meanings that they will encounter in print" (Smith, 2000, p. 647).

Traditional Music

Folk songs, country music, and commercials all appeal to the young child and develop and extend vocabulary. Music activities also develop listening skills, increase the attention span, improve comprehension and memory, and encourage the use of compound words, rhymes, and images. Feierabend (1990) recommends the use of traditional children's folk songs and rhymes because they "ensure a natural flow of musical language and textual content relevant to the young child's interests" (p. 15).

Folk songs from cultures around the world should also be included to help children as they begin to develop multicultural awareness and insights.

We know that music offers unique possibilities to expand and extend vocabulary. A rich vocabulary is a necessary skill for young children as they grow toward adulthood. A rich language may well be our most important achievement. This gift of language must be shared. The child delights in sharing language with receptive adults. To fully extend sensory experiences and expand the use of language, the adult cannot be a token listener. The young child quickly senses inattention and disinterest. The adult, too, must be imaginative and sensitive to mood and opportunity. Music is a natural and personal language. Those who work with children know that the languages of words, of music, of the body, and of gestures come naturally to most children.

Simple Tunes

Awareness is the key to language and music stimulation. Singing is often better than talking. The adult can make simple tunes:

- "Mary, put the box away."
- "Tommy, you can stand up tall."
- "Billy, let's cooperate."
- "Mary, Mary, brush your hair."

Children are true and avid imitators. After hearing an instruction, a simple melody, or a line from a book, their language exhibits fluency, ease, and color. For many children, words hold a special attraction. When blended with music and movement, the enchantment expands. Figure 7-1 lists several simple songs. These songs include repetition, songs that tell a story, and other topics that children enjoy.

WHOLE LANGUAGE

Much discussion today concerns psycholinguist Ken Goodman's "whole language," which places a strong focus on oral language experiences and reading aloud as a means of encouraging children to use their knowledge. The main structure of whole language is based on speaking, reading, and writing activities that are most naturally nurtured when children use words and concepts from their own experiences. Teachers avoid overemphasizing correct spelling and grammar. Instead, the emphasis is placed on supporting the child's self-expression. When working with emergent readers, teachers can record the child's words to share later or can write them

Figure 7-1 Examples of Simple Tunes

- "Polly Put the Kettle On" and "Here We Go 'Round the Mulberry Bush" are songs that include repetition and a chorus.
- "Miss Mary Mack, All Dressed in Black" and "She'll Be Comin' 'Round the Mountain" have repeated words and phrases that can be used to create an echo effect.
- "If You're Happy and You Know It" and "Old MacDonald Had a Farm" encourage children to make sound effects or animal noises.
- "Hush Little Baby" and "Humpty Dumpty" tell a story.
- "Do You Know the Muffin Man" engages children in a question-and-answer song or name game (Jackson, 1997).

on a chart or bulletin board. Teachers using the whole language approach do not change a child's words or dialect. The focus is always on the unique ways children express meaning within context or social situations. In other words, teachers do not break language into bits and pieces for study. Words in isolation or sounds in isolation have no meaning. Children do not need to practice isolated components of language, nor do they need to learn the parts and then put them back together and use them. They do need to learn language in many situations and with a variety of speakers (Brewer, 2001). Whole language programs are built on this belief that children should learn to read and write in the same natural way they learned to speak. Curriculum-related music, listening, songs, poems, and chants are used. Songs and poems are read aloud to internalize the rhythm and intonation of language. As we listen, we realize how musical speech is.

Stories and Singing

There are so many books in the world of children's literature that include songs, opportunities for movement and dance, and sometimes instrumentation. The literature selections in Figure 7-2 are recommended as developmentally appropriate for young children.

Singing and rhyming words can play an important role in the total language program for young children. They give children an opportunity to practice the correct and distinct pronunciation of words, the stress of vowel sounds, and the rhythmic flow of syllables and words. Humorous folk songs, in particular, with their nonsense syllables sung repetitively, provide a group activity in which children use their voices freely as they roll the sounds over their tongues. The songs in this text extend language skills as well as musical skill and enjoyment.

Figure 7-2   Stories That Sing

The following stories are recommended for young children.

Mama Don't Allow by Thatcher Hurd
  Live Oak Media, book and cassette edition, 2001

The Sound That Jazz Makes by C. B. Weatherford
  Walker and Company, 2000

Peanut Butter and Jelly: A Play Rhyme by Nadine Bernard
  Westcott/Bt Bound, 1999

Three Little Kittens by Paul Galdone
  Houghton Mifflin, book and cassette edition, 1999

Oh, A-Hunting We Will Go by John Langstaff
  Bt Bound, 1999

Musicians of the Sun by G. McDermott
  Simon and Schuster, 1997

The Lady with the Alligator Purse by Nadine Bernard Westcott
  Little, Brown, 1998

On Top of Spaghetti by Tom Glazer
  Goodyear, 1995

Making Sounds by J. Rowe and M. Perham
  Children's Press, 1993

Lizard's Song by George Shannon
  Mulberry Books, 1992

London Bridge Is Falling Down by Peter Spier
  Yearling Books, reissued 1992

I Make Music by E. Greenfield
  Black Butterfly Children's Books, 1991

Grandpa's Song by T. Johnston
  Dial Books for Young Readers, 1991

Old MacDonald Had a Farm by Glen Rounds
  Holiday House, 1989

The Wheels on the Bus by Maryann Kovalski
  Scott Foresman, 1990

Cat Goes Fiddle-i-fee by Paul Galdone
  Houghton Mifflin, 1988

Pop Goes the Weasel and Yankee Doodle by Robert
  Quackenbush
  Lippincott/Williams and Wilkins, 1988

I Know an Old Lady Who Swallowed a Fly by Colin and
  Jacqui Hawkins
  G. P. Putnam's Sons, 1987

The Complete Story of the Three Blind Mice by Paul
  Galdone
  Ticknow and Fields, 1987

The Balancing Act: A Counting Song by Merle Peek
  Clarion, 1987

Go In and Out the Window by the Metropolitan Museum
  of Art
  Henry Holt, 1987

*If You're Happy and You Know It: Eighteen Story Songs Set
  to Pictures* by Nicki Weiss
  Greenwillow Books, 1987

Over in the Meadow by Paul Galdone
  Prentice Hall for Young Readers, 1986

Go Tell Aunt Rhody illustrated by Aliki
  Macmillan, 1986

Sing a Song of Sixpence by Tracey Campbell Pearson
  E. P. Dutton, 1985

Hush Little Baby by Jeanette Winter
  Pantheon, 1984

Music, Music for Everyone by Vera Williams
  Greenwillow Books, 1983

Frog Went A-Courtin' by John Langstaff
  School and Library Binding, 1983

Roll-Over: A Counting Song by Merle Peek
  Houghton Mifflin/Clarion Books, 1981

The Friendly Beasts by Tomie de Paolo
  G. P. Putnam's Sons, 1981

Six Little Ducks by Chris Conover
  Thomas Y. Crowell, 1976

Skip to My Lou by Robert Quackenbush
  J. B. Lippincott, 1975

Over the River and Through the Wood by Lydia Maria Child
  Coward, McCann and Geoghegan, 1974

MUSIC AND READING SKILLS

As the young child matures, so does language, and the vocabulary expands as reading becomes a natural extension of language. We sometimes find the paradox of a child who ostensibly cannot read words but who can "read" music and respond to familiar words and melodies. Music is an excellent way to explore words and the concept of print. As "children listen and sing, they begin to realize that the print has meaning, and that there are similarities within the print, and the meaning (Fisher and McDonald, 2001).

Feierabend, Saunders, Getnick, Holahan (1998) report that there is "evidence to suggest that listening to songs repeatedly over an extended period of time contributes to an integration in long-term memory of words and music among preschool children" (p. 358). Researchers theorize that perhaps it is the multisensory approach—through movement, eyes, ears, and body coordination—coupled with the improvement in self-concept that makes the difference. It is the whole child who learns! Both reading and making music call for concentration, memory, and understanding of abstract concepts, and both are skills children prize and know are highly valued. It is the wise teacher who capitalizes on opportunities to spark reading.

To begin, we can set nursery rhymes or simple poetry to music, or place them in simple chants or choral verse. Country songs, ballads, pop tunes, and even carefully selected commercials are legitimate when reading enjoyment and skill are the goal. Words have meanings; words

Teachers and children need a cozy place to relax with books. Playing soothing, relaxing classical music can help create an intimate atmosphere.

open doors; words have power; words are personal; words are humorous; words tell us what we are. Words are ribbons of the future, and words set to music lead us there.

From nursery rhymes and simple poems we might progress to jingles, fingerplays, short prose stories, chant stories, jump-rope chants, and even haiku, which might use music as accompaniment. Or we might select a favorite tune of the children and fit original lines to that tune. It is rhythm, fluency, and attention-holding activity we seek to build. Whatever the ability of the child, participation is guaranteed. It is the rare adult who can resist the combinations described, and sharing enjoyment with children brings an added dimension to our participation. The following two chants focus on things children like to eat and children's birthdays. Change the words to include what your children think is best of all and insert the age of the children in your classroom into "Me."

Best of All

Lollipops and gum drops,
Choc'lets, bubble gum.
Lemon drops and licorice,
Oh, yum, yum!

Lollipops and ice cream,
Choc'let cake and pie,
Butterscotch, vanilla,
Oh, yum, yum!

Choc'let chips and M&Ms,
Gum balls, big and small,
Jello, pudding, sundaes, rolls,
Oh, I love them all!

Me

Today's my birthday;
I am four;
Growing bigger, too;
Cake and ice cream, gifts, and toys.
How old are you?

Today's my birthday;
I am five;
Growing taller, too;
Cookies, ice cream, cars, and boats.
How old are you?

Today's my birthday;
I am six;
Growing stronger, too;
Ice cream, chocolate, books and school.
How old are you?

All teachers and caregivers of young children need a well-stocked shelf of easy books, poetry, choral verse, and jingles. From these, they can choose selections to support vocabulary activities throughout the day, emphasizing the importance of the interrelationship of music, language, and reading in the daily life of the child. Reading skills are extended by simply learning a new song. Rote memorization, proper inflection, accenting, and syllabication are strengthened. As Lapp and Flood (1983) indicate, for syllabication in particular, children can clap the beat of a song, separating the words into correct syllables, then sing part of the song, leaving out certain syllables, words, or phrases. DeMicco and Dean (2002); Fisher and McDonald (2001); Moravcik (2000); Hildebrandt (1998) emphasize the importance of the interrelationship of music, language, and reading in the daily life of the child. McGirr (1994/1995) encourages teachers to remember that music and language are related modes of communication that share a number of characteristics. She writes:

> The music in language and the language in music support each other and young children's learning. Weaving language and music activities together through the use of quality children's literature provides an integrated, natural setting for meaningful learning. Language and music concepts develop simultaneously, along with creativity, imagination and critical thinking skills (p. 76).

Remember that recordings, tapes, jingles, and the like cannot take the place of an adult who enjoys both reading and music and displays this enjoyment to children. Children want to be like the primary adult in their lives. If that adult reads, sings, and is enthusiastic about these activities, the mood and example are contagious.

ESL and Non-English-Speaking Children

Sholtys (1989) offers valuable resources for teachers of non-English-speaking children. For example, to extend reading and language skills, the song "Jingle Bells" could lead to winter words, winter pictures, and winter poems about icicles, evergreens, snowmobliles, and more. He also suggests compiling a list of sound words such as *bang*, *boom*, *ring*, *buzz*, *rap*, *zoom*, *knock*, *clip-clap*, and *tick-tock,* all of which would be contributed by children. These sound words can also be coupled with instruments that make similar sounds.

Big Music Books

Another valuable resource available to teachers and children are *Big Music Books*. There are many delightful *Big Music Books* that are appropriate for young children and that will help you incorporate the concept of print into your music program. The following are excellent:

- Kovalsky, M. (1987). *The wheels on the bus.* New York: The Trumpet Club.
- Peek, M. (1985). *Mary wore her red dress and Henry wore his green sneakers.* New York: The Trumpet Club.
- Sweet, M. (1992). *Fiddle-i-fee: A farmyard song for the very young.* New York: The Trumpet Club.
- Weiss, N. (1987). *If you're happy and your know it.* New York: Greenwillow.
- Wescott, N. B. (1989). *Skip to my Lou.* New York: The Trumpet Club.

Early childhood educators who wish to create a stimulating and challenging environment for young children must include many opportunities for children to be thoroughly engaged in music and literacy activities. You will discover that music and reading are mutually supportive and beneficial to the learner. Imagination and creativity establish the bridge between the realms of music and reading.

MUSIC, SCIENCE, AND NUMBERS

The world is mysterious to young children. Their curiosity is limitless, and the need to know is imperative. "Why?" is a common question in households with young children. Everything must be experienced to be learned—being told does not suffice.

Music, science, and math go hand in hand. This is a natural combination for children. As we think about the integrated curriculum, it is important to remember all of the educational possibilities of weaving music, science, and mathematics throughout children's experiences and all parts of the classroom environment (Scholastic Early Childhood Today, 2003). Music and rhythm are a vital part of human culture. The integration of music into the general curriculum encourages students to become actively involved in their learning. For example, the rhythm, meter, measure, and pattern of familiar lyrics can help develop math and science skills while enhancing many other aspects of the curriculum (Rothenberg, 1996).

Music can be a real asset when it comes to teaching math. "Music is filled with patterns and that's what math is really about. You're not going to explain the intricacies of notes and scales to a three-year-old, but exposing a child to music now will help him learn these concepts later" (Gill, 1998, p. 40). One of the keys to success is exposing children to a wide variety of music, including country, classical, modern jazz, traditional blues, classic folk, and good old rock and roll. As children listen to and respond to the different rhythms they hear, the more patterns they are exposed to and the more they will recognize in the study of mathematics (James, 2000).

When selecting music with which to integrate science and numbers into the child's day, the problem becomes one of selecting from the wealth of resources available. Children are usually captivated by stars, comets, space, alien beings, space vehicles, bugs, worms, and reptiles. Use your imagination and those of the children to apply new lyrics about these things to a familiar melody or rhyme. Other songs may be based on these ideas:

- Animals
- Seasons
- Colors
- Plants
- Insects
- The child
- The body
- Autumn leaves

- Food
- Machines
- Indoors/outdoors
- Senses
- Travel
- Tools
- Growing up
- Sounds

We think of rainbows and prisms, "Pop Goes the Weasel," "Curious George," "Caps for Sale," and Rimsky-Korsakov's "Flight of the Bumblebee." We recall the classics *Ask Mr. Bear, Blueberries for Sale, Make Way for Ducklings,* and *Little Bear.* You might locate the Folkways recording *Songs of the Philippines* and sing "Pounding Rice." There are the sounds of nature: the music of birds, the wind in the trees, night sounds, and flowing water.

Many of us have known the following songs since childhood:

- "One, Two, Buckle My Shoe"
- "Sing a Song of Sixpence"
- "This Old Man"
- "Pop Goes the Weasel"
- "Eensy, Weensy Spider"

From the earliest stages, young children and adults count together and thrill to the mastery of numbers. Big, small, up, down, many, some, fat, thin, circle, square, nickel, dime—all follow a natural progression. Children quickly chant:

- "One, Two, Buckle My Shoe"
- "This Little Pig Went to Market"
- "Ten in a Bed"
- "Sing a Song of Sixpence"

Children gain a sense of power and feel a part of the adult world when they understand numbers. Music can be used to enhance children's understanding of mathematical concepts and skills. According to Gardner (1993), this integration is especially effective with children who have a strong sense of hearing and musical intelligence. When children are engaged in music activities, they are also developing reasoning skills, which are crucial for later learning as they develop concepts in areas like proportional reasoning and geometry (Grandin, Peterson, & Shaw, 1998). It is important for teachers to remember that activities that integrate music and mathematics do not require any specialized musical training. All you need is a set of rhythm instruments, a tape player or CD player, an object that can serve as a baton, and musical recordings that have different beats and rhythms (Johnson & Edelson, 2003).

The omnipresence of numbers in daily life may surprise you. Children notice signs, billboards, and their messages. Perhaps as adults we block them out—but young children do not! Theirs is a world of number, color, and newness. Look for numbers in your world, and transfer them to the world of the child through music.

MUSIC, MULTICULTURALISM, AND SOCIAL STUDIES

Music and social studies mesh easily. Perhaps in no other area of the curriculum is there such an abundance of songs that can add richness to the day. The National Standards for Music Education support the relationship between music, social studies, and other content disciplines. Content Standards 8 and 9, "Understanding relationships between music, the other arts, and disciplines outside the arts" and "Understanding music in relation to history and culture" (Consortium of National Arts Education Associations, 1994, pp. 28–29), address music and social studies in ways that apply to early childhood education (Barrett, 2001). The curriculum standards for social studies in the early grades "describe ways in which language, stories, folktales, music, and artistic creations serve as expressions of culture and influence behavior of people living in that culture" (National Council for the Social Studies, 1994, p. xiii).

Multicultural music can include songs, singing games and dances, instrumental music, stories, and poetry. Every area of social studies—history, geography, civics, economics, sociology, and anthropology—can be illustrated through music. The geography of our country is revealed through song. Our historic milestones are carried from generation to generation with music as we sing beautiful anthems like "America the Beautiful." When we sing this traditional anthem let us always remember that all human beings, no matter where their family originated, are members of the global village of America.

Songs from around the world help us learn about individuals, our similarities and differences, and what makes us all special. Counting songs, songs about color, musical stories, choral speaking, and action songs can be found in all the languages of the world and from all the cultures that speak these languages. Our enthusiasm, participation, flexibility, and willingness to learn songs from other cultures will encourage children to enlarge their musical repertoire.

Music from Around the World

Jenkins (1995) reminds us that every culture speaks through music. "Songs are rich with stories about the world, who people are, and how they live" (p. 41). With all the emphasis that is put on multiculturalism in education, early childhood educators must give young children the opportunity to hear and learn music of cultures other than their own. When teachers encourage children to listen to, experience, and sing traditional music of various cultures, children cannot help but gain new insight into those cultures through music (Hopton-Jones, 1995). This also helps children begin to develop a sense of cultural sensitivity. This does not come easily, nor does it come from being exposed to the "tourist approach" to multicultural music, as discussed in chapter 4. Teachers must be sure to include music from around the world as a part of their regular, daily music curriculum. Ethnic music resources are plentiful and increasingly available. Following is a Yoruba folk chant provided by our colleague Dr. E. Olaiya Aina. He used it with his children when he taught preschool in Nigeria. "This chant teaches children to love nature and animals," he explains. "It teaches color, comparison, and vocabulary. Children role play/dramatize by 'jumping and flying' like a bird as they chant the song. There is usually a lead person or child who chants the refrain of the song while others chant the chorus. Children love it!" (E. Aina, personal communication, 2003).

Yoruba Children's Chant

Yoruba Version
Eye meta tolongo waye
Chorus: Tolongo
Okan dudu bi aaro
Chorus: Tolongo
Okan riri bi osu,
Chorus: Tolongo
Soso firu bale
Chorus: Sooo
Soso firu bale
Chorus: Sooo

English Version:
Three birds were descending to Earth
Chorus: Tolongo
One of them as dark as the black dye
Chorus: Tolongo
One as white as the moon
Chorus: Tolongo
One has a tail so long
Chorus: Sooo
So long touching the ground!
Chorus: Sooo

Most early childhood classrooms have children from a number of different racial and ethnic backgrounds, but in some areas of the country, the classrooms are more homogeneous. Regardless of the cultural and ethnic makeup of

Nurturing music must be considered in the early years because of the richness it brings to a child's life.

your classroom, give your children the opportunity to develop a sensitivity to and understanding of the cultural diversity of today's world. Here in the United States, culturally diverse music can readily be found, so be careful that you don't overlook these rich sources of our musical heritage.

Gospel Music

Traditional gospel songs are sung by choirs, and solo voices are often accompanied by a variety of instruments ranging from piano or organ to rhythm instruments like drums and tambourines. Some of the more familiar gospel songs for Americans are "O Mary, Don't You Weep, Don't You Mourn," "Steal Away," "Wade in the Water," and "Nobody Knows the Trouble I've Seen." Figure 7–3 lists recommended recordings of African-American music and African-American gospel music. These are all available at your local music store.

Figure 7-3   Gospel Music Recordings

- *Africa to America: The Journey of the Drum.* Sounds of Blackness. Perspective Records.
- *Amazing Grace.* Aretha Franklin (with James Cleveland). Atlantic Records.
- *Peace Be Still.* Vanessa Bell Armstrong. Onyx International Records.
- *21 Greatest Hits.* Mahalia Jackson. Kenwood Records.
- *You Brought the Sunshine.* The Clark Sisters. Sound of Gospel Recordings.

Before we switch directions and move on to other topics, let's not forget that music is a global phenomenon and that no culture is without music (Blacking, 1973). Let's also remember Jenkins's concept of the global village.

PLANNING MUSICAL EXPERIENCES FOR YOUNG CHILDREN

The following plans have been developed as an aid for teaching music to children. You will note that the concept to be taught is stated first, followed by anticipated learning, a list of materials, and possible approaches. These plans are merely guides and can be used either where music is taught separately or as a part of the child's day. Feel free to introduce and carry out the lesson to suit your particular group of children.

Body Senses and Body Parts Awareness

Concept
Children can become more aware of body senses and body parts through songs and movement.

Learning
The children will

1. Identify some of the body senses and body parts
2. Sing about some of the functions of the body senses and body parts
3. Become more aware and appreciative of their bodies and what they can do

Materials

1. Songs: "All About Me" and "The Hokey-Pokey."
2. Recordings: *Getting to Know Myself* ("Touch" and "Turn Around") by Hap Palmer; *It's a Happy Feeling* ("Spare Parts") by Tom Thumb Records; and *Walter the Waltzing Worm* ("What a Miracle") by Hap Palmer.

Approach
Discuss the importance of the body senses. Name parts of the body involving the senses, such as the eyes, ears, nose, and mouth. Ask the children, "Why are these so important to us?" Show children pictures involving the body senses. Discuss.

Procedure

1. Sing the song "All About Me."
2. Have the children perform the appropriate movements to the song.
3. Ask the children to name and discuss other body parts and their functions. For example, the fingers can feel (touch); the tongue can taste (sense of taste).
4. Sing the songs, and perform the movements from the suggested recordings. (This may be extended over several days.)

ALL ABOUT ME

Source Unknown

Jack-in-the-Box

Concept

The power of springs to make sudden and bouncy movements

Learning

The children will

1. Discover that a mechanical spring, after being compressed and released suddenly, will produce a bouncy movement
2. Duplicate the same kind of springing action with their bodies
3. Discover that the muscles in their legs serve as springs to their bodies

Materials

1. Jack-in-the-box toy that plays the tune "Pop Goes the Weasel"
2. A spiral whisk, a "Slinky," or other objects having springs
3. Scalewise song: "Jack-in-the-Box" by Scott and Wood

Approach

Show the children the jack-in-the-box toy. Allow one of them to turn the handle and play the tune. (Jack pops up at the end of the song.) Ask, "What do you think makes Jack pop up? Let's find out."

Procedure

1. Permit each child to push Jack down in the box with his or her hand and then let him jump up again. (Do not put the lid down each time because that will take up too much time.) Let the children feel the springing movement. Ask, "What do you think is inside Jack that makes him pop up?" Some child will probably guess that Jack has something inside his body that makes him spring up.
2. Show the children different kinds of springs. A whisk composed of a spiral spring on a handle is a good example to use. Children can push down on the handle, let go suddenly, and see the springing action.
3. Sing the song "Jack-in-the-Box."
4. Have the children pretend that they are jacks-in-the-box.
5. Have them spring up on the words, "Yes! I will!"

Follow-up

1. "What did you do to make your body spring up like a jack-in-the-box?"
2. "Why did some of you go higher than the other boys and girls?"

Enrichment

Poem

Do you have something well hidden from view
That helps you jump when you tell it to?
Sometimes it helps you jump so high
You think you'll almost reach the sky!

JACK-IN-THE-BOX

LOUISE B. SCOTT

LUCILLE F. WOOD
Adapted by K. BAYLESS

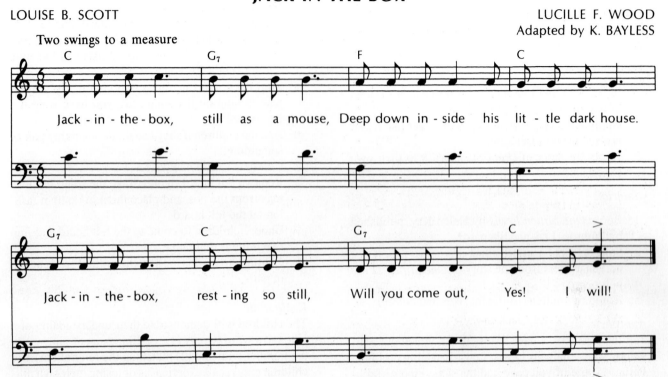

Jack - in - the - box, still as a mouse, Deep down in - side his lit - tle dark house.

Jack - in - the - box, rest - ing so still, Will you come out, Yes! I will!

"Jack-in-the-Box," from *Singing Fun* by Louise Binder Scott and Lucille Wood, copyright 1954 by Bowmar Publishing Corp. and used with their permission.

"Pairs"

Concepts

Pairs and sets of two

Learning

The children will

1. Identify a set of two and discover that a pair is a set of two things
2. Apply the concept of pairs and discover that a pair is a set of two similar items
3. Apply the story of *One Mitten Lewis* to their own experiences

Materials

1. Book: *One Mitten Lewis* by Helen Kay, published by Lathrop, Lee, and Shepard
2. Song: "Pairs," Upstarts, Inc.
3. Felt characters from the story of *One Mitten Lewis*
4. Felt board
5. Paired felt mittens (different sizes and colors)

Approach

Tell the children, "I have a story to tell you about a little boy whose name is Lewis. Lewis had a big problem. Perhaps some of you have had the same kind of problem that Lewis had. Let's find out."

Procedure

1. Tell the story of *One Mitten Lewis,* placing the felt characters on the felt board as the story is told.
2. After telling the story, discuss with the children some of their experiences of losing mittens.

3. Ask the children how many mittens it takes to cover both hands.
4. Tell the children there is a special word to describe two mittens that are alike and that it is used in a song they are going to learn. "Listen to the song while I sing it for you."
5. Sing the song. Encourage the children to participate in singing the song after you have sung it a few times.
6. Ask the children if they can think of another pair of something.
7. Continue to add new verses.
8. Remove felt board figures. Take the small felt mittens from the box and place them in random fashion on the felt board.
9. Choose children to come to the felt board and find two mittens that make a pair.
10. Continue to do this until all the mittens are matched in pairs.

Evaluation

The children will demonstrate their understanding of a pair and a set of two by (1) recalling pairs of things they are familiar with and (2) matching the felt mittens. The children may recall experiences of losing their own mittens and will understand how other people feel when they have lost something that belongs to them.

Enrichment

Poem:

"The Mitten Song" by Marie Louise Allen

PAIRS

Words and music by NANCY MACK
Arranged by K. BAYLESS

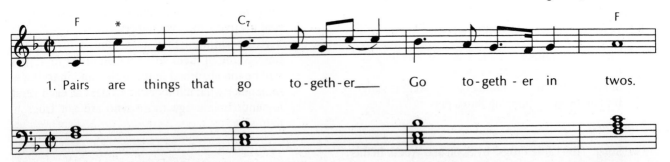

1. Pairs are things that go to-geth-er___ Go to-geth-er in twos.

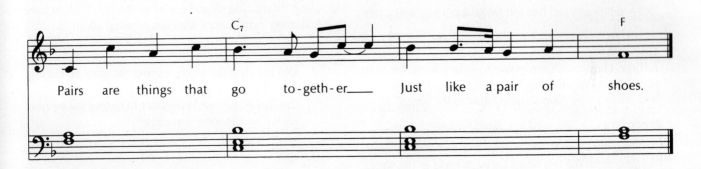

Pairs are things that go to-geth-er___ Just like a pair of shoes.

2. Eyes are things that go together   3. Twins are things that go together   4. Mittens are things that go together

Used by permission of Upstarts, Inc., from the publication "Wake Up Beautiful World," Mack and Blum (copyright 1974).
*If octave jump is too great, substitute (F) for (C).

"Ten Little Frogs"

Concept
Numbers as they apply to objects

Learning
After hearing the song, the children will

1. Identify the numerals 5, 4, 3, 2, and 1 as they correlate them with objects or people
2. Subtract 1 from each number as the song is sung
3. Imitate frogs by jumping into a pool

Materials

1. Song: "Ten Little Frogs" by Scott and Wood. In this lesson, the number is reduced to five for use with younger children.
2. A felt board and five felt frogs, a felt log, and a felt pool.

Approach
Tell the children, "I am going to sing a song for you about frogs. When I finish, let's see if you can tell us how many frogs there are altogether in the song."

Procedure

1. Sing the song. You or the children can remove a felt frog from the felt board for each verse of the song.
2. Ask children how many frogs are in the song.
3. Ask, "If we used children instead of frogs to act out the song, how many children would we need?"
4. Discuss with the children what could be used for a make-believe log and a make-believe pool.
5. Ask for five "frog" volunteers.
6. Tell the children they may sing with you this time. Many of them will not join in. At first, they will be too absorbed in the action and in trying to remember what number comes next as each verse is sung. Encourage those who are not frogs to help sing.

At the end of each verse, count the number of remaining frogs on the log. Do this until children get accustomed to "taking away" one frog each time. Songs using subtraction should not be used until children have had many experiences with songs using addition.

Evaluation

1. Did the children enjoy singing the song and acting it out?
2. Could the children remember to reduce the number each time the song was sung?

TEN LITTLE FROGS

LOUISE B. SCOTT

Adapted by K. BAYLESS

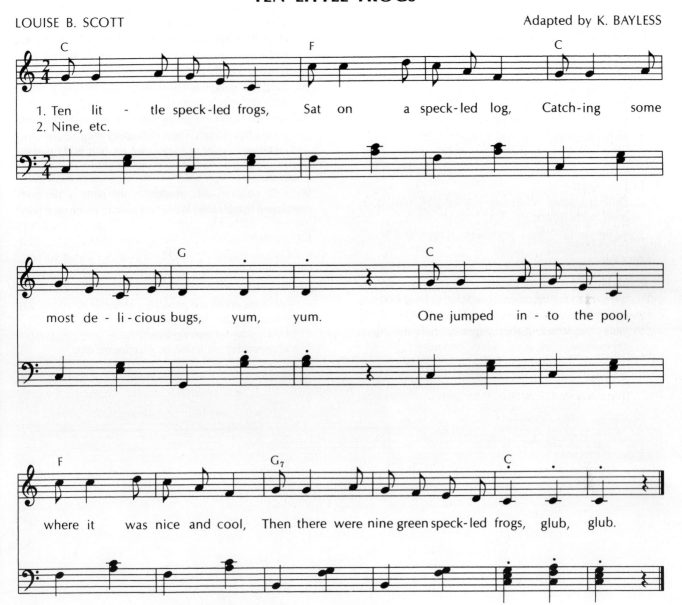

1. Ten lit - tle speck-led frogs, Sat on a speck-led log, Catch-ing some
2. Nine, etc.

most de - li-cious bugs, yum, yum. One jumped in - to the pool,

where it was nice and cool, Then there were nine green speck-led frogs, glub, glub.

Last verse
One little speckled frog, Sat on a speckled log,
Catching some most delicious bugs, yum, yum.
He jumped into the pool, Where it was nice and cool,
Then there were no green speckled frogs, glub, glub.

"Head, Shoulders, Knees, and Toes"

Concept
Naming and identifying parts of the body

Learning
The children will

1. Identify and name parts of the body as each part is mentioned in the song
2. Relate the parts of a doll's body to their own
3. Experience fast and slow tempo

Materials

1. Felt board
2. Doll character, miniature boy or girl, plus body parts made of felt
3. Action song: "Head, Shoulders, Knees, and Toes"

Procedure

1. Make up a short descriptive story about a doll or boy or girl figure, naming the parts of the body as you assemble them on the felt board. (The body parts mentioned in the song are head, shoulders, knees, toes, eyes, ears, mouth, and nose.)
2. Sing the song, pointing to the doll's body parts as they are mentioned in the song.
3. Block the board, and remove one part of the body. Have the children guess the part that is missing and name it. Continue to take turns. A child may help remove a body part.
4. Sing the song again, and have the children point to their own body parts.
5. As the children become familiar with the song, increase the tempo. They will enjoy singing the song faster and faster as they point to their body parts.

Evaluation
Were the children able to identify the parts of the body mentioned in the song? Were they able to name each part?

Enrichment

Poem

I look in the mirror and guess what I see,
My head, my ears, they're part of me.
And every day I wiggle my toes,
And sometimes you'll find me wiggling my nose.

HEAD, SHOULDERS, KNEES, AND TOES

Action song

Head, shoul-ders, knees, and toes, knees and toes. Head, shoul-ders, knees, and

toes, knees and toes and Eyes and ears and

mouth and nose, Head shoul-ders, knees and toes, knees and toes.

"Mister Wind"

Concepts

Rhythmic movement; wind

Learning

The children will

1. Discover that wind is air set in motion, has the power to carry and push things, and can be felt and heard but not seen
2. Use their imaginations to create their own movements stimulated by discussions about the wind

Materials

1. Pictures showing "winds" of different strengths at work. Include flying kites, wind blowing against an umbrella, storms, sailboats sailing in the water, branches of trees bending in the wind, and so on.
2. Poem: "Who Has Seen the Wind?" by Christina G. Rossetti
3. Rhythmic participation record: *My Playmate the Wind,* Young People's Records. (This record, which is presently out of production, is a valuable resource.)
4. Song: "Mister Wind" by K. Bayless and M. Ramsey

Approach

Read or recite the poem "Who Has Seen the Wind?"

Procedure

1. Show and discuss the wind pictures.
2. Have children blow on their hands. Help them discover that by using their mouths they are making a small wind.
3. Play the activity record *My Playmate the Wind.* Have children find their own spaces and move to the words and music.
4. At another time, permit children to find their own spaces and create their own movements stimulated by "word pictures," music, visuals, poems, records, and so on about the wind.
   (a) "Pretend that you are a tree. Your arms are the branches. How would you move your branches if the wind were blowing slowly and gently? If it were blowing very hard?"
   (b) "Now pretend you are holding onto an umbrella. Suddenly a gust of wind comes along. How would you hold your umbrella so it wouldn't get away from you?"
   (c) "The wind is strong and pushing hard on your back. How would you walk?"
   (d) "Pretend you are a kite. Use your arms and hands to show how the wind might blow you about in the sky."

Eloquence is in the eye of the beholder. Children use scarves or streamers to create the illusion of wind.

Evaluation

1. Were the children able to create their own rhythmic movements illustrating the effect of wind on people and things?
2. Did the children give examples of feeling and hearing the wind?

Enrichment

Poems

- "Wind Song" by Lillian Moore
- "The Wind" by Robert Louis Stevenson
- "Clouds" by Christina G. Rossetti

- "The North Wind Doth Blow"
- "To a Red Kite" by Lillian Moore

Songs

- "The North Wind" by K. Bayless
- "The Autumn Leaves" by A. Harwood, *The Spectrum of Music*

Records

- *Rustle of Spring* by Christian Sinding
- *Autumn Leaves* by Mercer et al.

MISTER WIND

Words and music by K. BAYLESS

1. Mis - ter Wind, you seem to be So mys - te - ri - ous to me. I can feel and— hear you too, But see - ing you I can - not do.

2
You are like a funny clown,
Twirling up and sometimes down,
But you help me fly my kite,
So Mister Wind, you are all right!!

FAVORITE SONGS AND RHYTHMS

Teachers and parents requested that many of the following songs and rhythms be included in this edition. Some selections were in the first, second, and third editions; many others are new. The songs have been transposed to keys suitable for the singing range of young children and can be used with children of various age ranges.

The songs and rhythms appear in a logical order, starting at the beginning of the school year and following the seasonal changes. Suggestions for their use are included with many. Others can be used for pure enjoyment and musical value.

Research indicates that there is a relationship between music and the development of reading skills.

The creativity of the arts and the joy of music
should be central to the education of every American child.
Richard Riley, former U.S. Secretary of Education

HAPPY SCHOOL SONG

Words by Janet Lee
Used by permission

Tune: Old Mac Donald

suggested verses:

2. with a *clap clap* or *(tap, tap)* here. . .
3. with a *shake shake* here. . .
4. with a *stomp stomp* here. . .
5. with a *hop hop* here. . .

TODAY IS MONDAY

Source unknown

1. To - day   is   Mon - day,   To - day   is

Mon - day,   Mon - day, string - beans   all   you   hun - gry   chil - dren,

Come and eat   it   up. 2. To - day   is   Tues - day,   To - day   is   Tues - day,

Tues - day, spa - ghet - ti,   Mon - day   string - beans,   All   you   hun - gry   chil - dren,

Come   and   eat   it   up.   To - day   is   Come   and   eat   it   up.

3. Wednesday, zoooop
4. Thursday, roast beef
5. Friday, fish
6. Saturday, chicken
7. Sunday, ice cream

(Note: As each verse is sung, repeat the other days of the week with their foods.)
Example of last verse:

Today is Sunday, today is Sunday   Wednesday, ZOOOOOP
Sunday, ice cream   Tuesday, spaghetti
Saturday, chicken   Monday, string beans
Friday, fish   All you hungry children
Thursday, roast beef   Come and eat it up.

Concepts: *recall of words and melody, sequencing*

MARY HAD A LITTLE LAMB

SARA JOSEPHA HALE

Traditional
Arranged by K. BAYLESS

1. Ma - ry had a lit - tle lamb, lit - tle lamb, lit - tle lamb,

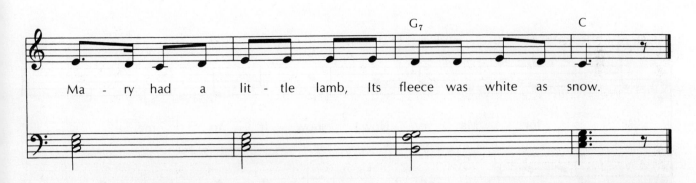

Ma - ry had a lit - tle lamb, Its fleece was white as snow.

2
And ev'ry where that Mary went,
Mary went, Mary went,
Ev'rywhere that Mary went,
The lamb was sure to go.

3
It followed her to school one day,
School one day, school one day,
It followed her to school one day,
Which was against the rule.

4
It made the children laugh and play
Laugh and play, laugh and play,
It made the children laugh and play,
To see a lamb in school.

"M" IS FOR MARY

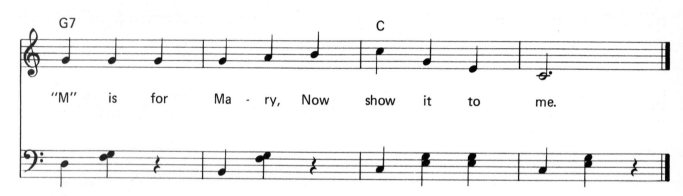

"M" is for Mary, I found it, you see,
"M" is for Mary, It's easy for me.

BINGO

Scottish song

Arranged by K. BAYLESS

There was a farm-er who had a dog, And Bin-go was his name - O. B - I - N - G - O, B - I - N - G - O, B - I - N - G - O, And Bin-go was his name - O

Suggestions

Sing the song through as written. Then repeat it and clap instead of singing the letter B in "B-I-N-G-O." On the next repetition, substitute clapping the letters B and I, etc. (This song is excellent for helping develop concentration.)

SWEETLY SINGS THE DONKEY

Traditional

Arranged by K. BAYLESS

Sweet - ly sings the don - key at the break of day.

If you do not feed him, this is what he'll say: He -

haw! He - haw! He - haw, he - haw, he - haw!

Musical concept: *adjusting voice to pitch differences (example: he-haw)*

WHO SEES SOMETHING RED?

Source unknown
Adapted by K. BAYLESS

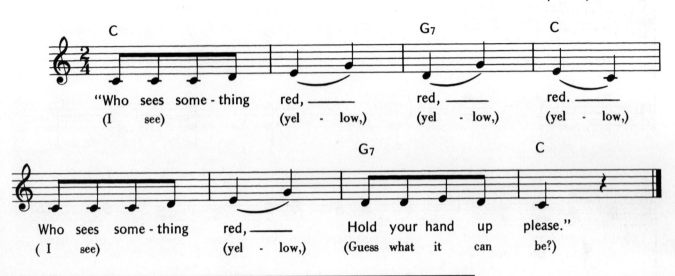

"Who sees some-thing red, ____ red, ____ red. ____
(I see) (yel - low,) (yel - low,) (yel - low,)

Who sees some-thing red, ____ Hold your hand up please."
(I see) (yel - low,) (Guess what it can be?)

Musical concept: steady, underlying beat (good for clapping or tapping)

COLOR GAME

Words and music by K. BAYLESS

Suggestion

Work with children to add extra verses. For example:

   If you have on brown, turn around

   If you have on black, step on a crack

   If you have on pink, make your eyes blink

   If you have on blue, touch your shoe

   If you have on white, go fly a kite

This delightful, musical playlet, "Superbrush and the Molars," is often used during dental health week. Encourage the children to create their own dialogue and sound effects. Tunes A and C are in the major mode, Tune B, the minor mode. Tune C has been transposed to a lower key to accommodate the younger voices.*

***Superbrush and the Molars** by Lois Roper*
Cast includes Villain (dark cape, child's play hammer, and sign saying "Mean Old Tooth Decay"), Superbrush (red cape and large cardboard toothbrush), and five Teeth (each child holds a large, white cardboard tooth with a colored smiling face).

Teeth sing Song A, "Happy Little Teeth."
Tooth 1 (stepping forward): "But here comes the bad guy." (Villain stalks in, stomps around, and waves hammer. He taps each Tooth lightly. As each is tapped, child turns the cardboard tooth over, hiding its smile.)
Chorus or group of children sing Song B, "Hee, Hee, Hee."
Teeth: "Help!"
Teeth 2 and 3: "Save us!"
Tooth 4: "Look, up in the sky!"
Tooth 5: "Is it a bird?"
Chorus or group of children: "No!"
Everyone: "It's Superbrush!"
Superbrush (bounds on stage, toothbrush held high): "I'll save you!" (He chases Villain around the stage. On the second time around, he touches the Villain with the toothbrush. Villain falls to the floor. With one foot on the victim, Superbursh raises his toothbrush.)
All sing Song C, "Toothsome Tune."

A. HAPPY LITTLE TEETH

*From INSTRUCTOR, February 1971 issue. Copyright © 1971 by Scholastic Inc. Reprinted by permission of Scholastic Inc.

B. HEE, HEE, HEE

*From INSTRUCTOR, February 1971 issue. Copyright © 1971 by Scholastic Inc. Reprinted by permission of Scholastic Inc.

C. TOOTHSOME TUNE

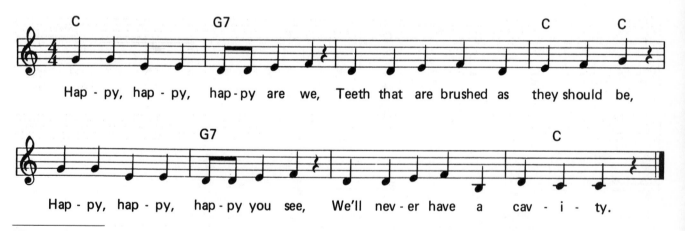

*From INSTRUCTOR, February 1971 issue. Copyright © 1971 by Scholastic Inc. Reprinted by permission of Scholastic Inc.

OVER IN THE MEADOW

South Appalachian folk song

Accompaniment by K. BAYLESS

I'VE GOT THAT HAPPY FEELING

Source unknown

2. I've got that happy feeling here in my feet (march in place).
3. I've got that happy feeling here in my hands (clap hands).
4. I've got that happy feeling all over me.

Suggestion

Have the children create other verses.

IF YOU'RE HAPPY

Traditional

Arranged by K. BAYLESS

2. If you're happy and you know it, stamp your feet.
3. If you're happy and you know it, nod your head.

4. If you're happy and you know it, swing around.
5. If you're happy and you know it, shout out loud!

Suggestion
Have the children create their own verses.

THE WHISPER SONG

Arranged by MARION WINTERS

By JOAN and ROGER BRADFIELD

BROWNIE SMILE SONG

HARRIET E. HEYWOOD

Melody by Ms. Heywood's Brownie
Girl Scout troop

1. I've some-thing in my pock-et. It be-longs a-cross my face, And I
2. I'm sure you could-n't guess it If you guessed a long, long while, So I'll

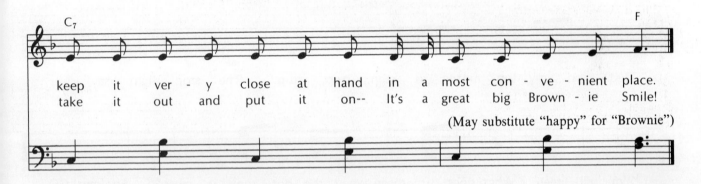

keep it ver - y close at hand in a most con - ve - nient place.
take it out and put it on-- It's a great big Brown - ie Smile!

(May substitute "happy" for "Brownie")

THE STOP LIGHT SONG

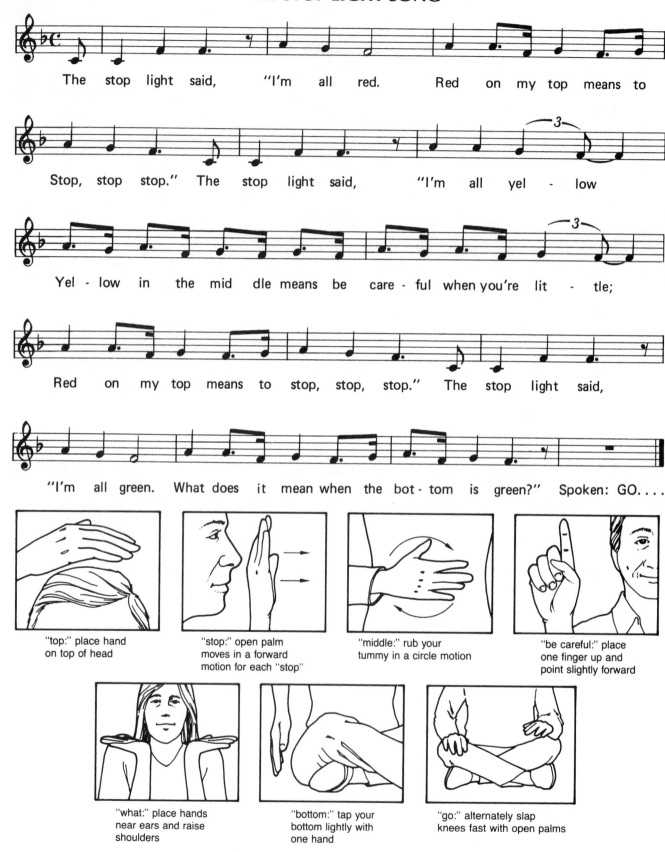

The stop light said, "I'm all red. Red on my top means to

Stop, stop stop." The stop light said, "I'm all yel - low

Yel - low in the mid - dle means be care - ful when you're lit - tle;

Red on my top means to stop, stop, stop." The stop light said,

"I'm all green. What does it mean when the bot - tom is green?" Spoken: GO....

"top:" place hand on top of head

"stop:" open palm moves in a forward motion for each "stop"

"middle:" rub your tummy in a circle motion

"be careful:" place one finger up and point slightly forward

"what:" place hands near ears and raise shoulders

"bottom:" tap your bottom lightly with one hand

"go:" alternately slap knees fast with open palms

By Bonnie Wendt Draeger. © 1985 from Paradiddles 1985 Music/Arts Review, P.O. Box 1348, Columbus, Indiana. Used by permission.

AUTUMN LEAVES

German folk tune
Words by Helen Myers Cornwell

VERSE

*1. Now the sum-mer is o-ver, There are leaves all a-round.

Au-tumn leaves, red and yel-low, Soft-ly fall to the ground.

REFRAIN

La lee la la la la la, La lee la la lee lie,

Au-tumn leaves of all col-ors, Tell-ing sum-mer good-by.

2
Now the summer is over,
And the leaves start to whirl.
Autumn leaves turn and tumble,
Chilly winds make them swirl. *Refrain*

3
Now the summer is over,
See the leaves ev'rywhere.
Autumn leaves make a carpet
Under trees dark and bare. *Refrain*

From WORLD OF MUSIC. © 1988 Silver Burdett & Ginn Inc. Used by permission.

*Transpose to key of C for ease of singing.

GOBBLE, GOBBLE, QUACK, QUACK

Source unknown
Arranged by K. BAYLESS

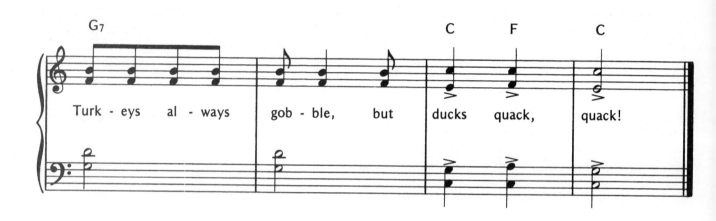

MR. TURKEY

Words and music by K. BAYLESS

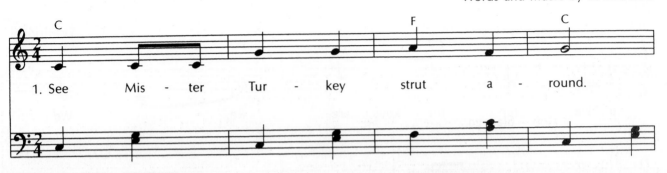

1. See Mis - ter Tur - key strut a - round.

Gob - ble, gob - ble, gob - ble, gob - ble is his fun - ny sound.

2
See Mister Turkey, he's so fat.
Wibble, wobble, wibble, wobble, round he goes like that.

FIVE FAT TURKEYS

Traditional

Five   fat   tur - keys   are   we,   We

slept   all   night   in   the   tree,   When   the   cook   came   a - round   we

could - n't   be   found,   So   that's   why   we're   here   you   see.

OVER THE RIVER

Traditional American song

1. O - ver the riv - er and through the wood, To Grand- fa - ther's house we
2. O - ver the riv - er and through the wood, Trot fast, my dap - ple

go,_____ The horse knows the way to car - ry the sleigh Through the
gray! ____ Spring o - ver the ground like a hunt - ing hound, For

white and drift - ed snow. O - ver the riv - er and
this is Thanks - giv - ing day! O - ver the riv - er and

through the wood, Oh how the wind does blow! _____ It
through the wood, Now Grand - mother's face I spy! _____ Hur -

stings the toes and bites the nose, As o - ver the ground we go. _____
rah for the fun, Is the pud - ding done? Hur - rah for the pump - kin pie! ____

THE NORTH WIND

M. RAMSEY

K. BAYLESS

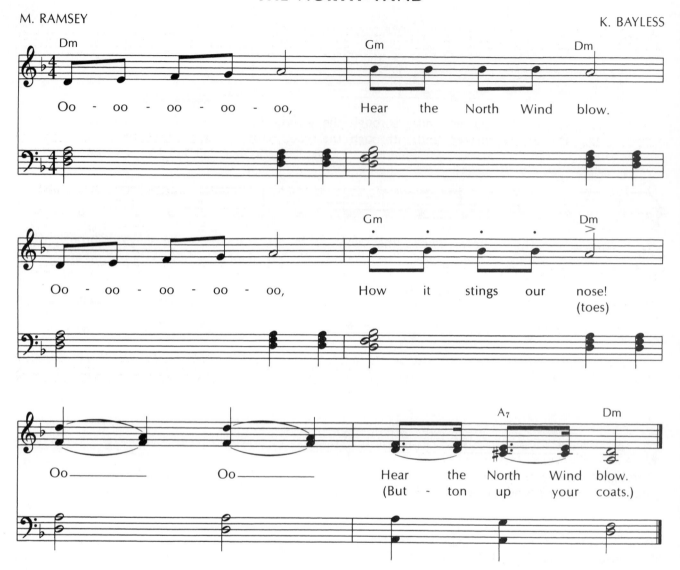

SIX LITTLE SNOWMEN

Source unknown

Six lit-tle men all made of snow,
Six lit-tle snow-men stand-ing in a row, Out came the sun and
stayed all day, One lit-tle snow-man melt-ed a-way.

or

2
Five little snowmen all made of snow
Five little snowmen standing in a row
Out came the sun and shined all day
One little snowman melted away, etc.

Snow
(To tune of "Row, Row, Row Your Boat")

Look, look, see the snow,
    See it falling down;
Swirling, swirling, swirling, swirling
    All around the town.

Look, look, see the snow,
    Cold and very white;
Swirling, swirling, swirling, swirling
    What a pretty sight!

Our Snowman
(Sung to the tune of "This Old Man")

Our snowman
Stands so tall.
We just made him from snowballs
With a big black hat to shade him from the sun.
Making him was so much fun!!

(SOURCE UNKNOWN)

AMERICA, WE LOVE YOU

Words and music by K. BAYLESS

Spoken cheer (optional): America, America, *We - love - you* !!!

A VALENTINE WISH

Words and music by K. BAYLESS

If I could be your Val - en - tine, You know what I would do, I'd

jump in - to my rock - et ship, and trav - el straight to you!

ONE RED VALENTINE

Source unknown
Adapted by K. BAYLESS

One red val - en - tine, Two red val - en - tines,

Three red val - en - tines four, I'll snip and cut and

col - or and paste, And then make twen - ty more.

LOVE SOMEBODY

American folk song

1. Love some-bod-y, yes I do; Love some-bod-y, yes I do;
Love some-bod-y, yes I do; Love some-bod-y, but I won't tell who.

2. Love somebody, yes I do;
   Love somebody, yes I do;
   Love somebody, yes I do;
   Love somebody, but you can't guess who.

A TISKET, A TASKET

Traditional
Adapted by K. BAYLESS

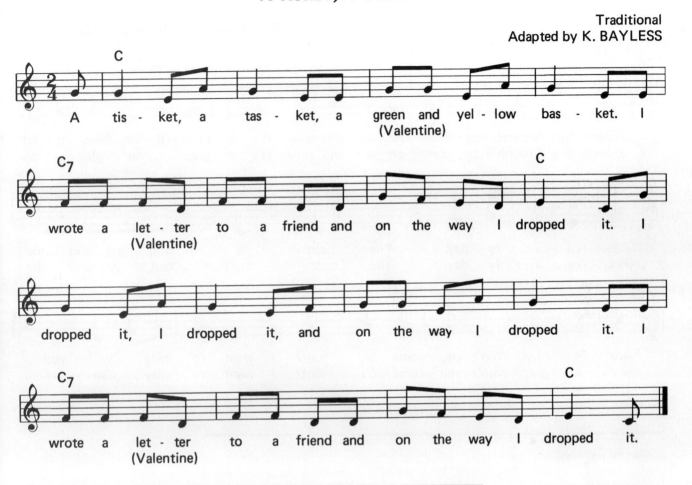

This favorite, play or party game can be adapted in many ways. For Valentine's Day, use a Valentine basket and have the child who is "It" drop a Valentine behind a child in the circle. The game proceeds like "Duck, Duck, Goose."

Musical concept: *sol-mi minor third—the international chant of childhood*

GROUNDHOG

Words and music by "Miss Jackie" Weissman
Used by permission

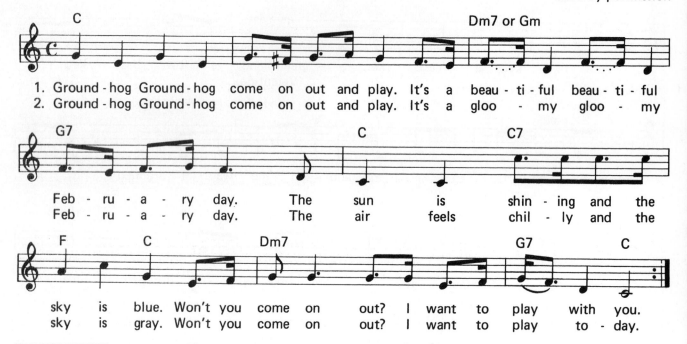

1. Ground-hog Ground-hog come on out and play. It's a beau-ti-ful beau-ti-ful
2. Ground-hog Ground-hog come on out and play. It's a gloo - my gloo - my

Feb-ru-a-ry day.   The sun   is   shin-ing and the
Feb-ru-a-ry day.   The air   feels   chil-ly and the

sky is blue. Won't you come on out? I want to play with you.
sky is gray. Won't you come on out? I want to play to-day.

Reprinted by permission of "Miss Jackie" Weissman.

Act out the following:

After verse 1: The groundhog climbs slowly out of his hole. He looks around and sees his shadow. "Help, help," he cries. "I see my shadow. I must go back into the ground for six more weeks of winter."

After verse 2: The groundhog climbs slowly out of his hole. He looks around, but he doesn't see his shadow. "Oh, I'm so happy. I don't see my shadow. Spring will soon be here."

Encourage children to be conscious of their own shadows when out in the sun. Do a lesson on shadows using artificial lighting.

SPRING IS HERE

K. BAYLESS

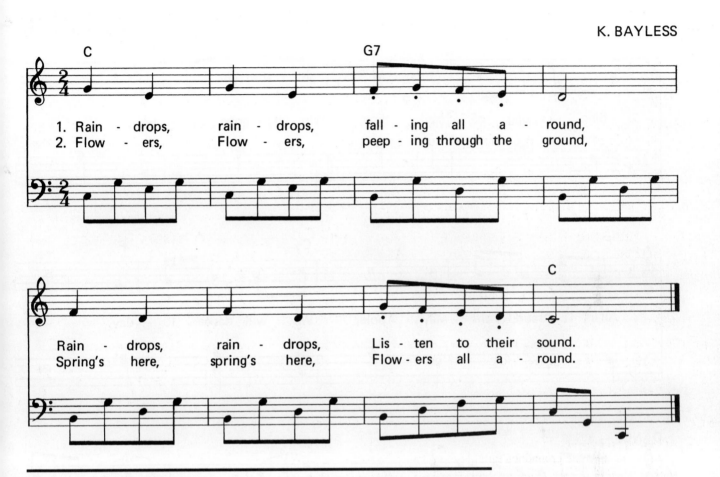

Have children sing marked notes staccato.

Musical concept: *sol-mi minor third*

MAYPOLE DANCE

Source unknown
Adapted by K. BAYLESS

Sing a song of May - time, Win - ter's gone a - way,

All a - round the May - pole, We will dance to - day.

DANCE

HOT POTATO

Traditional rhyme set to music
K. BAYLESS

One, po - ta - to, two po - ta - to, Three po - ta - to four,

Five po - ta - to, six po - ta - to, seven po - ta - to, more!

"Hot Potato" and "I Caught a Fish" are excellent examples of rhymes that can be sung. The scalewise progression makes them easy to sing. Older children love to jump rope while teachers and students sing or chant these very rhythmic rhymes.

I CAUGHT A FISH

Traditional rhyme set to music
K. BAYLESS

One, two, three, four, five, I caught a fish a - live,
Six, seven, eight, nine, ten, I let him go a - gain.

Why did you let him go? Be - cause he bit my fing - er so!

ONE ELEPHANT

Singing game

Chilean folk song
Arranged and adapted by K. BAYLESS

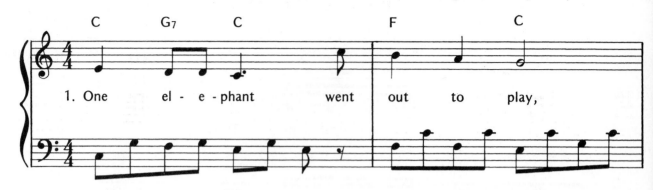

1. One el - e - phant went out to play,

All on a spi - ders web one day. He had such e-
(They)

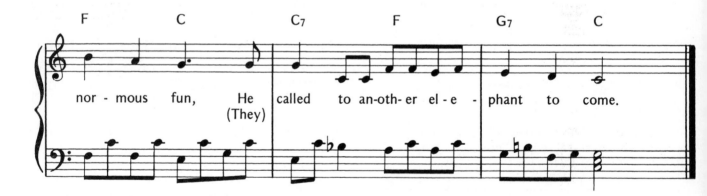

nor - mous fun, He called to an-oth- er el - e - phant to come.
(They)

2. Two elephants went out to play

3. Three elephants went out to play, etc.

Suggestions

After each verse is sung, have the children call out in singing fashion for the next
elephant to come. Have them sing "éléphant" (French for "elephant"). Sing the
syllables of the word *éléphant* as follows:

él - é - phant

One could also use the word for elephant in Spanish, Italian, or another language.
Children love calling for the next elephant in different languages.

JOHNNY WORKS WITH ONE HAMMER

Folk song

Arranged by K. BAYLESS

John - ny works with one ham - mer, one ham - mer, one ham - mer,

John - ny works with one ham - mer, Then he works with two.

2
Johnny works with two hammers,
two hammers, two hammers,
Johnny works with two hammers,
Then he works with three.

3
Johnny works with three hammers,
three hammers, three hammers,
Johnny works with three hammers,
Then he works with four.

4
Johnny works with four hammers,
four hammers, four hammers,
Johnny works with four hammers,
Then he works with five.

5
Johnny works with five hammers,
five hammers, five hammers,
Johnny works with five hammers,
Then he goes to sleep.

From *Finger Play* by Mary Miller and Paula Zajan. Copyright 1955, G. Schirmer, Inc. Used by permission.

Actions
Verse 1: Pound on right knee with right first in time with music.
Verse 2: Add left fist; pound on left knee.
Verse 3: Add right foot; tap on floor.
Verse 4: Add left left foot; tap on floor.
Verse 5: Add head; nod up and down. On words "goes to sleep," stop pounding, drop
       head, or lie down on floor and rest.

THIS OLD MAN

English singing game

This old man, he played one, He played nick-nack on my thumb,

Nick-nack, pad-dy whack, Give a dog a bone, This old man came roll-ing home.

2
This old man, he played two,
He played nick-nack on my shoe;
Nick-nack, paddy whack, Give a dog a bone,
This old man came rolling home.

3
This old man, he played three,
He played nick-nack on my knee;
Nick-nack, paddy whack, Give a dog a bone,
This old man came rolling home.

4
This old man, he played four,
He played nick-nack on my door; (Point to forehead.)

5
This old man, he played five,
He played nick-nack on my hive; (Fight the bees.)

6
This old man, he played six,
He played nick-nack on my sticks; (Hold up index fingers.)

7
This old man he played sev'n,
He played nick-nack up in heav'n; (Fly like angels.)

8
This old man, he played eight,
He played nick-nack on my pate; (Point to top of head.)

9
This old man, he played nine,
He played nick-nack on my spine; (Tap between shoulders.)

10
This old man, he played ten,
He played nick-nack once again;
Nick-nack, paddy whack, Give a dog a bone,
Now we'll all go running home.

THREE BLUE PIGEONS

American folk song

Arranged by K. BAYLESS

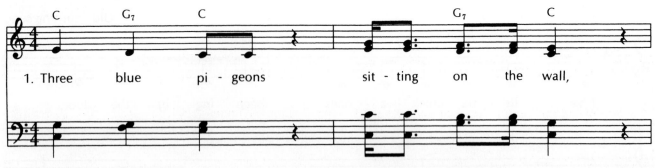

1. Three blue pi - geons sit - ting on the wall,

Three blue pi-_____ geons_____ sit - ting on the wall.

Spoken: One pigeon flew away. Whee-ee-ee-ee-ee!!

2
Two blue pigeons sitting on the wall,
Two blue pigeons sitting on the wall.
Spoken: Another one flew away. (or) The second one
flew away. Whee-ee-ee-ee-ee!!

3
One blue pigeon sitting on the wall,
One blue pigeon sitting on the wall.
Spoken: Another one flew away. (or) The third one flew
away. Whee-ee-ee-ee-ee!!

4
No blue pigeons sitting on the wall,
No blue pigeons sitting on the wall.
Spoken: One flew back. (or) The first one flew back.
Whee-ee-ee-ee-ee!!

5
One blue pigeon sitting on the wall,
One blue pigeon sitting on the wall.
Spoken: Another flew back. (or) The second one flew
back. Whee-ee-ee-ee-ee!!

6
Two blue pigeons sitting on the wall.
Two blue pigeons sitting on the wall.
Spoken: Another flew back. (or) The third one flew back.
Whe-ee-ee-ee-ee!!

7
Three blue pigeons sitting on the wall,
Three blue pigeons sitting on the wall.
Spoken: And now the pigeons *are all home!!*

Suggestion
Have the children be the pigeons, or use puppet pigeons on sticks to dramatize the song.

FIVE LITTLE CHICKADEES

Old counting song

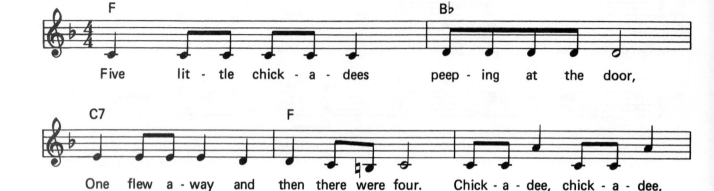

2
Four little chickadees sitting on a tree,
One flew away, and there were three,
(Refrain)

3
Three little chickadees looking at you,
One flew away, and then there were two,
(Refrain)

4
Two little chickadees sitting in the sun,
One flew away, and then there was one,
(Refrain)

5
One little chickadee left all alone,
He flew away, and then there were none,
(Refrain)

This is an excellent song to dramatize. Children can be the chickadees or can make chickadee puppets.

Movement concept: *flying*

FIVE LITTLE DUCKS WENT SWIMMING ONE DAY

Source Unknown

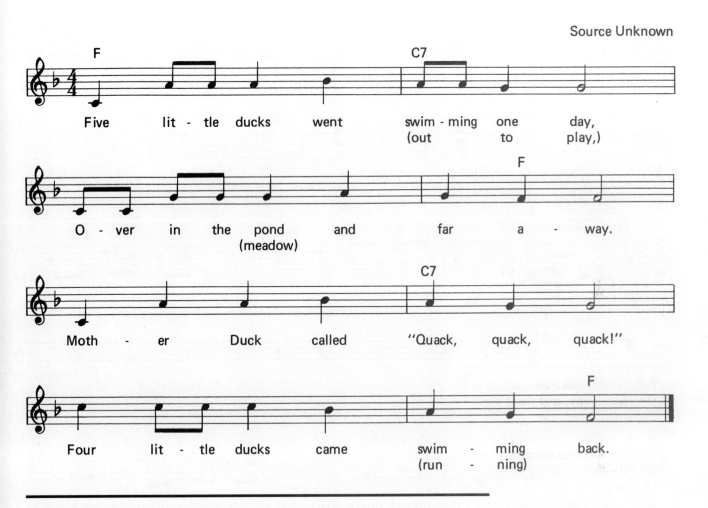

Continue singing the song until no little ducks come swimming (running) back.

Then, Father Duck said, "Quack, quack, quack" *(in a strong voice)* And five little ducks came swimming (running) back!

SIX LITTLE DUCKS

Folk song from Maryland

Arranged by K. BAYLESS

2
Down to the river they would go,
Wibble, wabble, wibble, wabble to and fro.
Refrain

3
Home from the river they would come,
Wibble, wabble, wibble, wabble, ho, hum, hum.
Refrain

ROLL OVER

Traditional American song

There were ten in the bed, And the lit - tle one said, "Roll
nine, etc.

o - ver, roll o - ver." So they all rolled o - ver and

1.–8.
one fell out. There were

9.
one fell out. There was

one in the bed, And the lit - tle one said, "Good - night!"

LITTLE FISH

D.R.G. and B.W.C.

W.E.S.

Lit - tle fish goes out to play, He wig - gles his fins, then swims a - way; He swims and swims in the wa - ter bright, He o - pens his mouth and takes a bite! Mmmmmmm! Tastes good!

"Little Fish" may be done without music as a fingerplay and choral speaking activity. When the children have learned it, they will enjoy singing the melody as they do the motions.

Put your left hand out, palm down, fingers together, thumb sticking out. Put your right hand on top of the left, palm down, thumb out. (See the fish with fins at his sides.) Wiggle your thumbs, then make the fish swim by moving hands up and down in unison. Now make the fish swim and wiggle his fins at the same time. Open his mouth. Keep the hands together but drop the left hand fingers and raise the right hand fingers. Rub tummy.

MY DOG RAGS

Unknown

Hand Motions

On words *flip-flop*, flip left hand over head, then right hand over head.

On words *wig-wag*, put hands together in back of you. Flip them to the left and then to the right of the body.

On words *zig-zag*, bend over, hands on hips. Bend the body to the left and then to the right.

I HAD A CAT

Kentucky folk song
Adapted by K. BAYLES

1. I had a cat and the cat pleased me, I fed my cat un-der yon-der tree. *(1. Refrain)* Cat goes fid-dle-i-fee.

(2. Refrain) Hen goes chim-my chuck, Cat goes fid-dle-i-fee.

(3. Refrain) Duck goes quack, quack, Hen goes chim-my chuck, Cat goes fid-dle-i-fee.

2. I had a hen and the hen pleased me, I fed my hen by yonder tree.
3. I had a duck and the duck pleased me, I fed my duck by yonder tree.

This is a cumulative song. Children add to each verse by renaming in reverse order what has been sung before.

Musical concept: *mi-re-do (3–2–1) intervals ("younder tree" and "cat goes fiddle-i-fee")*

Concept: *sequencing and memorization*

BARNYARD FAMILY

American folk song

Arranged by K. BAYLESS

1. I have a lit-tle roost-er by the barn – yard gate, And
that lit-tle roost-er is my play-mate, And that lit-tle roost-er goes
cock – a-doo-dle-doo, Doo-doo,__ doo-doo,__ doo-doo – dle doo.

2
I have a little hen by the barnyard gate,
And that little hen is my playmate,
And that little hen goes cluck, a-cluck-a-cluck,
Cluck-cluck, cluck-cluck, cluck-cluck-a-cluck.

3
I have a little duck by the barnyard gate,
And that little duck is my playmate,
And that little duck goes quack-a-quack-a-quack,
Quack-quack, quack-quack, quack-quack-a-quack, etc.

CROCODILE SONG

Old song

Source unknown
Adapted by K. BAYLESS

She sailed a - way on a bright and sun - ny day, on the
back of a croc - o - dile. "You see," said she, "He's as
tame as he can be as I float him down the Nile." The
Croc winked his eye as she waved a mer - ry bye,
Wear - ing a hap - py smile. At the end of the ride, the
la - dy was in - side, And the smile was on the croc - o - dile. (Clap - Clap).

Motions

Move one hand over the other arm in an up-and-down motion representing a sailing movement. Stroke one arm with the other hand so as to tame the crocodile. Wink the eye, and wave good-bye. Smile. On the words, "At the end of the ride, the lady was inside, and the smile was on the crocodile," open and shut hands (palms together) like a crocodile's mouth. Give two loud claps at the end of the song.

MAMMA KANGAROO

M. RAMSEY

K. BAYLESS

Bouncy

I am Mam-ma Kang-a - roo, Like to see me jump? I can take a great big leap up a - bove this hump. I am Mam-ma Kang-a - roo, Peek in - to my pock - et____.

This is ba - by Kang - a - roo, Sleep - ing in my pock - et____.

The Animals in the Zoo

(To the tune of "Here We Go Round the Mulberry Bush")

Look at the animals in the zoo, in the zoo, in the zoo,
See the different things they do, and we can do
    them too.

The elephant walks and swings his trunk, swings his
    trunk, swings his trunk,
The elephant walks and swings his trunk, and we can do
    it too.

The tall giraffe can stretch her neck, stretch her neck,
    stretch her neck,
The tall giraffe can stretch her neck, and we can do
    it too.

Monkeys swing on limbs of trees, limbs of trees, limbs of
    trees,

Monkeys swing on limbs of trees, and we can do it too.

Camels march like soldiers brave, soldiers brave, soldiers
    brave,
Camels march like soldiers brave, and we can do it too.

Bears stamp their heavy feet, heavy feet, heavy feet,
Bears stamp their heavy feet, and we can do it too.

The kangaroos go jump, jump, jump; jump, jump, jump;
    jump, jump, jump.
The kangaroos go jump, jump, jump, and we can do
    it too.

(As the song is sung, have children do the actions. Encourage them to add other verses.)

FROGGIE WENT A-COURTIN'

American folk song

Arranged by K. BAYLESS

2

He rode right up to Miss Mouse's door, uh huh, uh huh.
He rode right up to Miss Mouse's door, uh huh.
He rode right up to Miss Mouse's door,
Where he'd been many times before, uh huh, uh huh.

3

He took Miss Mousey on his knee, uh huh, uh huh.
He took Miss Mousey on his knee, uh huh.
He took Miss Mousey on his knee,
And said, "Miss Mousey will you marry me?" uh huh, uh huh.

4

"Without my Uncle Rat's consent, uh huh, uh huh. . .
I wouldn't marry the President," uh huh, uh huh.

5

"Where shall the wedding supper be?" uh huh, uh huh. . .
"Way down yonder in the hollow tree," uh huh, uh huh.

6

"What shall the wedding supper be?" uh huh, uh huh. . .
"Two green beans and a black-eyed pea," uh huh, uh huh.

7

First one in was a bumblebee, uh huh, uh huh. . .
Who danced a jig with a two-legged flea, uh huh, uh huh.

8

They all sailed off across the lake, uh huh, uh huh. . .
Got swallowed up by a big black snake, uh huh, uh huh.

9

There's corn and cheese upon the shelf, uh huh, uh huh. . .
If you want more verses just sing them yourself, uh huh, uh huh.

MISTER RABBIT

Southern folk song

Arranged by K. BAYLESS

1. "Mis - ter Rab - bit, Mis - ter Rab - bit, your ears might - y long!" "Yes, in - deed they're put on wrong."

Ev - 'ry lit - tle soul must shine, shine, shine.

Ev - 'ry lit - tle soul must shine. shine, shine.

2

"Mister Rabbit, Mister Rabbit, your coat's mighty gray!"
"Yes, indeed, 'twas made that way."
Ev'ry little soul must shine, shine, shine.
Ev'ry little soul must shine, shine, shine.

3

"Mister Rabbit, Mister Rabbit, your tail's mighty white!"
"Yes, indeed, I'm going out of sight."
Ev'ry little soul must shine, shine, shine.
Ev'ry little soul must shine, shine, shine.

JACK JUMPS UP, JACK STOOPS DOWN

Source unknown
Adapted by K. BAYLESS

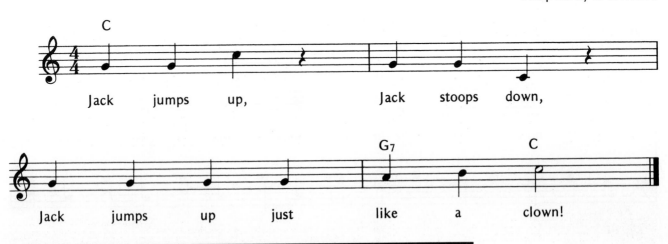

Jack jumps up, Jack stoops down,

Jack jumps up just like a clown!

Movement concepts: *jumping (springing with the legs); up-down*

MONKEY SEE, MONKEY DO

Traditional

If you clap, clap, clap your hands, The mon - key

claps, claps, claps his hands, Mon - key sees and

mon - key do, The mon - key does the same as you.

(Add other verses like, "If you stamp, stamp, stamp your feet," etc.)

This is a good song to help develop listening skills and skill in following directions.

Musical concept: *identical melodies in the first two phrases*

BOW, BELINDA

Traditional
Adapted

American game song
Arranged by K. BAYLESS

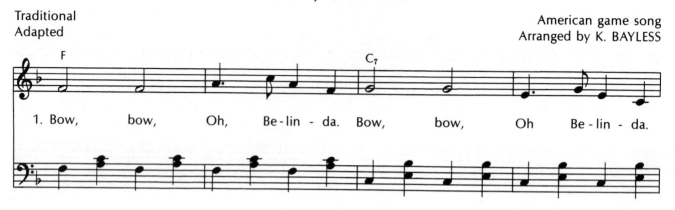

1. Bow,   bow,   Oh,   Be-lin-da.   Bow,   bow,   Oh   Be-lin-da.

Bow,   bow,   Oh   Be-lin-da.   Please   bow,   Be-lin-da.

2

One hand out, oh Belinda,
  or right hand out, oh Belinda,
One hand out, oh Belinda,
One hand out, oh Belinda,
One hand out before you.

3

Another hand out, oh Belinda,
  or two hands out, oh Belinda,
  or left hand out, oh Belinda,
Another hand out, oh Belinda,
Another hand out, oh Belinda,
Both hands out before you.

HOKEY POKEY

Traditional U.S. game song

Arranged by K. BAYLESS

2. You put your left foot in,
3. You put your right arm in,

4. You put your left arm in,
5. You put your whole self in,

GOING ON A PICNIC

Words and Music by Lynn Freeman Olson

1. Go - ing on a pic - nic, Leav - ing right a - way; If it does - n't rain we'll stay all day. 1. Did you bring the hot dogs? sal - ad?

Yes, I brought the hot dogs! Read - y for a pic - nic? Here we go!
sal - ad!

2. Did you bring the ice cream?
Yes, I brought the ice cream!
Did you bring the melon?
Yes, I brought the melon!
Ready for a picnic?
Here we go!

KEY IDEAS

1. Music is basic to the young child's day.
2. Enjoyment and appreciation are primary goals for including music in the young child's day.
3. Music enhances the flow of language as well as fluency and extension of language.
4. Research evidence indicates that there is a relationship between music and the development of reading skills.
5. Through careful selection of songs, science concepts can be extended and clarified.
6. Number learning can be enjoyed through the use of nursery rhymes and songs, jingles, and poetry.
7. Every area of the social studies curriculum can be expanded and illustrated through the use of songs.
8. Musical opportunities abound throughout the day and the curriculum. Seek them out.
9. Adults establish a musical environment through enthusiasm, participation, and flexibility.

SUMMARY

Music is a part of the daily lives of all children. Teachers and caregivers have virtually unlimited opportunity to seek out music resources to enhance the study of language, science, numbers, and social studies.

Research evidence supports the use of music to develop language, expand vocabulary, and enhance reading skills. Music naturally attracts the attention of children and leads to increased fluency in communication as they sing their favorite melodies.

Adults working with young children should seek out a wealth of music resources to incorporate into activities for children in their daily lives. Begin a collection of a broad variety of songs, chants, and poetry, and a collection of tapes, records, and texts.

QUESTIONS TO CONSIDER

1. List several songs that illustrate the basic concepts presented in the opening paragraphs of the chapter.
2. Music offers unique possibilities to expand and extend vocabulary. Select six songs that present unusual vocabulary that would appeal to children.
3. Write a lesson plan that integrates music and language arts.
4. Select at least two songs that might be used to integrate each of the following: music and math, music and science, music and social studies, music and reading skills, and music and art.
5. Prepare a bulletin board featuring music and one of the curriculum areas.
6. In your opinion, what is the best children's television program that incorporates music? Explain.
7. List your 10 favorite children's songs. What children's book could extend each one?

REFERENCES

Barrett, J. R. (2001). Interdisciplinary work and musical integrity. *Music Educators Journal, 87*(5), 27–31.

Blacking, J. (1973). *How musical is man?* Seattle, WA: University of Washington Press.

Brewer, J. A. (2001). *Introduction to early childhood education: Preschool through primary grades.* Boston: Allyn and Bacon.

Consortium of National Arts Education Associations. (1994). *National standards for arts education: What every young American should know and be able to do in the arts.* Reston, VA: Music Educators National Conference, 28–29.

DeMicco, D., & Dean, T. (2002). Mostly Mother Goose. *Journal of Youth Services in Libraries, 15*(2), 31–35.

Feierabend, J. M. (1990). Music in early childhood. *Design for Arts in Education, 91* (6), 15–20.

Feierabend, J. M., Saunders, T. C., Getnick, P. E., & Holahan, J. M. (1998). Song recognition among preschool-age children: An investigation of words and music. *Journal of Research in Music Education, 46*(3), 351–359.

Fisher, D., & McDonald, N. (2001). The intersection between music and early literacy instruction: Listen to literacy! *Reading Improvement, 38*(3), 106–115.

Gardner, H. (1993). *Multiple intelligence: The theory in practice.* New York: Basic Books.

Gill, J. (1998). Add a little music. *Parent and Child, 5*(4), 40–45.

Grandin, T., Peterson, M., & Shaw, G. (1998). Spatial-temporal versus language-analytical reasoning: The role of music in training. *Arts Education Policy Review, 99,* 11–15.

Hildebrandt, C. (1998). Creativity in music and early childhood. *Young Children, 53*(6), 68–74.

Hopton-Jones, P. (1995). Introducing the music of east Africa. *Music Educators Journal, 82*(3), 26–30.

Jackson, H. L. (1997). *Early childhood curriculum: A child's connection to the world.* Albany, NY: Delmar.

James, A. R. (2000). When I listen to music. *Young Children, 55* (3), 36–37.

Jenkins, E. (1995). Music is culture. *Scholastic Early Childhood Today, 9,* 40–41.

Johnson, G. L., & Edelson, R. J. (2003). Integrating music and mathematics in the elementary classroom. *Teaching Children Mathematics, 9*(8), 474–479.

Lapp, D., & Flood, J. (1983). *Teaching reading to every child* (2nd ed.). New York: Macmillan.

McGirr, P. I. (1994/1995). Verdi invades the kindergarten. *Childhood Education, 71*(2), 74–79.

Moravcik, E. (2000). Music all the livelong day. *Young Children, 55*(4), 27–29.

National Council for the Social Studies. (1994). *Expectations of excellence: Curriculum standards for social studies.* Washington, DC: Author.

Rothenberg, B. S. (1996). The measure of music. *Teaching Children Mathematics, 2*(7), 408–410.

Scholastic Early Childhood Today. (2003). Early childhood mathematics: Promoting good beginnings. *Scholastic Early Childhood Today, 17*(4), 15–16.

Sholtys, K. C. (1989). A new language, a new life. *Young Children, 44*(3), 76–77.

Smith, J. (2000). Singing and song writing support early literacy instruction. *The Reading Teacher, 53,* 646–649.

Zinar, R. (1983). *Music in your classroom.* West Nyack, NY: Parker.

SONG COLLECTIONS

Cohn, A. L. (1993). From sea to shining sea: A treasury of American folklore and folk songs. New York: Scholastic

Weikart, P. S. (1997). Movement plus rhymes, songs and singing games. (2nd ed.). Ypsilanti, MI: High/Scope Press.

RECORDINGS

Nursery Days (CD)
Woody Guthrie
Smithsonian Folkways Recordings, Washington, DC (1992)

Songs Children Love to Sing (CD)
Thomas Moore
Thomas Moore Records, Charlotte, NC (2000)

Rise and Shine (CD)
Raffi
Rounder Records, Cambridge, MA (1996)

Kids in Motion: Songs for Creative Movement (CD)
Greg Scelsa and Steve Millang
Young Heart Music, Huntington Beach, CA (1995)

Birds, Beasts, Bugs, and Fishes (Little and Big) (CD)
Pete Seeger
Smithsonian Folkways Recordings, Washington, DC (1998)

CHAPTER EIGHT

Remembering the Importance of Music in All Our Lives

It gives a soul to the universe, wings to the mind, flight to the imagination, a charm to sadness, gaiety and life to everything. It is the essence of order and leads to all that is good, just, and beautiful, of which it is the invisible, but nevertheless dazzling, passionate, and eternal form.

Plato

As an early childhood teacher, you will be a part of an exciting and rewarding profession. You will be in the unique position of making children's lives richer and more fulfilled. No matter what your talents, you can use your personal experiences with music to teach music and to integrate musical experiences into the daily lives of your children.

You have learned a great deal about the development of children. You have read and practiced ways in which you can help children sing, play instruments, move and dance, listen to music, and create music. You have also learned how to provide children with meaningful activities that reflect the diversity of our society.

One of the most important things you can do through musical experiences is to help your children learn to value music as an important part of their lives. An important goal of music education is that young children develop sensitivity to the expressive qualities of music while developing their musical responsiveness, involvement, and appreciation of music beyond the doors of their classroom.

DEVELOPING AN APPRECIATION OF MUSIC

Music is a vital part of every child's education because music constitutes a universal language of the senses and emotions that is fundamental to the human experience. Music enables us to reflect, record, and nurture awareness, understanding, and appreciation of cultural and ethnic diversity while providing knowledge, skills, and understanding of ourselves, our community, and the world. Music education also promotes the development of the whole child as it fosters the creative process, critical thinking, problem solving, self-awareness, and communication. It is through the study of music that children gain knowledge, skills, and understanding that will enable them to participate productively, as individuals and as members of society, in their future workplaces and in their communities at large (South Carolina Visual and Performing Arts Framework, 1993). The next section describes some things that you can do to encourage your children to appreciate the breadth and depth of musical experiences.

Live Performances

One of the best ways to broaden children's views and appreciation of music is to invite a guest to visit your classroom to sing or play an instrument. Children are apt to be better listeners if, at first, they can listen to a live performance. "Often, local symphony orchestras or high school groups prepare special programs for children. Some of these programs introduce the instruments of the orchestra and help children listen for their sounds; others

present musical stories that children will enjoy" (Brewer, 2001, p. 399).

Seeing the instrument while it is being played will help children associate it with its sound. Young adult performers usually relate well to children and often inspire them to want to play instruments when they get older. In some communities, operettas and musicals that are appropriate for young children are produced. These help immensely to build good listening skills while providing much enjoyment for the children. If your community does not have an orchestra or another performing group, ask your fellow teachers and parents to recommend someone who plays an instrument. Even if no professional musicians are available to perform for your children, there has to be someone in your school or community who plays an instrument! Sometimes, all you need is a parent to come into your school to play the piano or strum a guitar for a sing-along. You might even consider learning to play the recorder yourself so that you can pipe tunes for your children.

Once your children have seen a live performance, they are usually more interested in hearing music being played or sung on a recording. By the time children are 4 or 5, they are ready to sit attentively for a short performance or to listen to a recording. They may even begin to recognize the sounds of certain instruments!

Musical Stories

Music that has a story connection is a good way to introduce and review some of the instruments of the orchestra. *Peter and the Wolf* by Prokofiev and "The Dance of the Sugar Plum Fairy" from *The Nutcracker Suite* by Tchaikovsky are wonderful recordings that can be used to ask children to describe the images, ideas, or moods that the music evokes. Other good pieces are the *Grand Canyon Suite* by Ferde Grofe and Camille Saint-Saens's "Danse Macabre." Entire pieces or suites need not be listened to at one time. One section of a piece may be enough, depending on the age, interest, and musical appreciation of the children.

Background Music

Background music can create a desirable atmosphere or establish an appropriate mood in the classroom. Although some teachers feel that background music is distracting, most believe that quiet orchestral music, lullabies, or a selection like Saint-Saens's "The Swan" are appropriate for rest time, for example. "Sea Gulls" by Hap Palmer has become a favorite recording to use for quiet relaxation. The entire recording is designed to provide soothing instrumental music as a background for resting. You may recall reading in chapter 1 about the little girl who, after listen-

Children enjoy an old-fashioned sing-along with their teacher playing the piano.

ing to selections from *Madame Butterfly,* came up to her teacher and said that the lady's voice made her sleepy! Had quiet background music not been playing, she would have missed this wonderful exposure to "sleepy" music.

Children sometimes like to listen to a favorite story recording during rest time. Recordings of poetry, nursery rhymes, and folk music are other favorites of many children. Music from around the world is also a good choice during rest time. Two popular recordings, available on CD, are "The Fairy Dance: Myth and Magic in Celtic Songs and Tunes" and "Japan: Ensemble of Traditional Instruments of Japan." Background music that contains loud tones and fast tempos is too stimulating and should be avoided at rest time.

During free play, background music can influence the noise level of the room. Soft, soothing music may have a quieting effect on the room, whereas music with words or loud music can cause a room to be noisy and uncomfortable.

There are many good stories in music recordings on the market today. The same is true for appropriate background music to play in your classroom. Children enjoy both types of recordings. However, since children's tastes are so diverse, you should have a wide variety of vocal recordings, classical music, and musical stories from which children can choose.

BUILDING A MUSIC LIBRARY

While you are still a student and before you begin student teaching is a good time to begin a collection of recordings. We all have our own favorite genres, but I encourage you to think beyond what you normally listen to and begin exploring music that is either new or unfamiliar. Experiment

with classical music, and listen to selections by Bach or Mozart. Listen to jazz played and sung by Louis Armstrong. Buy a CD featuring the sitar, mridanga, or kanjira. "Sunada: Music from the Classical Tradition of South India" by the great Karaikudi Subramaniam and "Ancient Egypt: A Tribute Composed and Performed by Ali Jihad Racy" are good choices. Use the Internet to research artists and composers, but do not download pirated music. Just because you can get it for free doesn't make it right.

MUSIC EDUCATION: MUSIC FOR A LIFETIME

The most important element of music education is not the number of activities you design or the methods of implementation you use. What is most important is that you provide a musical environment in which children know they can reach and explore their musical potential.

The creative teacher with a conscious interest in the processes involved in music education "needs to see herself not as one who 'gives' art [music] to students (as tourists 'do' the Louvre), but as one who can open up windows on the world to students as well as to herself" (Dimondstein, 1974, p. 303).

You have discovered firsthand what it feels like to be in an environment that encourages musical thinking, and you have experienced an atmosphere that gives you time to enjoy musical activities. Now you are faced with a choice. You must decide, from your own experiences and for your own professional and personal reasons, how you will go about the task of introducing children to music. How will you structure the environment to give your children the time and freedom to become involved in music?

How will you break away from the confines of having the "music teacher" as the sole source of music for your children? What experiences will you design to help your aspiring musicians understand the value of music in all our lives and to use that understanding in the learning process? For all of us who are charged with enhancing the quality of life for young children, how will we experience movement in dance, feel the imaginary force of the wind on our bodies, capture melody in singing, create an original beat or rhythm, or recall the intimate moments when humming a lullaby? Think about these things, and remember that you do not have to be innately talented to sing, play a musical instrument, dance, or move to the mood of the music. What you have to be is open to exploration.

Give yourself and your children permission to give form to sensory perceptions, to take risks with creativity, and to respond to all musical experiences. Be sensitive and aware of your musical potential and the musical efforts of your children. Joy and pleasure, for all of you, wait to be discovered.

You have come to the end of this book but certainly not the end of your musical journey. Our hope is that your musical experiences, your understanding of the characteristics of young children, and your application of theory to practice have been filled with personal and professional meaning. We hope that all of your experiences will encourage you to continue this magnificent adventure, both for your own musical growth and for the children who look to you for guidance. Acknowledge the talents and musical abilities of your children, and open a pathway for them to fill their lives with music.

When music brings this kind of joy to our lives, the world becomes an even better place.

*The woods would be very silent if no birds sang
except those that sang best.*

Henry David Thoreau

REFERENCES

Brewer, J. (2001). *Introduction to early childhood education: Preschool through primary grades* (4th ed.). Needham Heights, MA: Allyn & Bacon.

Dimondstein, G. (1974). *Exploring the arts with children.* New York: Macmillan.

South Carolina Visual and Performing Arts Framework. (1993). Columbia, SC: South Carolina State Board of Education.

APPENDIX A

Music from Around the World

HI-YO-WITZI (Morning Song)

Melody and Words by Chief White Eagle
(North American Indian) Abridged

Hi - yo hi - yo - wit - zi nai - yo,

Hi - yo hi - yo - wit - zi nai - yo.

Hi - yo nai - yo hi!

HI YO HI YO IP SI NI YAH
(HAPPY SONG)

Navajo

A. Hi   yo,   hi   yo ip   si   ni   yah,

Hi   yo,   hi   yo ip   si   ni————   yah,

Hi————   yo,   hi   yo ip   si   ni   yah,

Hi————   yo,   hi   yo ip   si   ni   yah,

Hi   yo,   hi   yo!

ALOUETTE

French Canadian

A - lou - et - te, gen -tille A - lou - et - te,
a - lu - ɛt - tə ʒã - tij a - lu - ɛt - tə

A - lou -et - te, Je te plu -me- rai. 1. Je te plu - me -rai la tête,
a - lu ɛt tə, ʒə tə ply -mə - re ʒə tə ply - mə -re la tɛt

(Teacher)
Fine F

(Children)
C₇

(Teacher)
F C

(Children)

C₇ *D.C. al Fine*

Je te plu - me - rai la tête, Et la tête, et la tête, Oh!
ʒə tə ply -mə - re la tɛt ɛ la tɛt ɛ la tɛt o

2. Le bec (lə bek)—the beak 4. Le dos (lə do)—the back 6. Le cou (lə ku)—the neck
3. Le nez (lə ne)—the nose 5. Les pattes (le pat)—the feet *Note:* la tête (la tet)—the head

CHIAPANECAS

Mexican folk tune

Arranged and adapted by K. BAYLESS

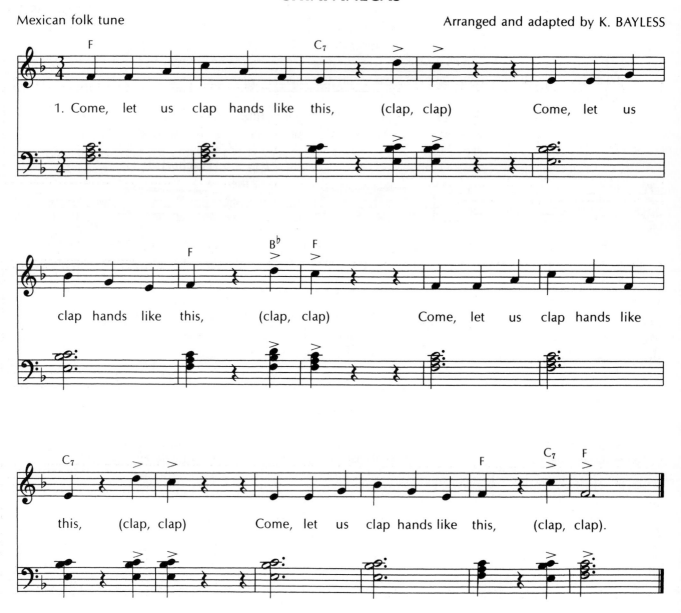

2. Come, let us stamp feet like this, (stamp, stamp)

HANUKKAH LATKES*

FREDA BRECK

Not too fast

From *The Magic of Music* Book One, Copyright © 1965 by Ginn and Company. Reprinted by permission of Pearson Education, Inc.

*A *latke* is a potato pancake customarily eaten during Hanukkah.

LIGHT A LITTLE CANDLE

Adapted from a folk melody

ROSE ENGEL
JUDITH BERMAN

Light a lit - tle can - dle, Ha - nuk - kah will come;

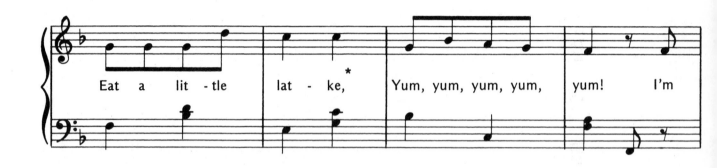

Eat a lit - tle lat - ke,* Yum, yum, yum, yum, yum! I'm

count - ing on my fin - gers and I'm count-ing on my thumb,___

Just how man - y days till Ha - nuk - kah will come!

MY DREYDL*

My Top

S. S. Grossman

S.E. Goldfarb

1. I have a lit - tle drey - dl, I made it out of clay; And
When it's dry and read - y Then drey - dl I shall play. O
drey - dl, drey - dl, drey - dl, I made it out of clay; O
drey - dl, drey - dl, drey - dl, Now drey - dl I shall play.

*A *dreydl* is a four-sided top with a Hebrew character on each side.

EL COQUÍ
(THE FROG)

Puerto Rican

El co - quí sings a lul - la - by soft- ly.   I can hear el co -
quí all night long;   Though I fall fast a - sleep when it's bed- time,
In my dream comes his sweet lit- tle song: Co - quí, Co - quí, Co -
quí, quí, quí, quí!   Co - quí, Co - quí, Co - quí, quí, quí, quí!

THE LITTLE STICK

Folk Song from South America
English Version by Verne Muñoz
Arranged by Pablo Garcia Todoña

LOOBY LOO

Old English folk game

Arranged by K. BAYLESS

Here we dance Loo - by Loo, Here we dance Loo - by light,
(go)

Here we dance Loo - by Loo, All on a Sat - ur - day night. I

put my right hand in, I put my right hand out, I

give my right hand a shake, shake, shake, And turn my - self a - bout.

2. left hand   3. right foot   4. left foot   5. head right in   6. whole self

SANDY MALONEY

English singing game

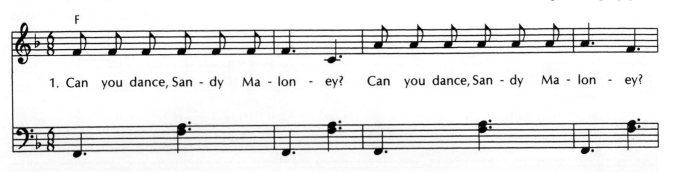

1. Can you dance, San-dy Ma-lon-ey? Can you dance, San-dy Ma-lon-ey?

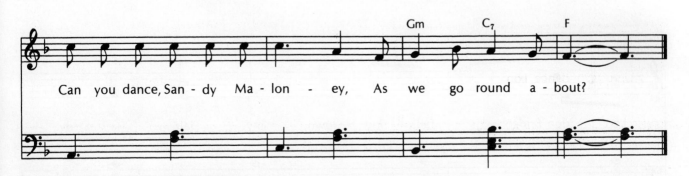

Can you dance, San-dy Ma-lon-ey, As we go round a-bout?

2

Put both your hands on your shoulders,
Put both your hands on your shoulders,
Put both your hands on your shoulders,
And turn you round about.

Chorus
Here we dance, Sandy Maloney,
Here we dance, Sandy Maloney,
Here we dance, Sandy Maloney,
As we go round about.

3

Put your hands behind you,
Put your hands behind you,
Put your hands behind you,
As we go round about.

Chorus

Suggestion:
Allow the children to create additional verses.

LONDON BRIDGE

Mother Goose

English singing game
Arranged by K. BAYLESS

1. Lon - don Bridge is fall - ing down, fall - ing down, fall - ing down,

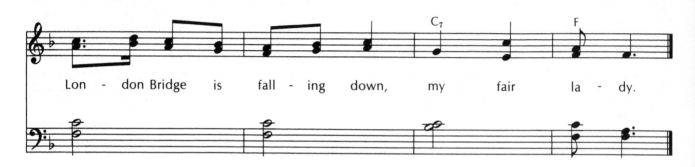

Lon - don Bridge is fall - ing down, my fair la - dy.

2. Build it up with iron bars,
3. Iron bars will bend and break,
4. Build it up with gold and silver,
5. Gold and silver I've not got,
6. Here's a prisoner I have got,

7. What'll you take to set him free,
8. One hundred pounds will set him free,
9. One hundred pounds we have not got,
10. Then off to prison he must go,

Two children are chosen to make an arch; they raise their arms above their heads to make a bridge for the other children to pass under. These two children secretly decide which one represents silver and which one gold. The other children then pass under the bridge as the song is sung. At the words "My fair lady," the bridge falls. The child who is caught is asked which he prefers, gold or silver. This child then stands behind the one who represents his choice. The game continues until all the children have been chosen.

FIVE LITTLE BUNS

Traditional English song

Arranged by K. BAYLESS

1. Five lit-tle buns in a bak-er's shop, Nice and round with sug-ar on the top, A-

long came a (boy) with a pen-ny one day, And bought a sug-ar bun and took it right a-way.
        (girl)

AIKEN DRUM

Traditional
Scottish

1. There was a man lived in the moon, lived in the moon, lived in the moon, There

was a man lived in the moon, and his name was Ai-ken Drum.

Chorus: And he played upon a ladle, a ladle, a ladle,
And he played upon a ladle, and his name was Aiken Drum.

2. And his hat was made of cream cheese, etc.
3. And his shirt was made of good roast beef, etc.

FRÈRE JACQUES

French

Frè - re   Jac - ques,   Frè - re   Jac - ques,
frɛ - rə   ʒa - kə   frɛ - rə   ʒa - kə

Dor - mez - vous?   Dor - mez - vous?
dɔr - me   vu   dɔr - me - vu

Son - nez   les   ma - ti - nes,   Son - nez - les   ma -
sɔ - ne   le   ma - ti - nə   sɔ   ne   le   ma -

ti - nes,   Din,   din,   don!   Din,   din,   don!
ti - nə   din   dɛ̃   dʒ̃   din   dɛ̃   dʒ̃

Translation:
  Are you sleeping, Are you sleeping, Brother John, Brother John?
  Morning bells are ringing, Morning bells are ringing,
  Ding, Ding, Dong, Ding, Ding, Dong.

LES PETITES MARIONNETTES
(Little Puppets)

French folk song

English version by JUDITH GREEN
Arranged by K. BAYLESS

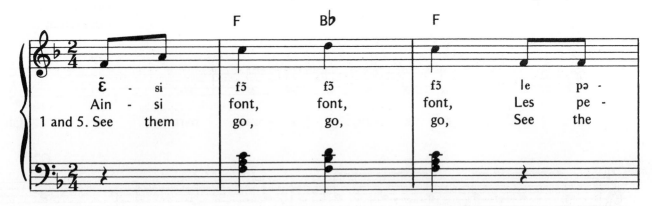

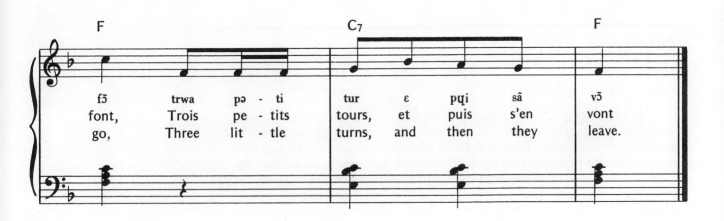

2

See them move their heads,
See the little marionettes;
See them move their heads,
Three little nods, and then they
  leave.

3

See them move their arms,
See the little marionettes,
See them move their arms,
Three little claps, and then they
  leave.

4

See them move their legs,
See the little marionettes;
See them move their legs,
Three little jumps, and then they
  leave.

GO AWAY PARTNER

Source unknown

German singing game
Adapted by K. BAYLESS

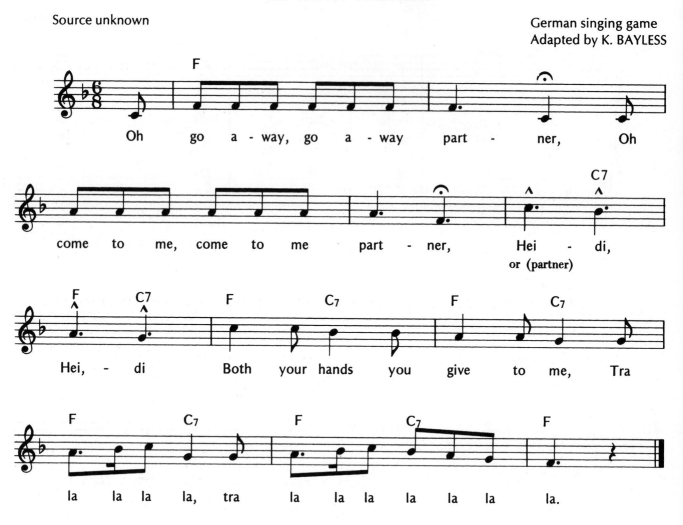

Oh go a - way, go a - way part - ner, Oh

come to me, come to me part - ner, Hei - di,

or (partner)

Hei, - di Both your hands you give to me, Tra

la la la la, tra la la la la la la la.

Formation:

O Boy
X Girl

XO   XO
O
X

Four boys and four girls stand in formation, facing partners. Raise arms and hands with palms out toward the partner. On the words "Oh go away, go away partner," the arms and palms are moved forward and back in rhythmic movement, keeping the palms toward the partner. On the words "Oh come to me, come to me partner," the palms are turned toward the player, and the rhythmic movements are repeated. On the words "Both your hands you give to me," partners join hands and dance in a circle until the end of the song. At this point, the inside group of four children remain in position. The group of children on the outside move clockwise to the next partner, and the song is then repeated. (*Note:* It is easier to use this kind of formation when only the outside group changes partners.)

DANCE FROM HANSEL AND GRETEL

Germany

This song and dance from *Hansel and Gretel* is one of the most popular selections for young children. The singing range is really too wide for young children since it goes from middle C to high F, but because the song is so beloved by children, it is included in our collection.

SEE THE LITTLE DUCKLINGS

German folk tune

See the lit - tle duck - lings, swim - ming here and there,

Heads are in the wa - ter, tails are in the air.

HOW D'YOU DO, MY PARTNER?

Swedish singing game

Arranged by K. BAYLESS

Children stand in a circle, facing the center. One child stands in the center and skips to a child in the circle. They shake hands, then join hands and skip around the inside of the circle. Other children clap hands. The song is repeated with the two children choosing new partners.

DINOSAUR DIET

Slovak folk tune
Adapted words

Long a - go a di - no - saur* lived in our own state, He
had a health - y ap - pe - tite, and this is what he ate:
Green leaves and tops of trees, small plants and tall weeds;
What a fun - ny di - et! I would - n't like to try it.

*Instead, substitute a particular type if desired: bron-to-saur-us, pter-o-dac-tyl.

From *ABC Music Series Book*, copyright © 1959. Used by permission of D.C. Heath and Company.

STODOLA PUMPA

Czech folk tune

Sto-do - la,   sto-do - la,   Sto-do - la pump-a,   sto-do - la pum - pa.   Sto-do - la   pum - pa,

Sto-do - la,   sto-do - la,   sto-do - la   pum - pa,   sto-do - la   pum - pa,   pum, pum, pum.

Suggestions:
Slap each knee once for each "stodola." Clap twice for each "pumpa." Clap for each
"pum" at the end of the song.

KOLYADA (Yuletide)

Ukrainian folk tune

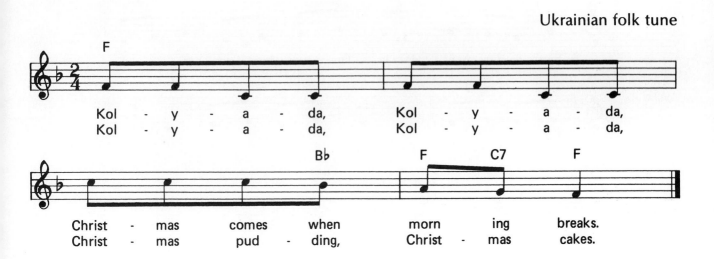

Kol - y - a - da,   Kol - y - a - da,
Kol - y - a - da,   Kol - y - a - da,

Christ - mas   comes   when   morn   ing   breaks.
Christ - mas   pud - ding,   Christ - mas   cakes.

LADYO, LADYO

Old Swiss melody

Down the moun-tain side we go, La - dy - o, La - dy - o.
We feel hap - py all day long, La - dy - o, La - dy - o.

Gai - ly through the drift - ing snow, La - dy, La - dy - o.
Come and lis - ten to our song, La - dy, La - dy - o.

Musical concept: *Children can learn to control the voice by "yodeling" on the word Ladyo.*

SAN SERENI

Spanish

San Se - re - ní de la bue - na, bue - na vi - da,

San Se - re - ní de la bue - na, bue - na vi - da, A-

sí, a - sí, a - sí, a - sí, a - sí, a - sí.

TRES PAJARILLOS

L. W.   L. W.

U - no, dos, tres, u - no, dos, tres, Tres pa - ja - ri - llos,
One, two, three, one, two, three, Three lit - tle birds,

tres pa - ja - ri - llos, Can - tan a - sí, can - tan a - sí,
three lit - tle birds Sing like this, sing like this,

Pip - a - ri - a - ri - a, Pip - a - ri - a - ri - a, Can - tan a - sí, can - tan a - sí.
Peep - a - ree - a - ree - a, Peep - a - ree - a - ree - a, Sing like this, sing like this.

Suggestion:
Select C, D, and E from the resonator bells. Help the children find the melody
patterns using these pitches. Play the patterns on the bells, and determine which
move up and which move down.

TANGALAYO

Source unknown

West Indian song

Tan - ga - lay - o!   Come lit - tle don - key

come; Tan - ga - lay - o!   Come lit - tle don - key

come   My don - key walk, my don - key balk, my don - key

has   a   fun - ny   talk!   My don - key   go,   my don - key

stop,   my don - key   look   and   then   he   drop!

KYE KYE KULE

African

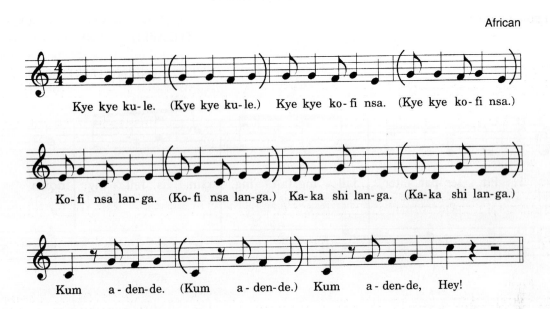

Kye kye ku-le. (Kye kye ku-le.) Kye kye ko-fi nsa. (Kye kye ko-fi nsa.)

Ko-fi nsa lan-ga. (Ko-fi nsa lan-ga.) Ka-ka shi lan-ga. (Ka-ka shi lan-ga.)

Kum a-den-de. (Kum a-den-de.) Kum a-den-de, Hey!

OJO MA R Q

Nigerian folk song

Written and sung by OMOTE AWANI

O Jo Ma r ǫ   O Jo Ma r ǫ   I tur a lo ję

O Jo Ma r ǫ   O Jo Ma r ǫ   I tur a lo ję

Pronunciation Key:
Ojo, as in *old Joe*; ã, as in *apple*; I, as in *eat*; u, as in *soothe*; a, as in *apple*, ǫ, as in *up*; ę, as in *set*; o, as in *old*.

This is a song about rain. It means "Rain please fall. You are refreshing."

JAPANESE RAIN SONG

Lightly

Japanese folk song contributed by
ELIZABETH CLURE and HELEN RAMSEY
English words by ROBERTA McLAUGHLIN
Arranged by ALBERT DeVITO

1. Pit - ter -pat - ter, fall - ing, fall - ing, rain is fall - ing down.

Moth - er comes to bring um - brel - la, Rain is fall - ing down.

Refrain:

Pi chi, pi chi, cha pu, cha pu, ran, ran, ran.

2. Underneath the dropping willow stands a little child.
No umbrella, child is weeping, rain is falling down.

AFTER SCHOOL

Grace Boynton

Chinese Folk Melody

School is out as the sun goes down;

Books in my bag I go through the town,

Home are my par - ents who smile at me

I make a nice low bow like this you see.

From *The Pogoda*, copyright 1946 by the Cooperative Recreation Service, Inc.

KOOKABURRA

Australia

Written by M. SINCLAIR

Kook - a - bur - ra sits on an old gum tree, _____

Mer - ry, Mer - ry King of the bush is he, _____ Laugh, Kook-a - bur - ra,

Laugh, Kook-a - bur - ra, Gay your life must be.

Music Terminology
and
Approaches to Music Education

MUSICAL CONCEPTS

The musical concepts presented below will help parents and teachers as they expand on and enrich the music experiences of their preschool or kindergarten-age children. For most children, this will be just the beginning of their understanding of music. Children's awareness of musical concepts should grow out of their natural experiences with music. Parents and teachers can plan for and guide these discoveries. Most of the musical selections throughout this book include one or more of the following concepts.

I. Melody
   A. Direction: discover whether the melody of a song moves up or down
   B. Pitch differences (high-low): respond to high or low sounds

II. Rhythm
   A. Steady beat: respond to a steady beat of music by tapping, clapping, or playing percussion instruments
   B. Tempo (fast-slow): experience songs, both fast and slow; move in response to music that gets faster or slower
   C. Rhythm patterns: echo simple rhythm patterns and repeat them by clapping or playing a percussion instrument; recognize repeated patterns in a song
   D. Rhythmic activities: walk, run, gallop, skip, and hop (locomotive movements) and bend, push, pull, reach, and sway (nonlocomotive movements) to music

III. Form
   A. Beginning and ending: learn to respond to beginnings and endings of music; start when the music begins, and stop when it comes to an end; draw a "map" of the song in the air, from beginning to end
   B. Two-part song (AB or ABA): respond in one way to one section or part of the music and in a different way to the other
   C. Individual or group (call and response): imitate musical tone calls or phrases
   D. Verse and refrain: recognize the difference between a verse and a refrain

IV. Tone color
   A. Instruments: begin to identify instruments by sight and sound; begin with strings, winds, and percussion; be exposed to different methods of playing instruments, such as blowing, striking, and bowing

    B. Natural and environmental sounds: experience clapping, snapping, whistling, and tongue-clicking. Identify different environmental sounds, such as trains, sirens, machines, owls, and other animals.

    C. Voices: recognize the difference in men's, women's, and children's speaking and singing voices

    D. Dynamics (soft-loud): recognize the difference between loud and soft in music; recognize when music gets louder and softer

V. Texture-harmony

    A. Have the experience of adding harmony to a song by playing simple bell parts, or strumming on an Autoharp®.

    B. Have opportunities to hear songs with and without accompaniment

GLOSSARY

accent A stress or emphasis given to certain notes.

beat The audible or visual markings of the metrical divisions of music. Also, a pulse that can be heard or felt in music.

direction The upward or downward movement of a melody.

duration The length of time that sound persists (short or long).

dynamics The loudness or softness of sounds in music.
    crescendo Gradually growing louder.
    diminuendo Gradually growing softer.
    forte (f) Loud.
    fortissimo (ff) Very loud.
    mezzo forte (mf) Moderately loud.
    mezzo piano (mp) Moderately soft.
    pianissimo (pp) Very soft.
    piano (p) Soft.
    sforzando (sf) Forcefully.

fermata (⌢) The sustaining of a note, chord, or rest for a duration longer than the indicated time value, with the length of the extension at the performer's discretion.

form Scheme of organization that determines the basic structure of a composition. Often designated by letters (AB form, ABA form, etc.).

harmony The simultaneous combination of tones (sounding at one time).

interval The difference in pitch between two tones.

measure Music contained between two vertical bars.

melody The succession of single tones (moving upward or downward) in a musical composition.

ostinato A short rhythmic or melodic pattern that is repeated.

pentatonic scale A five-tone scale (do, re, mi, sol, la). It can begin on any tone.

phrase A division of a composition—a "musical sentence." Commonly, a passage of four or eight measures.

pitch The highness or lowness of a tone.

rest A sign (symbol) in music indicating an interval of silence.

scale A succession of ascending or descending tones arranged according to fixed intervals.

staccato Short, detached sound.

steady beat Regular, even pulsation.

tempo The speed or rate of beats in music.
    accelerando Gradually getting faster.
    allegretto Moderately fast.
    allegro Fast.
    andante Moderately slow.
    andantino Slightly faster than andante.
    largo Very slow.
    lento Slow.
    presto Very fast.

timbre The quality of a sound (voice or instrument).

tonal music Music that has a "home base"—that is, music that is written in a particular key.

tone color The sound that makes an instrument or voice different from another.

GRAND STAFF AND PIANO KEYBOARD

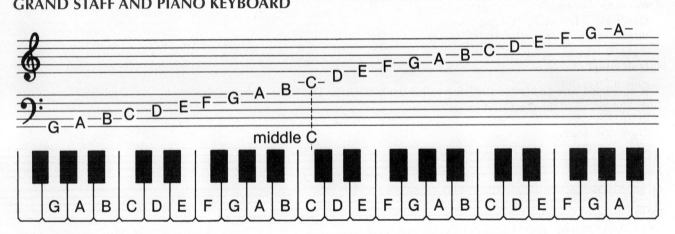

MUSIC FUNDAMENTALS

Staff

Music is written on a staff that consists of five lines and four spaces. Notes are placed upon the staff to indicate *pitch*, which is the highness or lowness of tone.

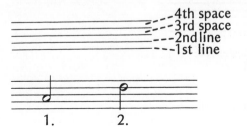

To indicate where a note is located, the lines and spaces are always counted from the bottom of the staff up to the top, as shown above:

1. This note is in the second space.
2. This note is on the fourth line.

When a note is below the third line, the stem goes up on the right side of the head. When the note is on the third line, the stem can go in either direction, but if the note is above the third line, the stem extends down on the left side, as follows:

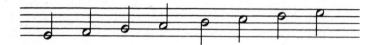

Letter Names

The first seven letters of the alphabet are used to name the lines and spaces. These are used consecutively and repeatedly to correspond with all the white keys on the piano.

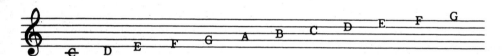

Great Staff

The combined bass and treble staffs are called the great staff. The letter names of the lines and spaces of the great staff are as follows:

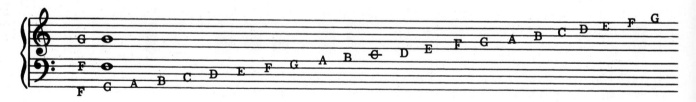

Clefs

For vocal and piano music, the treble and base clefs are used almost exclusively. Middle C has the same pitch in each of these clefs.

Treble or G Clef locates the
pitch G above Middle C.

Bass or F Clef locates the
pitch F below Middle C.

When making the treble clef sign, be sure the two lines of the sign cross on the fourth line of the staff and the G line or second line is crossed three times.

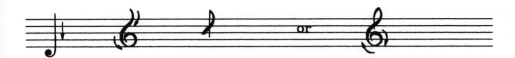

Other Terms

1.   2.   3.   4.   5.

1. *Bars.* Lines drawn vertically through the staff are called *bars.*
2. *Double bars.* These are used at the end of a composition to indicate the completion of a composition.
3. *Measure.* The music contained between two bar lines is one measure. The rhythm of the music is measured.
4. *Accent marks.* These are used for accent or emphasis.
5. *Tie.* The curved line connecting two or more notes of the same pitch (in the same place on the staff) is called a *tie.* The note is sounded or played once and held for the duration or value of all the notes.

6.   7.   8.   9.   10.   11.

6. *Slur.* The curved line connecting two or more notes of different pitch is called a *slur.* One word or syllable of a word is sung on the two or more tones.
7. *Repeat signs.* Two dots before a bar indicate that the music of the preceding section is to be repeated. Go back to the preceding double bar or, in case there is no double bar, go back to the beginning and continue to the end or the sign "Fine."
8. *Fermata (hold).* The note under this sign is to be held longer than usual, the length of time dependent on the interpretation being given the music.
9. *Sharp.* This sign in front of a note indicates a tone one-half step, higher than the normal pitch of that tone (next adjacent key on the piano or bells).
10. *Flat.* This sign indicates a tone one-half step lower than the normal pitch.
11. *Natural.* This sign removes the effect of a sharp or flat or takes away the sharp or flat.

a.   do   di   ti   te   ti

b.   la   le   fa   fi   fa

a. Placed before a flatted note, the natural has the same effect as a sharp and raises that tone one-half step higher than the pitch represented by the flatted note.
b. Placed before a sharped note, the natural has the same effect as a flat and lowers that tone one-half step below the pitch represented by the sharped note.

12. *Half step.* A step is a unit for measuring distance in music. The tone nearest to any given tone, either above or below, is a half step from the given tone. The half steps that occur normally on the staff are between B and C (*12a*) and E and F (*12b*). As another example, on the keyboard the half steps are from white key G to black key G# (*12c*) and from white key A to black key A♭ (*12d*).

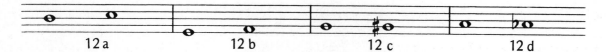

13. *Whole step.* A whole step consists of two half steps. On the keyboard the whole steps are from a white key to the next white key or from a black key to the next black key (except from B to C and from E to F).

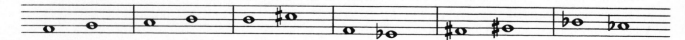

14. *Chromatic.* Sharps, flats, or naturals (other than those in the signature) placed before notes in a composition are called *chromatics* or *accidentals.* When sharps, flats, or naturals are used in a measure of music, they affect only the same note when repeated in the same measure. The measure bar automatically cancels these accidentals.

Notes and Their Corresponding Rests

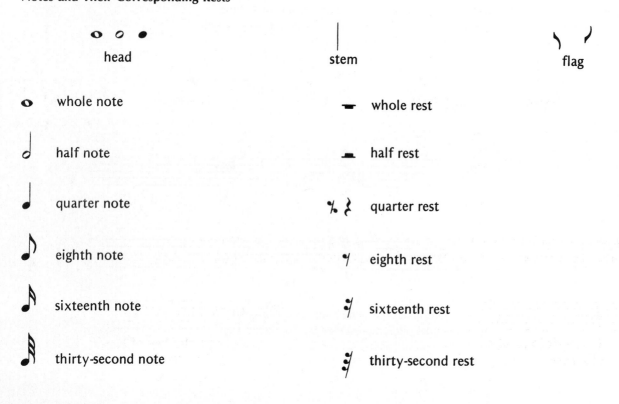

| | head | | stem | | flag |

𝅝	whole note	▬	whole rest	
𝅗𝅥	half note	▬	half rest	
𝅘𝅥	quarter note	𝄽	quarter rest	
𝅘𝅥𝅮	eighth note	𝄾	eighth rest	
𝅘𝅥𝅯	sixteenth note	𝄿	sixteenth rest	
𝅘𝅥𝅰	thirty-second note	𝅀	thirty-second rest	

Placement of Rests on the Treble Staff

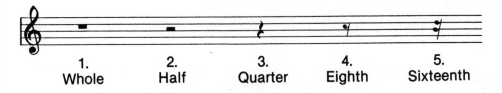

1.	2.	3.	4.	5.
Whole	Half	Quarter	Eighth	Sixteenth

1. The whole rest is placed down from the fourth line of the staff.
2. The half rest is made up from the third line.
3. The quarter rest is started in the third space and goes down into the second space.
4. The flag of the eighth rest is made in the third space and on the left side of the stem.
5. The flags of the sixteenth rest are made on the third and fourth lines and on the left side of the stem.

Dotted Notes

A dot following a note adds one half of the value of the note. The most commonly found dotted notes are:

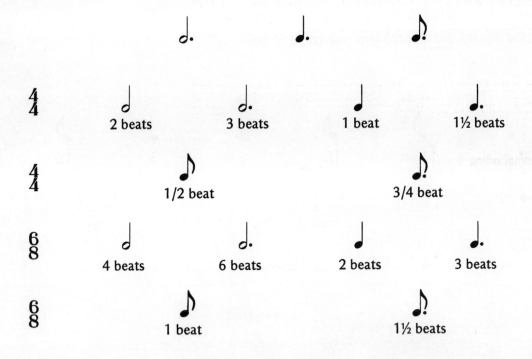

Signature

The term *signature* includes the clef sign, sharps or flats, and numbers. The sharps or flats indicate the *key signature*. The numbers indicate the *time* or *meter signature*.

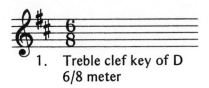

1. Treble clef key of D
   6/8 meter

2. Bass clef key of E♭
   4/4 meter

Rules for Meter (Time) Signatures

Meter signatures are numerical indications of the regular recurrence of a beat or pulse. They are composed of two numbers placed one above the other. The upper figure tells the number of beats in a measure. The lower figure tells the kind of note that receives one beat.

Examples of Meter Signatures

$\frac{4}{4}$ $\frac{3}{4}$ $\frac{2}{4}$ The 4 on the bottom means that the <u>quarter</u> note gets one count or beat.

C means common time, the same as $\frac{4}{4}$ time.

| 4 beats | 2 | 1 beat | 1/2 | 1/4 | 3 | 1½ | 3/4 |

$\frac{3}{8}$ $\frac{6}{8}$ The 8 means that the <u>eighth</u> note gets one count or beat.

| 4 beats | 2 | 1 beat | 1/2 | 6 | 3 | 1½ |

Typical complete measures of these meter signatures are:

Finding the Key of a Song

Songs are written in various keys. The key of a song is determined by the scale tones used. Thus a song in the key of C uses the tones in the scale of C:

Key of C

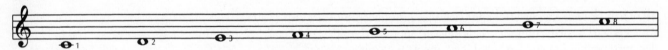

In this scale, the pitch of C is considered to be the key center or the pitch that begins and ends the scale series, and in this scale it is given the number 1. In the C scale, the pitch of D is number 2, E is number 3, F is number 4, G is number 5, A is number 6, B is number 7, and C again is number 8, or the octave of 1. In the scale of C, none of the pitches is either sharped (#) or flatted (♭), so in a song in the key of C no sharps or flats are shown at the beginning of the song.

Songs in other keys show key signatures that use sharps or flats because they are based on scales that have to use pitches either sharped or flatted. Thus a song in the key of G, the tones of which are derived from the scale of G, has to use a sharp (F#) in its signature because in the scale of G this pitch (F) has to be sharped:

Key of G

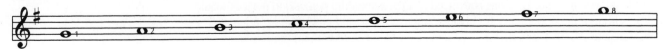

This sharp is placed on the staff after the clef sign. In each case, the key signature denotes the pitch considered to be the key center for the song. The pitch so considered is always given the number 1.

To play or sing a song in its proper key setting, it is important to be able to tell from the key signature in what key the song is to be played or sung. The technique of determining the key from a given key signature is not difficult.

In songs having flats in their signatures, call the line or space of the staff on which the last flat (the one to the far right of any others shown) is placed "four" (4) and count downward each consecutive line or space of the staff until the line or space number one (1) is reached. The pitch for that line or space of the staff is then the key center *(x)* or key tone (keys of B♭, E♭, A♭, and D♭):

Key of F   B♭   E♭   A♭   D♭

In songs having only one flat in in their signature, call the line of the staff on which it is placed "4," and count down to 1 (key of F above).

To find the key of songs with sharps, move up one line or space of the staff from the last sharp, which is the one to the far right of any others shown in the key signature. If the last sharp is located on a line, the key center will be located on the next space. If the last sharp is located in a space, the key center will be located on the next line:

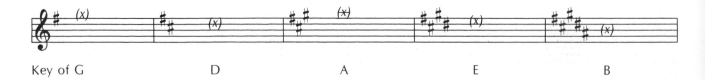

Key of G   D   A   E   B

APPROACHES TO MUSIC EDUCATION

The Orff Approach

The Orff, or Orff-Schulwerfe, approach was introduced by Carl Orff (1895–1982), a well-known German composer. This musical approach emphasizes the use of specially designed percussion and keyboard instruments for young children.

Orff was influenced by Dalcroze's thinking, by the surge of interest in physical education and gymnastics, and by the advent of a new kind of dancing that has since become known as modern dance. Orff, like Dalcroze, had a great interest in the theater. He opened a school for gymnastics and dance in 1924 and combined the study of music with gymnastics. This fusion became the key to his concept of music education. Orff began to create music for the young dance students in his school. By 1948, he had developed an educational system specifically for music.

The contrast and variation of rhythm are the primary elements in Orff's style of musical composition, and percussion instruments that produce this rhythm naturally play a primary role in these works. Thus Orff invented new percussion instruments to meet his demand for novel effects. These unique instruments distinguish Orff's approach from others. They are easy to play and are of excellent quality. Since rhythmic responses are so natural to the young child, Orff was convinced that these melodic percussion devices would allow children the opportunity for creative improvisation and ensemble experience. The child memorizes pitch and rhythmic patterns with facility and without inhibition.

Orff felt that children should play instruments from memory and that the study of piano should come only after the development of other musical skills. Drill is to be avoided. Orff believed that a gradual progression from speech patterns to rhythmic activities to song was the best and most natural for the child. The playing of instruments follows. Children try out and play various rhythm patterns and melodic and ostinato figures on instruments. Orff felt the instruments provide a comprehensive and sound musical foundation for the child.

Originally, Orff based his approach on German folklore and children's music. (Orff's music for children is now available in English-language adaptations.) Teachers might substitute American folk music and children's songs in the pentatonic mode. These songs can be accompanied by the Orff instruments. The prized Orff instruments are manufactured in Germany but can be readily obtained in the United States. Although the teacher must be fairly well trained and the instruments are rather expensive, the Orff approach is used successfully throughout the United States.

We have been very impressed with the range of possibilities in using the Orff instruments. Teachers are encouraged to pursue the Orff approach in more depth. Today, the Orff Institute, established in 1963 in Salzburg, offers training in the Orff approach for teachers from many parts of the world. Music schools throughout America can provide information on the Orff approach.

The Suzuki Method

The Suzuki method, or talent education, was developed by Dr. Shinichi Suzuki, a violinist and Japanese language teacher. The approach received worldwide recognition and acclaim when 3-, 4-, and 5-year-old children demonstrated their ability to play demanding sonatas and concertos on their miniature violins. Suzuki's method of instruction employs a psycholinguistic approach. The child learns to respond to and repeat music in the same manner that he learns to speak his native tongue, playing first by ear rather than by reading notes. Suzuki regards two elements as being very important in his method: "(1) The child must be helped to develop an ear for music. (2) From the very beginning, every step must by all means be thoroughly mastered" (Suzuki et al., 1973, p. 12).

The Suzuki method requires close supervision by the parent and the teacher. The student must listen, practice, and perform. The parent is asked to attend each weekly lesson and to supervise daily practice sessions. Parental involvement not only ensures that the student follows the teacher's instructions, but gives encouragement and praise for the child's efforts. The children have the opportunity to play for each other in informal recitals. Frequent opportunities to play before an audience build a child's self-confidence.

The Suzuki method now encompasses the instruction of piano, cello, flute, and viola as well as violin. Although each particular instrument has its own music repertoire, Suzuki's basic techniques, principles, and philosophy still apply. Many schools today are employing the Suzuki method and instrumental technique, which relies primarily on the human ear.

Obviously, each approach discussed here offers a unique musical experience to the young child. Whatever approach feels most comfortable to the teacher will be the most successful one for the students.

Resources for Teachers
in Early Childhood Classrooms

PROFESSIONAL ORGANIZATIONS, NEWSLETTERS, AND JOURNALS

Organizations

Association for Childhood Education
International (ACEI)
11141 Georgia Ave.
Suite 200
Wheaton, MD 20902

Educational Resources Information Center/Early Childhood
Education (ERIC/ECE)
805 W. Pennsylvania Ave.
Urbana, IL 61801

National Association for the Education of Young Children
(NAEYC)
1834 Connecticut Ave., N.W.
Washington, DC 20009

National Association for Music Education
Music Educators National Conference (MENC)
1902 Association Dr.
Reston, VA 22091

Newsletters

ERIC/ECE Newsletter
805 W. Pennsylvania Ave.
Urbana, IL 61801

Report on Preschool Programs
Capitol Publications, Inc.
1300 N. 17th St.
Arlington, VA 22209

Journals

Child Development
Society for Research in Child Development
University of Chicago Press
5801 Ellis Ave.
Chicago, IL 60637

Childhood Education
Association for Childhood Education International
11141 Georgia Ave.
Suite 200
Wheaton, MD 20902

Children Today
U.S. Department of Health, Education, and Welfare
Office of Child Development
Children's Bureau
Superintendent of Documents
U.S. Government Printing Office
Washington, DC 20402

Merrill-Palmer Quarterly of Behavior and Development
Merrill-Palmer Institute
71 E. Ferry Ave.
Detroit, MI 48202

Music Educators Journal
Music Educators National Conference
1902 Association Dr.
Reston, VA 22091

Young Children
National Association for the Education of Young Children
1834 Connecticut Ave., N.W.
Washington, DC 20009

SOURCES FOR ORDERING INSTRUMENTS

Children's Book and Music Center
2500 Santa Monica Blvd.
Santa Monica, CA 90404

Lyons Band
PO Box 1003
Elkhart, IN 46515

Oscar Schmidt/Music Education Group
230 Lexington Dr.
Buffalo Grove, IL 60090

Rhythm Band, Inc.
PO Box 126
Fort Worth, TX 76101

BOOKS ON MAKING INSTRUMENTS

Make Your Own Musical Instruments
Muriel Mandell and Robert E. Wood
Sterling Publishing
419 Park Ave. S.
New York, NY 10016

Music and Instruments for Children to Make and *Rhythms, Music, and Instruments to Make*
John Hawkinson and Martha Faulhaber
Albert Whitman
560 W. Lake St.
Chicago, IL 60606

Simple Folk Instruments to Make and Play
Ilene Hunter and Marilyn Judson
Children's Book and Music Center
2500 Santa Monica Blvd.
Santa Monica, CA 90404

SONGS FOR LISTENING AND MUSIC APPRECIATION

It has often been said that the tastes of young children can be shaped by the music we play for them. For children to appreciate music of quality, they need to hear the music played repeatedly. A list of recordings that develop listening skills and music appreciation follows.

"Air on the G String" (Bach)
"Aragonaise" from *Le Cid* (Massenet)
"Ballet of the Unhatched Chicks" (Moussorgsky)
"Barcarolle" from *Tales of Hoffman* (Offenbach)
"Berceuse" (Chopin)
"Bridal Chorus" from *Lohengrin* (Wagner)
Carnival of the Animals (Saint-Saëns)
Children's Corner Suite (Debussy)

"Clown" from *Marionettes* (MacDowell)
"Country Gardens" (Granger)
"The Dancing Doll" (Poldini)
"Danse Macabre" (Saint-Saëns)
"Dance of the Ballerina" from *Petrouchka* (Stravinsky)
"Entrance of the Little Fauns" (Pierné)
"The Flight of the Bumblebee" (Rimsky-Korsakov)
"Golliwog's Cakewalk"(Debussy)
Grand Canyon Suite (Grofé)
Hansel and Gretel (Humperdinck)
"The Happy Farmer" (Schumann)
"Hornpipe" from *Water Music* (Handel)
"Knight of the Hobby Horse" (Schumann)
"Leap Frog" from *Children's Games* (Bizet)
"March Militaire" (Schubert)
"March of the Little Lead Soldiers" (Pierné)
"March of the Toys" (Herbert)
Mother Goose Suite (Ravel)
Nutcracker Suite (Tchaikovsky)
"Of Tailor and a Bear" (MacDowell)
Peer Gynt Suite No. 1 (Grieg)
Peter and the Wolf (Prokofiev)
"Pizzicato" (Delibes)
"Polka" (Shostakovich)
Scenes from Childhood (Schumann)
"The Skater's Waltz" (Waldteufel)
"Sleighride" (Anderson)
The Sorcerer's Apprentice (Dukas)
"The Swan" from *Carnival of the Animals* (Saint-Saëns)
"Sweet Dreams" (Tchaikovsky)
Symphony No. 94 in G Major ("Surprise") (Haydn)
"To a Water Lily" (MacDowell)
"Toy Symphony" (Haydn)
"Waltzing Doll" (Poldini)

MUSIC THAT HIGHLIGHTS MUSICAL INSTRUMENTS

The selected recordings below highlight particular instruments.

"Anvil Chorus" from *Il Trovatore* (Verdi)
   Tambourine, triangle
Carnival of the Animals (Saint-Saëns)
Piano, double bass, strings, flute, clarinet, xylophone
"Dance of the Sugar Plum Fairy" (Tchaikovsky)
Celesta
New World Symphony, second movement (Dvořák)
English horn
"Nocturne" from *A Midsummer Night's Dream* (Mendelssohn)
French horn, cello, bassoon
Peter and the Wolf (Prokofiev)
Oboe, bassoon
"Prelude and Fugue in G Major" (Bach)
Organ

"Stars and Stripes Forever" (Sousa)
Piccolo
"The Swan" (Saint-Saëns)
Cello, piano
"Trumpet Voluntary in D" (Purcell-Clark)
Trumpet
"Waltz of the Flowers" (Tchaikovsky)
Harp
"The White Peacock" (Griffes)
Flute

MUSIC FOR MOVEMENT

The following classical recordings are recommended for use with movement.

Creative Dancing
"Danse Macabre" (Saint-Saëns)
Nutcracker Suite (Tchaikovsky)

Hopping
"Ballet of the Unhatched Chicks" (Moussorgsky)

Jumping/Leaping
"Aragonaise" from *Le Cid* (Massenet)
"Leap Frog" from *Children's Games* (Bizet)

Marching
"American Salute" (Gould)
"Children's March" (Goldman)
"Entrance of the Little Fauns" (Pierné)
"March" from *Nutcracker Suite* (Tchaikovsky)
"March Militaire" (Schubert)
"March of the Little Lead Soldiers" (Pierné)

Running
"The Ball" from *Children's Games* (Bizet)
"Catch Me" from *Scenes from Childhood* (Schumann)
"Tag" (Prokofiev)

Skipping/Galloping
"Gallop" from *The Comedians* (Kabalevsky)
"Knight of the Hobby Horse" from *Scenes from Childhood* (Schumann)
"The Wild Horseman" from *Album for the Young* (Schumann)

Sliding/Gliding
"The Skater's Waltz" (Waldteufel)
"The Swan" from *Carnival of the Animals* (Saint-Saëns)
"Waltz on Ice" from *Winter Holiday* (Prokofiev)

Swaying/Rocking
"Barcarolle" from *Tales of Hoffman* (Offenbach)
"To a Water Lily" (MacDowell)
"Waltz" from *Six Piano Pieces for Children* (Shostakovich)
"Waltz of the Dolls" (Delibes)

Tiptoe
"Dance of the Little Swans" from *Swan Lake* (Tchaikovsky)

Walking
"Bourree" (Telemann)
"Gavotte" (Handel)
"Walking Song" from *Acadian Songs and Dances* (Thomson)

Whirling
"Clowns" (Kabalevsky)
"Impromptu—The Top" from *Children's Games* (Bizet)
"Tarantella" from *The Fantastic Toy Shop* (Rossini-Respighi)

CHILDREN'S BOOKS ABOUT MUSIC

Amazing Grace (1993)
M. Hoffman
New York: Scholastic
With encouragement from her grandmother, Grace discovers that she can play Peter Pan in the school play.

A Very Young Musician (1991)
J. Krementz
New York: Simon and Schuster
This is the story, illustrated with photographs, of a boy who is learning to play the trumpet.

Ben's Trumpet (1979)
Rachel Isadora
New York: Mulberry Books
Ben has an imaginary horn that he plays for his family and friends. One day the trumpet player from the Zig Zag Jazz Club introduces Ben to a real horn.

Carnival of the Animals (1971)
Camille Saint-Saëns
Tokyo: Gokkin
Various instruments impersonate animals. For example, the double bass impersonates an elephant, and the cello, a swan.

Clap Your Hands (1992)
L. B. Cauley
New York: G. P. Putnam's Sons
Rhyming text instructs the listener to find something yellow, roar like a lion, give a kiss, tell a secret, spin a circle, and more.

Frère Jacques (1973)
Barbara Schook Hazen
New York: J. B. Lippincott
A monk has a terrible problem with oversleeping, especially when it is his turn to ring the morning bells. The problem is finally solved by a young choir boy. Includes words and music to the song.

Frog Went A-Courtin' (1955)
John Langstaff
New York: Harcourt, Brace and World
Langstaff made one story out of the different versions of the ballad that are sung in various parts of America.

From Head to Toe (1997)
Eric Carle
New York: Harper Collins
Animals invite children to imitate them as they stomp, wriggle, thump, and clap.

Grandpa's Song (1991)
T. Johnson
New York: Dial Books
A little girl helps her forgetful grandfather by singing him a favorite song.

Hush, Little Baby (1976)
Margot Zemach
New York: E. P. Dutton
A beautifully illustrated book of the popular folk song.

Lentil (1940)
Robert McCloskey
New York: Viking Press
Lentil wants to sing but cannot. When he opens his mouth, only strange sounds come out. He cannot whistle either. Lentil saves up enough money to buy a harmonica and saves the day when the band members' lips all pucker up and they can't play their instruments for Colonel Carter. The people give Lentil a warm welcome.

Musical Max (1990)
Ruth Kraus
New York: Simon and Schuster
When Max decides to put away his instruments, it drives the neighbors as crazy as when he was practicing.

Music, Music for Everyone (1984)
Vera Williams
New York: Mulberry
Rosa earns money to help out her mother when her grandmother is sick. Rosa's accordion is a great addition to the Oak Street Band.

Musicians of the Sun (1997)
Gerald McDermott
New York: Simon and Schuster
In this retelling of an Aztec myth, Lord of the Night sends Wind to free four musicians that the Sun is holding prisoner, so they can bring joy to the world.

Over in the Meadow (1957)
John Langstaff
New York: Harcourt, Brace and World
The text is Langstaff's version of an old rhyme for children. Not a traditional folk song.

Over the River and Through the Wood (1974)
Lydia Maria Child
New York: Coward, McCann and Geoghegan
An illustrated version of the favorite Thanksgiving song.

Peter and the Wolf (1971)
Sergei S. Prokofiev
Tokyo: Gokkin
Morristown, NJ: Silver Burdette (U.S. distributor)
In this classic of music literature, each character is represented by an instrument.

Really Rosie (Reissued 1999)
Lyrics by Maurice Sendak, music by Carole King
New York: Ode/CBS Records
Includes "Chicken Soup with Rice" and other songs.

Six Little Ducks (1976)
Chris Conover
New York: Thomas Y. Crowell
One little duck leads his friends into mischief in this adaptation of an old camp song.

Something Special for Me (1983)
Vera B. Williams
New York: Greenwillow
The story of Rosa, who takes money from a jar and can't decide what she wants to buy. She finally decides on a small used accordion and loves it.

Song and Dance Man (1989)
Stephen Gammell
New York: Alfred Knopf
Grandpa demonstrates for his visiting grandchildren some of the songs, dances, and jokes he performed when he was a vaudeville entertainer.

The Boy Who Loved Music (1979)
David Lasker
New York: Viking Press
This book, based on the true story of a boy who played horn in the orchestra of Prince Nicolaus Esterhazy, is beautifully illustrated and filled with humor.

The Fox Went Out on a Chilly Night (1961)
Peter Spier
Garden City, NY: Doubleday
An old folk song beautifully illustrated.

The Little Band (1991)
J. Sage
New York: Margaret K. McElderry Books
Everyone is delighted by the little band as it marches through town.

The Philharmonic Gets Dressed (1986)
Karla Kuskin
New York: Harper Collins
The musicians of the orchestra are shown going about their daily routine and preparing for an evening concert.

The Sound that Jazz Makes (2000)
C. B. Wetherford
New York: Walker
The story of the origins of jazz. Illustrations complete this history, which links jazz's African and American roots.

The Willow Flute: A North Country Tale (1975)
D. William Johnson
Boston: Little, Brown
Lewis Shrew goes out into the white woods to gather twigs for
  his stove. He finds a musty old room in a house. As he
  searches throughout the house, he finds a willow flute amid
  the wreckage on the floor. As he begins to play, winter
  disappears and spring returns.

There Was an Old Woman
Retold and illustrated by Sims Taback
New York: Simon and Schuster
A recent version of the cumulative song about the old lady
  who swallows a fly.

Learning Autoharp® and Guitar for the Classroom

A PRACTICAL APPROACH TO LEARNING TO PLAY THE AUTOHARP

The Autoharp® is a relatively easy instrument to learn to play. The best way to become proficient in playing it is to learn the location of the bars and chords and then spend a great deal of time just playing and singing.

Care and Tuning

The Autoharp should receive the same kind of treatment that one would give a fine piano or other instrument. Dampness and sudden changes of temperature will affect its playing qualities. When it is not in use, keep it in a box or case and store it in a dry place of even temperature.

The instrument should be tuned frequently to keep it in perfect tune. This is not difficult to do if one has a good sense of pitch. It should either be tuned to a well-tuned piano, to some other instrument with a fixed pitch (such as an accordion), or to a pitch pipe. If one person plays the corresponding key on the piano while the other person tunes the Autoharp, the tuning can be done in approximately 10 minutes.

Middle C should be tuned first, and the lower and higher octaves tuned in unison with it. In the same manner, continue to tune the other strings. The tuning tool should be placed on each peg and turned *slowly* with either the right or left hand, either clockwise or counterclockwise, until the tone produced by the string matches the tone of the corresponding key of the piano or other instrument. With the other hand, pluck the string with the thumbnail while turning the tuning tool. By turning the tool clockwise, the pitch of the string will be raised. Turning the tool counterclockwise lowers the pitch. When one is first learning to tune the Autoharp, it is most helpful to have one person playing the note on the piano while an-

other person does the tuning. Continued practice in tuning the Autoharp should make one's ear more sensitive to changes in pitch.

When checking to see if the Autoharp is out of tune, press down the bars, one at a time, and slowly draw the pick across the strings to locate the string or strings that are out of tune with the chord. Usually, only a few strings will be out of tune at one time.

For optimum results, it is extremely important to keep the instrument in tune. If one does not have a good ear for pitch, ask a music teacher or some other musical person for help.

Autoharp Chording

This chart indicates the primary chords as they appear in the various Autoharp keys:

Key*	Tonic I	Subdominant IV	Dominant V_7	Tonic I
C major	C	F	G_7	C
F major	F	$B^\flat$	C_7	F
G major	G	C	D_7	G
D minor	D_m	G_m	A_7	D_m
A minor	A_m	D_m	E_7	A_m

* Play the chord progressions in each key until you feel familiar with their individual qualities.

The primary chords on the Autoharp—the I, the IV, and the V_7 in any of the keys—are played in the following manner. When the index finger is placed on the I chord of a given key, the middle finger falls on the V_7 chord and the ring finger on the IV chord of that key. For example, place the index finger on the F major bar. This would be the I chord in the key of F. The middle finger would fall on the C_7 bar (the V_7), and the ring finger would fall on the $B^\flat$ major bar (the IV chord).

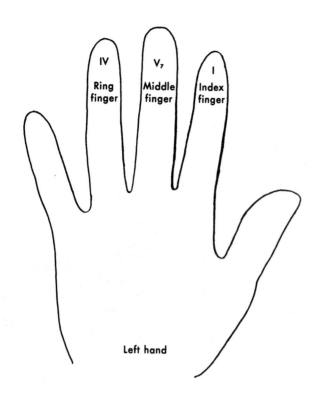

The chart below indicates the chord markings for the 12-bar Autoharp, the system used in this appendix:

Bar label*	Chord produced	See note†
G Min.	G minor	G_m
B♭ Maj.	B♭ major	B♭
A Sev.	A seventh	A_7
C Sev.	C seventh	C_7
D Min.	D minor	D_m
F Maj.	F major	F
E Sev.	E seventh	E_7
G Sev.	G seventh	G_7
A Min.	A minor	A_m
C Maj.	C major	C
D Sev.	D seventh	D_7
G Maj.	G major	G

* On the Autoharp, "Maj" stands for the word *major* and "Min" stands for the work *minor*. In a song, a chord marking followed by a small *m* indicates that the chord is a minor one. A chord is considered major if it is not followed by a small letter.

† The letters and signs shows in this column are the same ones that are generally found in guitar chords on sheet music.

Variations in Strumming Technique

Variations in rhythm or accent can be accomplished by strumming in different ways.

To strum rhythmically, one must be acquainted with the time or meter signature found at the beginning of every song. Some of the more commonly used meter signatures are 2/4, 3/4, 4/4, and 6/8. The top number always indicates the number of beats or counts in each measure; the lower number indicates what kind of note or rest receives one beat or one count. For example, in 2/4 time the top number 2 shows there are two beats in each measure, and the lower number 4 shows that a quarter note (♩) receives one count. In 6/8 time, the top number 6 shows there are six beats in each measure; the lower number 8 shows that an eighth note (♪) receives one count.

Chord markings for the songs in this book, placed above the music staff, are changed when the melodic line requires it. Additional chords are to be strummed between chord changes according to the rhythm of the song and the strumming patterns desired by the player. Press down one of the bar buttons with the index finger of the left hand, and strum with the right. Following are several suggested variations in strumming patterns:

- *2/4 time.* One or two strokes per measure, depending on the tempo and style of the song. For one stroke per measure, strum on beat 1 and count silently on beat 2. For two strokes per measure, strum on both beats, 1 and 2.
- *3/4 time.* One long, accented stroke or one long, accented and two short strokes, depending on tempo and style of the song. Strum one long, accented, full stroke, and count silently on beats 2 and 3, or strum one long, accented, full stroke from the bass strings up and two short, unaccented strokes on the higher-pitched strings.
- *4/4 time.* One, two, or four strokes to the measure, depending on the tempo and style of the song. For one full stroke to a measure, strum on beat 1 and count silently on beats 2, 3, and 4. For two full strokes to a measure, strum on beats 1 and 3 and count silently on beats 2 and 4. For four strokes to a measure, use short strokes on all 4 beats.

Guitars can also be strummed to mimic the banjo and harp.

- *Banjo quality.* Sharp, short strokes from the bass strings up or the higher-pitched strings down or stroking in both directions. The player can best decide on the desired length of stroke. A plastic pick is sometimes desirable to obtain the banjo effect.
- *Harp quality.* Full, long strokes from the bass strings up, using most or all of the strings. One may also achieve the harp quality by strumming in both directions on the strings for certain desired effects. By strumming on the left side of the bars, one can obtain a realistic harplike effect. Play smoothly without accent and only fast enough to keep the rhythmic pattern flowing.

- *Broken rhythms.* A combination of short and long strokes in either direction. If one can "feel" certain rhythmic patterns, it is usually not difficult with experimentation and practice to strum these patterns on the Autoharp.

When practicing the strumming patterns, press down firmly one bar button at a time with the fingers of the left hand. Strum with the right hand, using an easy, flowing action. The left-handed person may find it easier to reverse these positions. It is possible to obtain an endless variety of rhythm patterns by experimentation.

When playing the Autoharp, always try to strum it in such a way to help create a mood that is appropriate to the song being played or sung.

FINGERING CHART FOR THE GUITAR

The Guitar and Its Parts

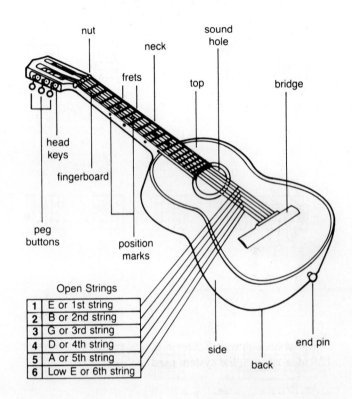

Open Strings

1	E or 1st string
2	B or 2nd string
3	G or 3rd string
4	D or 4th string
5	A or 5th string
6	Low E or 6th string

Guitar Fingering Chords Common to the Music in This Book

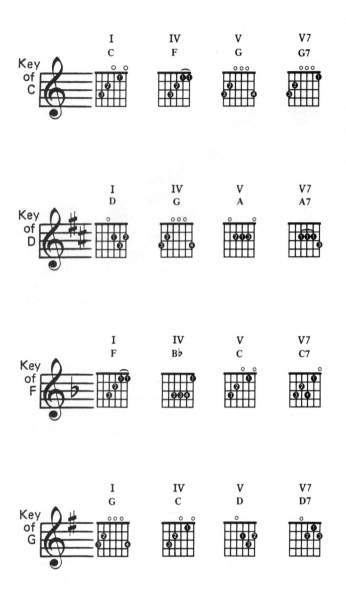

1   means first finger (forefinger)
2   means second finger
3   means third finger
4   means fourth finger
T   means thumb

The small circle (o) used on the diagrams indicates that those strings are to be played "open"—that is, they are not fingered.

A string that has no marking is not played. A slur ⌢ connecting two or more numbers on the diagrams means that those strings are to be pressed by one finger.

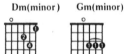

Instruments for the Classroom

PERCUSSION, MELODY, AND CHORDING INSTRUMENTS

The following percussion, melody, and chording instruments are suitable for use with young children:

Percussion Instruments

Rhythm sticks	Gong
Tone blocks	Drums, small and large
Wood blocks	Bongo drums
Temple blocks	Tom-tom drums
Tambourines	Maracas
Triangles	Claves
Finger cymbals	Coconut shells
Cymbals	

Melody Instruments

Piano	Step bells
Melody bells	Xylophone
Resonator bells	

Chording Instruments
Autoharp®
Guitar
Ukulele

Drums

A drum is a versatile instrument to have in the home and classroom. A good drum is basic to any rhythm program for young children. One can make it do so many things. It can be played to tell when it is time to clean up the room or to call the children in from play. The syllables of a name can be tapped out on a drum. One can play loudly or softly, fast or slowly, on this "friendly" instrument.

Drums can be purchased or made, and it is recommended that a variety of sizes and kinds be made accessible. Each drum should differ in pitch so that children have the opportunity to hear and distinguish different levels of pitch. If possible, arrange several different drums close together, in a semicircle for example, so that children can discover the different sounds the drums produce as they tap one, then another. Children will soon discover that the drum produces different sounds depending on how, where, and with what they strike it. In good weather, the children can collect the drums and take them outside to experiment with them. When this kind of opportunity is provided, children can accompany their rope-skipping games and create rhythms of their own. Parents and teachers are beginning to use some of the interesting drums from different parts of the world, such as the Orient, Africa, and some of the Latin American countries.

Rhythm Sticks

Rhythm sticks, two slender pieces of hardwood approximately 12 inches long, are good basic instruments for keeping time when marching, singing, or accompanying another instrument or a record. One stick from the pair is usually notched. A scraping sound can then be produced when the smooth stick is scraped across the stick that is notched. Sticks can be made from doweling. When making rhythm sticks, be sure the type of wood used produces a good tone quality.

Wood Blocks

Two pieces of square- or rectangular-shaped wood with handles are used for this instrument. The size of the wood and the weight of the wood should fit the age of the children using the instrument. Some wood blocks are too heavy and large for younger children. The instrument can be played by tapping or sliding one wood block against the other.

Sand Blocks

Sand blocks are made from sandpaper attached by staples to the sides of two wooden blocks, approximately 2½ × 4 inches each. Choose size and weight according to the age of the children using them. Sand blocks are much easier to use if they are equipped with handles or holders. They are played by rubbing one sandpaper block against the other.

Tone Blocks

A small block of wood, hollowed out with a cut on each side, and a wooden mallet make up the tone block. It is played by striking the mallet above the cut opening. This produces a hollow, resounding tone. When played correctly, the instrument provides a good underlying beat for musical selections.

Wrist Bells

Sleigh bells, which should be of good quality, are mounted on a strap. The instrument is worn on the wrist or ankle and produces an effective sleigh bell sound to accompany songs and dances.

Jingle Bells on Handles

Generally, a single bell is mounted on the end of a handle. The instrument is held in one hand and shaken in time to music.

Tambourines

Six or more pairs of jingles are mounted in the instrument's shell. The plastic shell head comes in different sizes. The instrument may be shaken or struck with the hand, knee, or elbow, producing an interesting jingling effect.

Triangles

The triangle consists of a steel rod bent into a triangular shape, open at one corner, and struck with a small, straight, steel rod. We suggest that this instrument be purchased, since most homemade triangles have rather poor tone quality. The instrument is held by a holder and struck with a metal rod. It may also be played by placing the rod inside the triangle and striking it back and forth against the sides.

Maracas

Maracas are gourd or gourd-shaped rattles filled with seeds or pebbles. The instruments are shaken to produce rhythmic effects and can be played singly or by holding one maraca in each hand.

Castanets

Castanets are a pair of concave pieces of wood, which may be held in the palm of the hand and clicked together or attached to a handle for easier use by small children. The sound makes an interesting accompaniment for dancing.

Finger Cymbals

Two small cymbals with finger holders are held with each hand and struck together. The instrument also may be played by placing the loop holder of one cymbal over the thumb and the loop of the other cymbal on the middle finger. The two finger cymbals are then struck together.

Hand Cymbals

Concave plates of nickel, silver, bronze, or brass produce a sharp, ringing sound when struck. Cymbals may be played in pairs by striking one against the other or singly by striking one cymbal with a drumstick.

Autoharp®

This string instrument has buttons or bars that, when depressed by the finger, dampen all the strings needed for the desired chord. It can be played by strumming or plucking. The number of bars on Autoharps varies; the most common types have 12 or 15. People with little or no musical training can learn to play the Autoharp in a relatively short time.

Melody Bells

Melody bells are arranged like notes on the piano keyboard and are mounted on a frame. The bells are played with mallets. Sets come in various ranges.

Step Bells

These bells are mounted on an elevated frame, include chromatic tones, and come in various ranges. Some frames are collapsible, allowing easy storage. Children can easily see whether the melody moves up or down.

Resonator Bells

Mounted individually on a block of wood or plastic, these bells are arranged in a luggage case. Mallets are used to play the bells. The keyboard is similar to the piano keyboard. Each bell may be removed from its case and played individually. These are excellent for use by both child and teacher.

Song Index

Subject Index

Accelerando, 227
Accent, 14, 226
Accent marks, 229
Action
    children and, 3
    songs, 13–14
Affective aspect development, 3
African American music, 64
Afro-Caribbean rhymes, 82
Age appropriate learning. *See* Developmentally appropriate practice
Allegretto, 227
Allegro, 227
Alliteration, fingerplays and, 14
Andante, 227
Andantino, 227
Appreciation, of music, 194–195
Attention span, music activities and, 120–121
Auditory stimulation, of infants, 25–26
Autoharp®,17, 250
    care and tuning of, 243
    chording on, 243–244
    presenting new songs with, 103
    resonator, 106
    variations on strumming technique on, 244–245
Axial (nonlocomotor) movement, 108

Background music, 194–195
Balance, 12
Ballads, 122
Bars, 229
Beanbags, for use in creative movement, 20
Beat, 226
    establishing, 109–110
    steady, 227
Bells, 15
    jingle bells on handles, 250
    melody, 250

Montessori, 106
    resonator, 15, 17, 106, 250
    step, 250
    wrist, 250
Bending, 12
Big Music Books, 124
Bodily-kinesthetic learning, 5, 78
Body awareness, dance movements and, 11
Body percussion, 105

Caribbean ring dances, 82
Castanets, 250
CDs
    CD players, 106
    four- and five-year-olds and, 110
Chanting, 41, 43–44, 122, 123
Child-appropriate learning. *See* Developmentally appropriate
        practice
Children. *See also* specific age groups
    creativity of, 2
    egocentric nature of, 3
    imaginations of (*See* Imagination)
    shy, 3
Chromatic, 230
Classical music, 15–19
Claves, 16
Clefs, 228
Commercials, 120–121
Communication
    movement as, 81
    music as, 81–82
    nonverbal, 4
    through music, 120
Competencies, of teachers, 2
Comprehension, music activities and, 120–121
Concertinas, 16